Footprint Handbook

Venezuela

BEN BOX

This is
Venezuela

Venezuela is where the Andes meet the Caribbean. The Orinoco river separates the great plains from the table-top mountains of the Gran Sabana, where waterfalls tumble into the forest and lost worlds are easy to imagine.

Lying at the heart of the country – geographically and spiritually – are the *llanos* (plains), a vast area of flat savannah the size of Italy that is home to an immense variety of exotic birds, mammals and reptiles, including caiman, anacondas, anteaters, pumas, jaguars and giant otters. These plains flood seasonally, but when the waters retreat, the animals share their territory with cattle and the *llanero* cowboys, renowned for their hospitality towards visitors.

If the sea is more to your taste, head for the country's seductive coastline – the longest in the Caribbean. Venezuela's waters have some of the best (and least known) dive sites in the region. Pick of the bunch are Islas Los Roques, an archipelago of emerald and turquoise lagoons and dazzling white beaches.

At the other end of the country, the Amazon is home to humid rainforests and rare plants and animals, as well as over 20 different ethnic groups. This part of Venezuela is very much frontier territory and remains as wild and untamed as it was when the country received its first foreign visitor back in 1498. So overwhelmed was Columbus by what he saw that he described it as "Paradise on Earth".

Ben Box

Best of
Venezuela

top things to do and see

❶ Henri Pittier National Park

From the steep forested slopes of the cordillera to the sandy shores of the Caribbean, Venezuela's oldest national park has a huge diversity of habitats, making it a haven for migratory birds. Discover hidden beaches, hike through dense rainforest, snorkel in a lagoon or kayak through mangroves; all within two hours of the capital. Page 45.

❷ Catatumbo

The fabulous lightning displays over this swampy delta have earned it the name, the 'Lighthouse of Maracaibo'. With optimum conditions of heat and humidity combined with wind caused by the Andes, the resulting storms are a real spectacle of nature. Page 63.

❸ Sierra Nevada National Park

A stone's throw from the adventure sports capital of Mérida is Venezuela's highest and most spectacular mountain range. A paradise for hiking, climbing, canyoning and paragliding, it's also one of the last refuges of the Andean condor and spectacled bear. Pages 79 and 81.

❹ Los Llanos

The rivers and marshes of the Orinoco plains are one of the best places in Venezuela to see wildlife. In the rainy season, the flat grassy landscape transforms into a vast wetland. It's also the traditional home of the *llaneros* (cowboys) and their distinctive *joropo* music. Page 92.

❺ Mochima National Park

With some of Venezuela's most accessible
Caribbean beaches, this park is an
important tourist destination. Boat trips
run to the tiny offshore islands that dot
the coast, while high cliffs and montane
forest harbour a wealth of wildlife. It's a
great place to swim, snorkel, dive or hike.
Page 103.

❻ Los Roques

Some 160 km north of Caracas in the middle of the Caribbean Sea, the entire archipelago of Los Roques is protected as a national park. Undeveloped and largely uninhabited, there's little to do except gawp at the idyllic white-sand beaches and turquoise lagoons or snorkel among the coral reefs that teem with underwater life. Page 125.

❼ Angel Falls

The world's highest waterfall is Venezuela's most famous attraction: the dramatic jet of water tumbling off the table-top *mesa* into the deep canyon below is a remarkable sight. Hidden deep in the lost world of Canaima National Park, with no access by road, the challenge of getting there is half the experience. Page 135.

Red howler monkey

Route planner

One to two weeks

beaches, waterfalls, mountains and plains

A two-week visit would allow time on the beaches of either the eastern or western coasts, and a visit to the interior. If time is short there are flights between most cities and Caracas for the first or last leg of your trip.

East of Caracas is **Parque Nacional Mochima**, with some excellent beaches and a multitude of islets. Further east are unrivalled beaches on the **Paria Peninsula**, as well as **Isla de Margarita**, one of the country's principal tourist destinations. From the coast, take a bus to historic **Ciudad Bolívar** and then fly to the **Gran Sabana**, among whose wonders are the **Angel Falls**. There are many other falls in this region and a few places to stay, the most popular being **Canaima Camp** on a lagoon on the Río Carrao.

West of Caracas, some 320 km west of the capital, is the **Parque Nacional Morrocoy**, with many islands close to the shore. North of Morrocoy is the historic town of **Coro**, surrounded by sand dunes, and the **Paranaguá Peninsula**. From here, head south by road to the **Andean Sierra Nevada** where the main centre for adventure is **Mérida**. It has plentiful accommodation and tour companies, who can arrange treks, climbing and excursions to **Catatumbo** on Lake Maracaibo and to ecotourism ranches on the plains to the east.

Three to four weeks

diving, exploring and trekking

With an extra week or two, you could spend some time diving and relaxing on the beautiful archipelago of **Islas Los Roques**, reached by plane from Caracas. Then explore the west coast and sierras. Travel west to east from the Andes across the **Llanos** to **Ciudad Bolívar**, from where you can explore the **Gran Sabana**, not just at **Canaima**, but also from the road south to **Santa Elena de Uairén**. Where Venezuela meets Brazil and Guyana is **Mount Roraima**; to reach its summit is one of the country's most adventurous excursions.

When to go

The climate is tropical, with changes between the seasons being a matter of wet and dry, rather than hot and cold. Temperature is determined by altitude. The dry season in Caracas is December to April, with January and February the coolest months (there is a great difference between day and night temperatures at this time). The hottest months are July and August. The Caribbean coast is generally dry, and rain is particularly infrequent in the states of Sucre, in the east, and Falcón, in the northwest.

The lowlands of Maracaibo are very hot all year round, but especially so from July to September. South of the Orinoco, in the Gran Sabana and Parque Nacional Canaima, the dry season is November to May. The best time to visit Los Llanos is just after the rains, when the rivers and channels are still full of water and the humidity is not too high.

In the Andes, the dry season is October to May; this is the best time for climbing or hiking. The days are clear, but the nights are freezing cold. The rains usually begin in June, but in the mountains the weather can change daily. High season, when it is advisable to book in advance, includes Carnival, Easter, 15 July to 15 September and Christmas to New Year.

Fact file
Location 105000° N, 669667° W
Capital Caracas
Time zone GMT -4½ hrs
Telephone country code +58
Currency Bolívar fuerte (BsF)

Weather Caracas

January	February	March	April	May	June
☀ 25°C 17°C 16mm	☀ 26°C 18°C 18mm	☀ 27°C 18°C 12mm	☁ 27°C 20°C 59mm	☁ 27°C 21°C 80mm	☁ 26°C 20°C 139mm

July	August	September	October	November	December
☁ 26°C 20°C 121mm	☁ 26°C 20°C 124mm	☁ 27°C 20°C 114mm	☁ 26°C 20°C 123mm	☁ 26°C 19°C 73mm	☁ 25°C 18°C 42mm

What to do

from birdwatching to fishing to scuba diving

Venezuela is an excellent destination for adventure sportsand other specialist interest activities. Mérida in the Andes is the main centre for climbing, trekking and paragliding. Good areas for wildlife tours and birdwatching are the Llanos as well as many national parks such as Henri Pittier and Catatumbo, near Lake Maracaibo. The Caribbean coast and islands are perfect for diving, yachting and fishing.

Birdwatching and wildlife

The Henri Pittier national park is accessible from Caracas and is a birders' paradise. Roughly 40% of Venezuela's species can be spotted here including eagles and kites.

Lying at the heart of the country – geographically and spiritually – are the Llanos (plains), a vast area of flat savannah the size of Italy. This is home to an immense variety of birds, exotic mammals and reptiles. The plains flood during the wet season and visitors can explore the rivers and inlets in canoes. During the dry season, from December to April, the animals have to leave the depths of the swamps in order to seek water. This is the time when rarer mammals such as jaguars, pumas and giant otters can be more easily seen.

Ecotourism and Hatos

Llanero cowboys have a renowned hospitality towards visitors and you can stay on one of the many luxurious *hatos* – former cattle ranches – or rough it on a budget tour from Mérida in the Andes. An alternative to travelling independently or arranging a tour from Mérida is to stay at a tourist ranch. Most are in Apure state and can be reached from Barinas or San Fernando de Apure. Today many of the ranches are owned by the government.

Fishing

Venezuela boasts some of the best sports fishing in the world today. Though deep-sea fishing has been the focus of the country's international reputation, closer to shore there is other quarry, such as tarpon, barracuda, bonefish, ladyfish, snook, blue fish, kingfish, wahoo, jack crevalle, blue runner and yellowfin tuna.

Freshwater fishing is also excellent in Venezuela. Fishing trips can be made to the Llanos (see under Rafting, page 13) and the many lakes in the Sierra Nevada de Mérida offer great fishing for brown trout. The season runs from mid-March to September. As most lakes are within national parks you will need a permit from Inparques. Lake Camatagua, the Guri Dam and Uraima Falls are renowned for the peacock-bass fishing.

Horse riding

At the main tourist spots such as Pico El Aguila and Laguna Mucubají it is possible to rent the small criollo horses for a couple of hours. For those looking for more serious horse riding with healthy Quarter-mixed horses, there is Hacienda El Vaho close to Santo Domingo and Finca Yegua Blanca close to Tabay.

Mountain biking

The popularity of this sport has increased dramatically over the past years. Several operators rent out bikes for one or more days and explain where you can go and what to do on your own. Expect to pay US$10-25 for a day's biking (check brakes and gears before setting out); or US$35-70 for organized tours. Jají and its surroundings and the *páramo* are good places for one- or two-day options.

Mountaineering and trekking

The main area for mountaineering and trekking in Venezuela is the Andean mountains around Mérida. The Sierra Nevada de Mérida, in particular, and also the Sierra de la Culata offer many and varied possibilities for novices and experienced climbers and trekkers alike. There are, however, many other hiking trails throughout the country. Take the appropriate equipment and be especially aware of the dangers of altitude sickness if you are hiking high in the Sierra Nevada. Pico Bolívar is Venezuela's highest peak, at 5007 m, and it attracts climbers from all over the world. Pico Humboldt is the second highest mountain in Venezuela, at 4944 m. It's visited all year round, with its northeast and west faces being preferred by climbers.

The best time for climbing or trekking in the Andes is the dry season, from October to May, with clear days and freezing cold nights. The summer runs from December to May; the rains begin in June and continue until October or November, though there's always a chance that the weather will change from one day to the next. During the summer the days are clear and the nights very cold, with minimum temperatures of minus 10-15°C on the high peaks. August is the coldest month on the peaks.

One of the most popular treks in Venezuela is Mount Roraima, the flat-topped table mountain, or *tepuy*, in the extreme southwest of the country. Roraima straddles three countries – Venezuela, Brazil and Guyana – and they meet in a triple-point on the top. Over 3000 people per year take the six-day trek from Paraitepuy to the summit and back.

Paragliding and hangliding

Mérida is situated in a valley surrounded by high mountains. About one-third of them are accessible over land or by cable car. Depending on the time of day there is always one spot from where you can fly and soar on the thermals.

Rafting and kayaking

The best time for rafting is during the rainy season from May to November, and sometimes till December. On the southeastern slopes of the Sierra Nevada National Park, some three to five hours away from Mérida, you'll find unspoiled, virgin rivers flowing down to the flatlands. Here, the water temperature is very agreeable, with a temperature of around 30°C.

Scuba diving

As you would expect of a country with the longest coastline in the Caribbean, scuba diving in Venezuela is wonderful, with some of its sites ranking right up there with the better-known and highly acclaimed Bonaire and the Cayman Islands. Venezuela also has the advantage of still being relatively unknown. The coast offers many and varied diving sites and, in addition to the underwater flora and fauna, you can explore sunken shipwrecks from the colonial era.

Large parts of the coastline are protected as marine-based national parks Los Roques is an archipelago of over 300 tiny islands lying north of La Guaïra; Morrocoy is in the state of Falcón on the western coast; and Mochima lies between Puerto La Cruz and Cumaná on the eastern coast. As well as these national parks, there are hundreds of other potential sites, the best of which are found around the islands.

Where to stay

from ultra-luxurious hotels to posadas

Hotels and posadas

Using the new Simadi exchange rate (or the parallel market – see Money, page 176), value for money is quite high. For the thrifty, there are foreign-run, no-frills places catering for backpackers. The major cities, Isla Margarita, Los Roques, Guayana and Amazonas have higher room rates (eg US$20-60). Rooms are cheaper without air conditioning. In the Andean region prices are lower, starting at around US$5-10 per person. If comfort and cleanliness is what you are after, the price of a basic three-star (Venezuelan 'four star') air conditioned hotel room, private bath and breakfast will be in our $$-$ range, depending on location and whether it's a hotel or posada. A prior reservation will not guarantee you a room. If you can, insist on seeing the room before paying; if you don't, you will probably be given the worst possible room.

A group of 20 posadas, mostly in the west of the country, have joined together under the banner **El Circuito de la Excelencia**, www.circuitodelaexcelencia.com, to offer high-quality, distinctive lodging, food and service. **Casa Tropical** ① *CC Paseo Las Mercedes, Sector La Cuadra, Local 26, Caracas, T212-993 2939,*

Price codes

Where to stay
$$$$ over US$150
$$$ US$66-150
$$ US$30-65
$ under US$30

Price of a double room in high season, including taxes.

Restaurants
$$$ over US$12
$$ US$7-12
$ US$6 and under

Prices for a two-course meal for one person, excluding drinks or service charge.

www.casa tropical.com.ve, offers interesting accommodation in seven properties on the central coast, in Ciudad Bolívar, Canaima and Amazonas.

Camping

Camping in Venezuela is risky because of crime. Camping, with or without a vehicle, is not possible at the roadside. If camping on the beach, for the sake of security, pitch your tent close to others.

Guides

Elizabeth Kline's Guide to Camps, Posadas and Cabins in Venezuela 2013-14, published every two years or so (US$35, purchasing information from klineposada1944@ gmail.com) is incredibly detailed and doesn't pull its punches. *La Guía Valentina Quintero* also covers the whole country, suggesting routes, where to stay and eat, published biannually, www.valentinaquintero.com.ve.

Food
& drink

Food

There is excellent local fish (such as *pargo* or red snapper, *carite* or king fish), crayfish, small oysters and prawns. Although it is a protected species, turtle may appear on menus in the Península de Paraguaná as *ropa especial*. Of true Venezuelan food there is *sancocho* (vegetable stew with meat, chicken or fish); *arepas*, bland white maize bread; toasted *arepas* served with various fillings or the local salty white cheese, are cheap, filling and nutritious; *cachapas*, a maize pancake wrapped around white cheese; *pabellón*, of shredded meat, beans, rice and fried plantains; and *empanadas*, maize-flour pies of cheese, meat or fish. At Christmas there are *hallacas*, maize pancakes stuffed with chicken, pork and olives, boiled in a plantain leaf. A *muchacho* (boy) on the menu is a cut of beef. *Ganso* is not goose but beef. *Solomo* and *lomito* are other cuts of beef. *Hervido* is chicken or beef with vegetables. On the Península de Paraguaná roast kid (*asado de chivo*) and kid cooked in coconut are served. *Contorno* with a meat or fish dish is a choice of chips, boiled potatoes, rice or yuca. *Caraotas* are beans; *cachitos* are filled croissants. *Pasticho* is what Venezuelans call Italian lasagne. The main fruits are bananas, oranges, grapefruit, mangoes, pineapple and pawpaws. *Lechoza* is papaya, *patilla* water melon, *parchita* passion fruit, and *cambur* a small banana. Excellent strawberries are grown at Colonia Tovar, 90 minutes from Caracas, and in the Andes. Delicious sweets are *huevos chimbos* (egg yolk boiled and bottled in sugar syrup) and *quesillo*, made with milk, egg and caramel. **Note** Venezuelans dine late!

Drink

Venezuelan rum is very good; recommended brands are Cacique, Pampero and Santa Teresa. There are four good beers Polar (the most popular, sold as Polar, Ice, Solera and Solera Light), Regional, Cardenal and Zulia (a *lisa* is a glass of keg beer; for a bottle of beer ask for a *tercio*). Brazilian *Brahma* beer is brewed in Venezuela. There is a good local wine in Venezuela. The Polar brewery joined with Martell (France) to build a winery in Carora. **Bodegas Pomar** also sells a champagne-style sparkling wine. Look out for Pomar wine festivals in March and September. Liqueurs are cheap, try the local *ponche crema*. Coffee is very cheap (*café con leche* is milky, *café marrón* much less so, *café negro* is black); it often has sugar already added, ask for "sin azúcar". Try a *merengada*, a delicious drink made from fruit pulp, ice, milk and sugar; a *batido* is the same but with water and a little milk; *jugo* is the same but with water. A *plus-café* is an after-dinner liqueur. *Chicha de arroz* is a sweet drink made of milk, sugar and vanilla. Fruit juices are very good, ask for "jugo natural, preparado en el momento" for the freshest juice.

Restaurants

As with lodging, eating out is cheap if you change dollars using Sicad 2. Midday used to be the best time to find a three-course *menú ejecutivo* or *cubierto*, but increasingly many places offer only à la carte, quoting scarcity of supplies. Minimum price for a basic meal is US$2, not including drinks. Hotel breakfasts are likely to be poor. It is better and cheaper in a *fuente de soda* and cheaper still in a *pastelería* or *arepería*. See page 14, for our restaurant price guide.

ON THE ROAD
Food and drink glossary

Drinks bebidas
beer cerveza
coffee café
milk leche
mineral water agua mineral
tea té
wine vino

Fish pescados
bass robalo
catfish bagre
dolphin (fish) dorado
grouper mero
red snapper pargo
trout trucha
tuna atún

Fruits frutas
avocado aguacate
banana cambur

blackberry mora
coconut coco
guava guayaba
papaya lechosa
passion fruit parchita
pineapple piña
strawberry fresa
tamarind tamarindo
watermelon patilla

Meat carne
bacon tocineta
chop chuleta
goat chivo
ham jamón
hamburger hamburguesa
lamb cordero
liver hígado
pork cerdo/cochino
ribs costillas
sausage chorizo/salchicha

tenderloin lomito
tongue lengua

Seafood mariscos
crab cangrejo
lobster langosta
octopus pulpo
shrimps camarones
squid calamares

Vegetables legumbres
black bean caraota
carrot zanhoria
coleslaw criolla
french fries papas fritas
lettuce lechuga
mushrooms hongos
peas arveja
rice arroz
salad ensalada

Essential Caracas

Finding your feet

Maiquetía airport is 28 km from Caracas; if you're arriving or leaving at night, you are advised to stay in one of the nearby hotels on the coast rather than travelling to/from the city. For those travelling by bus, there are three main terminals in different parts of the city, each serving different regions of the country.

In the centre, each street corner has a name addresses are generally given as 'Santa Capilla y Mijares', rather than the official 'Calle Norte 2, No 26'. Modern multi-storeyed edifices dominate and few colonial buildings remain intact. A 10-km strip from west to east, fragmented by traffic-laden arteries, contains several centres Plaza Bolívar, Plaza Venezuela, Sabana Grande, Chacaíto, Altamira, La California and Petare. The Avila mountain is always north.

Getting around

The metro is air-conditioned, clean, safe, comfortable and quick, although poorly signed and often packed, especially at rush hours. It is supplemented by numerous bus services (again, crowded at rush hour), cable cars and taxis. Only ever use official taxi cabs or private taxis owned by your hotel.

Tip...
Saturday and Sunday mornings and public holidays are bad for travel into/out of Caracas.

When to go

Caracas has a pleasant Caribbean climate, although it can be hot and humid from June to September. If you're in the city on 3 May, look out for festivities associated with the Velorio de la Cruz de Mayo, which is still celebrated with dances and parties in some areas.

Tip...
Many museums are closed on Monday and at lunchtime.

Security

Safety in Caracas has deteriorated in recent years and crime rates and kidnappings have risen significantly. You should be on your guard as soon as you arrive there are many pirate taxis and rip-off merchants at the international airport. It is best not to arrive in Caracas at night. Avoid certain areas, such as all western suburbs from the El Silencio monument to Propatria; the areas around the Nuevo Circo and La Bandera bus stations; the area around the *teleférico*; Chapellín near the Country Club, and Petare. It is not advisable to walk at night in the city, except in the municipality of Chacao (Altamira, Chacao and Los Palos Grandes) and in Las Mercedes. Street crime is common, even armed robbery in daylight. Carry handbags, cameras and other valuables on the side away from the road, as motorcycle bag-snatchers are notorious. Police checks are frequent, thorough and can include on-the-spot searches of valuables; bribes are sometimes asked for. See also Safety, page 179.

Caracas

Founded in 1567, Caracas is situated in a rift in thickly forested mountains which rise abruptly from a lush green coast to heights of 2000 m to 3000 m. The capital lies in a small basin at 960 m, which runs some 24 km east and west. For all its Caribbean appeal, it is not the gentlest of introductions to South America. Some enjoy its pleasant, year-round climate, its parks and cosmopolitan nightlife. Others are drawn to see firsthand the Bolivarian revolution in action. But others find this city of three million people, loud, congested and unsettling. By way of escape, there are several nearby excursions to mountain towns, the colonial district of El Hatillo, the Parque Nacional El Avila/Waraira Repano, beaches and Los Roques, a beautiful Caribbean atoll reached by a short flight.

Best for
Excursions ▪ Museums ▪ Nightlife ▪ Parks

Plaza Bolívar and around

The shady **Plaza Bolívar**, with its fine equestrian statue of the Liberator and pleasant colonial cathedral, is still the official centre of the city, though no longer geographically so. The **Capitolio Nacional**, the National Assembly, consists of two neoclassical-style buildings, the **Legislative Palace** and the **Federal Palace** ⓘ *Tue-Sun, 0900-1100, 1400-1600*. The Elliptical Salon has some impressive paintings and murals by the Venezuelan artist Martín Tovar y Tovar. The present **Cathedral** dating from 1674 has a beautiful façade, the Bolívar family chapel and paintings by Michelena, Murillo and an alleged Rubens 'Resurrection'. Bolívar was baptized in this Cathedral, and the remains of his parents and wife are here. The **Museo Sacro** ⓘ *Plaza Bolívar, de la Torre a Gradillas, Tue-Sun 1000-1700*, has colonial religious paintings and images, plus an art gallery, handicrafts, café and bookshop. Concerts and other cultural events are held at weekends.

The **Consejo Municipal** (City Hall) on Plaza Bolívar contains three **museums** ⓘ *all open Tue-Fri 0930-1200, 1500-1800; Sat and Sun 0930-1800*. The first features a collection of paintings by Emilio Boggio, a Venezuelan painter; the Raúl Santana

① Caracas

Where to stay 🛏
1 Avila
2 Eurobuilding
3 Paseo Las Mercedes

Restaurants 🍴
2 La Castañuela
3 La Montanara
4 Mokambo

Museum of the Creole Way of Life has a collection of miniature figures in costumes, all handmade by Raúl Santana; and the Sala de Arqueología Gaspar Marcano, exhibits ceramics, mostly discovered on the coast.

Casa Natal del Libertador ⓘ *Sur 1 y Este 2, Jacinto a Traposos, opposite Plaza El Venezolano, T541 2563, Tue-Fri 0900-1600, Sat, Sun and holidays 1000-1600, free*, is a fascinating reconstruction of the house where Bolívar was born on 24 July 1783. Interesting pictures, furniture and murals tell Bolívar's life story. The first house, of adobe, was destroyed by an earthquake. The second was later pulled down. The **Museo Bolivariano** is next door and contains the Liberator's war relics.

San Francisco ⓘ *Av Universidad y San Francisco (1 block southwest of Plaza Bolívar)*, the oldest church in Caracas, rebuilt 1641, should be seen for its colonial altars. **Santa Teresa** ⓘ *between La Palma and Santa Teresa, just southeast of the Centro Simón Bolívar*, has good interior chapels and a supposedly miraculous portrait of Nazareno de San Pablo; there are popular devotions here on Good Friday.

Panteón Nacional and around

The remains of Simón Bolívar, the Liberator, lie here in the **National Cemetery** ⓘ *Av Norte y Av Panteón, Tue-Sun 0900-1200, 1330-1600*. Every 25 years the

Bars & clubs 🎵
5 Juan Sebastián Bar

President opens Bolívar's casket to verify that the remains are still there. The tomb of Francisco Miranda (the Precursor of Independence), who died in a Spanish prison, has been left open to await the return of his body; likewise the tomb of Antonio José de Sucre, who was assassinated in Colombia.

Museo Histórico Fundación John Boulton ⓘ *Final Av Panteón, Foro Libertador, Casa N 3, next to the Panteón Nacional, T0212-861 4685, www.fundacionboulton. com, Tue-Sat 1000-1600*, contains good collections of 19th-century art and objects, furniture, maps, metals and coins and objects and documents relating to the life of Simon Bolívar.

San Bernardino

A delightful house in the beautiful suburb of San Bernardino houses the **Museo de Arte Colonial** ⓘ *Quinta Anauco, Av Panteón, San Bernardino, T0212-551 8190, www.quintadeanauco.org.ve, Tue-Fri 0900-1200 and 1400-1600, Sat-Sun and holidays 1000-1600, US$0.50*. It was built in 1720 and was formerly the residence of the Marqués del Toro. Everything from the roof to the carpet has been preserved and the house contains a wealth of period furniture and sculpture and almost 100 paintings from the colonial era.

2 Caracas centre

Where to stay		
1 Alex	4 El Conde	
2 Avila	5 Limón	
3 Dal Bo Hostel		

Restaurants
1 Bar Basque
2 Café Casa Veroes
4 La Cita

Parque Central

There are two good museums located at the **Parque Central**, a jungle of concrete edifices between Avenida Bolívar and Avenida Lecuna. The **Museo de Arte Contemporáneo** ① *Parque Central, Cuadra Bolívar, T0212-573 8289, www.fmn.gob. ve, Tue-Fri 0900-1700, Sat-Sun 1000-1700, free,* has some 3000 works on display, including modern sculptures and works by, among others, Miró, Chagall, Matisse and Picasso; it's one of the finest collections of modern art in South America. The **Museo de los Niños** ① *Parque Central, next to east Tower, Nivel Bolívar, T0212-575 0695, www.maravillosarealidad.com, Mon-Fri 0900-1700, Sat-Sun and holidays 1000-1700, US$1.40, children US$1.20,* is an extremely popular and highly sophisticated interactive science museum.

Plaza de los Museos

Parque Los Caobos is a peaceful place to wander if you are visiting the **Plaza de los Museos**, which is located at the western end of the park. Nearby is the **Bosque de las Esculturas**, an open-air sculpture exhibition. **Museo de Bellas Artes** ① *Plaza de los Museos, www.fmn.gob.ve, free, Mon-Fri 0900-1600, Sat-Sun and holidays 1000-1700,* is the oldest museum in Caracas, designed by Carlos Raúl Villanueva. It contains a permanent collection of contemporary and 19th-

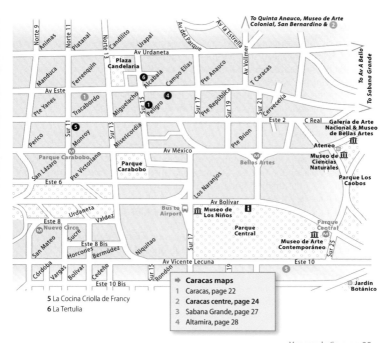

5 La Cocina Criolla de Francy
6 La Tertulia

century works by mainly Venezuelan and South American artists and also has a good café surrounded by outdoor sculptures. Adjacent is the **Galería de Arte Nacional** ⓘ *T0212-576 8707, www.fmn.gob.ve, Mon-Fri 0900-1700, Sat-Sun and holidays 1000-1700*, which displays the history of Venezuelan art and also houses the **Cinemateca Nacional** ⓘ *www.cinemateca.gob.ve*, an arts and experimental cinema complex. **Museo de Ciencias Naturales** ⓘ *Plaza de los Museos, Los Caobos, T0212-577 5103, www.fmn.gob.ve, Mon-Fri 0900-1700, Sat-Sun and holidays 1030-1800*, has archaeological (particularly pre-Columbian), zoological and botanical exhibits, plus interesting temporary shows.

University and botanic gardens

Universidad Central de Venezuela ⓘ *Ciudad Universitaria, near Plaza Venezuela, www.ucv.ve*, is one of the most successful expressions of modern architecture in Latin America. Designed by Carlos Raúl Villanueva, it was declared a World Heritage Site by UNESCO in 2000. Among its important works of art are Floating Clouds by Alexander Calder in the auditorium, murals by Victor Vasarely, Wilfredo Lam and Fernand Léger, and sculptures by Jean Arp and Henri Laurens.

   Jardín Botánico ⓘ *near Plaza Venezuela, entrance by Ciudad Universitaria, daily 0830-1630*, has collections of over 2000 species; 10,000 trees from 80 species grow in the arboretum alone. Here is the world's largest palm tree (*Corypha sp*) and the elephant apple tree with its huge edible fruit.

Sabana Grande *See map opposite.*

East of Plaza Venezuela, the mid-town neighbourhood of Sabana Grande is bisected by the pedestrianised Boulevard Sabana Grande (actual name Avenida Abraham Lincoln), which connects with eastern Caracas. It has been cleaned up in recent years and is now a popular commercial district filled with shops, eateries and a book market – a great place to observe everyday Caraqueño life.

Eastern Caracas

The safest and most fashionable area of the city lies to the east of Sabana Grande in an area known as the 'golden belt of Caracas'. It includes Country Club, Las Mercedes, Valle Arriba, Chacao, La Castellana, Altamira, Los Palos Grandes and Sebucán, and it has the best hotels and residential districts. **Plaza Alfredo Sadel** is an open space where public events take place all year round. It's on Avenida Principal of Las Mercedes, an old residential neighbourhood that has been transformed into an exclusive commercial zone.

   Plaza Bolívar de Chacao ⓘ *Av Mohedano, entre Ribas y Páez*, marks the spot where the town of Chacao was born, in the grounds of the Hacienda San Diego. Opposite is Iglesia San José, its patron saint. It's a popular meeting place and a stage for art exhibitions and folklore shows. **Plaza Francia** ⓘ *Av Francisco de Miranda, entre Av Luis Roche y Av San Juan Bosco, Altamira*, commonly called Plaza Altamira, is a well-known landmark with an obelisk, a fountain and a Metro station. **La Estancia** ⓘ *just along from the Altamira metro exit, www.pdvsalaestancia.com*, is a cultural centre with good exhibitions, regular activities and events including free yoga and music. It is set in a lovely park with beautiful trees and manicured lawns, the perfect place to escape from the hectic city. **Plaza Los Palos Grandes** ⓘ *3a Av entre 2a y 3a Transversal, Los Palos Grandes*, at the heart of the fashionable neighbourhood of the same name, has a library, a coffee shop and mural. It is a good place to start a tour of the area and has an open market on Saturdays.

Parque Nacional del Este (officially Parque Gerneralísimo Francisco de Miranda) ⓘ *Tue-Sun, 0530-1700 for joggers, 0830-1700 for others, Miranda metro station*, is the largest park in Caracas and a popular place to relax, especially at weekends. It has a boating lake, cactus garden, tropical birds, some caged animals and reptiles as well as the **Humboldt Planetarium** ⓘ *T0212-234 9188, www.planetariohumboldt. com*. **Museo de Transporte** ⓘ *Parque Nacional del Este (to which it is connected by a pedestrian overpass), T0212-234 2234, www.automotriz.net/museo-del-transporte, Sun 0900-1700,* has a large collection of locomotives and old cars.

West of the centre

The refurbished **Parque Ezequiel Zamora/El Calvario**, west of El Silencio, with the Arch of Confederation at the entrance, has a good view of Centro Simón Bolívar. It has a small Museo Ornitológico, botanical gardens and a picturesque chapel. Near here is the Cuartel 4 de Febrero (4-F), the barracks in 23 de Enero district, also known as the Cuartel de la Montaña. It is now home to the **Museo de la Revolución Bolivariana**

3 Sabana Grande

➡ **Caracas maps**
1 Caracas, page 22
2 Caracas centre, page 24
3 **Sabana Grande, page 27**
4 Altamira, page 28

Where to stay 🛏
2 Crillón
3 Cristal
4 Gran Meliá
5 Nelson's Place
7 Plaza Palace

Restaurants 🍴
1 Da Guido
6 Jaime Vivas
7 La Huerta

Bars & clubs 🍸
9 El Maní Es Así

① T0212-672 1719, Tue-Sun 1000-1600 (take a taxi, sketchy neighbourhood), the final resting place of the body of President Hugo Chávez, who died in March 2013. His body is entombed within a sombre, temperature-controlled marble sarcophagus. A 2-km Bulevar de la Dignidad will connect El Calvario with the site of the museum via the Plaza 4 de Febrero.

4 Altamira

Caracas maps
1 Caracas, page 22
2 Caracas centre, page 24
3 Sabana Grande, page 27
4 Altamira, page 28

Where to stay 🛏
3 Caracas Palace
4 Chacao & Suites
5 La Floresta
6 Pestana Caracas
7 Renaissance
8 Residencia Montserrat
9 The VIP

Restaurants 🍴
1 Amapola
2 Aprile
3 Arabica Coffee Bar
4 Arepa Factory Tradicional
5 Avila Burger
7 Catar
8 Chez Wong
9 Come a Casa
10 El Alazán

11 El Presidente
12 Miga's
14 St Honoré

Bars & clubs 🍸
15 360° Rooftop Bar

Other parks and urban excursions

At the foot of the Avila mountain, the **Parque Los Chorros** ⓘ *Tue-Fri 0830-1630, Sat-Sun 0830-1800, take bus from Los Dos Caminos station to Lomas de Los Chorros*, has impressive waterfalls and forest walks.

Paseo Los Próceres ⓘ *Metro Los Símbolos*, not far from the Escuela Militar, is a monument to the Venezuelan Independence heroes and is popular with walkers, runners and cyclists. The densely wooded **Parque Caricuao** ⓘ *Tue-Sun 0900-1630; take metro to Caricuao Zoológico, then 5-min walk up Av Principal La Hacienda,* is at the southwest end of the Metro line, and part of Parque Nacional Macuro. It makes a pleasant day out.

El Hatillo ⓘ *take a bus or taxi from central Caracas, about 20-30 mins' drive, depending on traffic*, once a separate village now subsumed by the city sprawl, is one of the few places in Caracas that has retained its colonial architecture. Built around a central plaza, its peaceful streets of multi coloured houses offer a fine selection of cafés, restaurants, shops and small galleries. It is a wonderful spot to escape from the city and to shop for handicrafts, but it's busy at weekends. It holds an annual international music festival, usually in October, but dates vary.

Listings Caracas *maps p22, p24, p27 and p28*

Tourist information

The main tourist office is **Corpoturismo** (Parque Central, Torre Oeste, p 35, 36 y 37, T0212-576 5696). Online local guides in Spanish include http://laguiadecaracas.net, www.guiacaracas.com and www.ciudadccs.info. Information can also be found on the Alcaldía's website, www.caracas.gob.ve.

Where to stay

The cheapest hotels are in the downtown area, but this is not a safe part of town at night, or even in the day with a backpack. Sabana Grande, which has a wide range of hotels, is not safe after 2000. If you don't want to stay in the suburbs or centre, spend a little more and go to the upmarket Chacao, Altamira, La Castellana districts (all easily reached by metro), where it is relatively safe to stroll around during the day. There are hotels on the coast, close to the airport, if you do not want to go into the city. If you book from abroad, make sure you receive written confirmation before beginning your journey.

Central area

The cheapest hotels are around the Nuevo Circo bus terminal (not a safe area). Plaza Bolívar and its surrounding streets are busy by the day, but by night are deserted and unsafe.

$$$ Alex
Ferrenquín esq la Cruz, T0212-578 0437, www.hotelalex.com.ve.
A modern, new high-rise option boasting a bold contemporary lobby with tropical aquariums, 100 rooms on 14 floors with crisp furnishings and funky carpets, TVs, Wi-Fi, gym, small pool, and restaurant.

$ Dal Bo
Av Sur 2 y Av Universidad, esq
San Francisco, T0424-215 0799,
www.dalbohostal.hostel.com.
Cosy hostel with small dorms, 1½ blocks
from Plaza Bolívar, on 1st floor of an
old building. Wi-Fi, tourist info, console
games and Blu-Ray DVDs. A sociable
option. Prices are in US dollars, payment
in dollars or euros only.

$ El Conde
Av Sur 4 esq El Conde, T0212-862 2007.
Elegant old hotel, well located for those
wanting to stay in the historic centre,
but the rooms are very run-down. It's
also hard to get a reservation. Own
restaurant and bar.

$ Limón
Av Lecuna, Frente Parque Central,
T0212-571 6457, Bellas Artes metro.
Recently remodelled red-brick building
with a restaurant attached. Safe, parking,
well located for museums and galleries.

San Bernardino
This residential area is 2 km north of
Bellas Artes metro.

$$ Avila
Av Jorge Washington, T0212-555 3000,
www.hotelavila.com.ve.
Founded by Nelson Rockerfeller in
1942, now a bit past its heyday but still
a pleasant and tranquil retreat set in
lush tropical gardens. Most staff speak
English and German, there are fans,
mosquito screens, pool, Metrobus
nearby, a good restaurant and poolside
bar, and travel agency. A 20-min drive
from the centre.

Sabana Grande/Chacaíto
This is a busy area with restaurants and
shops, but most close by early evening
and it is unsafe to be out after 2000
when crowds and atmosphere change.
The western fringes of Sabana Grande
around Plaza Venezuela should be
avoided entirely after sunset.

$$$$ Gran Meliá
Av Casanova y El Recreo, T0212-762 8111,
www.gran-melia.com/en.
Beyond the ugly concrete 1970s exterior,
the Gran Meliá boasts a sumptuous
marble lobby, James Bond staircases and
glittering crystal chandeliers. However,
it is past its heyday. Variety of rooms and
good facilities including business centre,
gourmet buffets, restaurants, fitness
centre (at extra cost), spa, pool area,
piano bar.

$$ Nelson's Place
C El Recreo, Edif 6, p 2, Apt 623,
www.nelson. com.ve, or www.agelvis.
com (contact by email).
By prior reservation only, Nelson Agelvis
has 1 excellent fully furnished apartment
complete with Wi-Fi, cable TV, kitchen,
and lounge, and 1 economical
room, both conveniently located in
a residential block next to El Recreo
shopping mall. Exceptional hospitality,
attention and travel information. A
comfortable introduction to Caracas.
Prices in dollars. Highly recommended.

$$ Plaza Palace
Av Los Mangos, Las Delicias, T0212-762
4821, plaza_palace_hotel@hotmail.com.
A secure building located on a quiet
residential street. Amenities include
parking and business facilities. Helpful,
English spoken.

Chuao/Las Mercedes

An upmarket commercial district southeast of the centre and Sabana Grande, no metro station.

$$$ Eurobuilding Hotel & Suites

C La Guarita, Chuao, T0212-902 1111, www.hoteleuro.com.

A modern 5-star hotel that's part of an international chain. It has a well-furnished all-suite wing, large pool, gym, spa, barber, restaurants, weekend rates.

$$$-$$ Hotel Paseo Las Mercedes

CC Paseo Las Mercedes, Las Mercedes, T0212-993 1244, www.hotelpaseolasmercedes.com.ve.

Located in the shopping mall with fine restaurants and bars on the doorstep. Comfortable, spacious rooms with good service.

Chacao, Altamira, La Castellana

These 3 districts, east of Gran Sabana and the centre, are adjacent to each other, and are a respectable commercial and residential zone.

$$$ Caracas Palace

Av Luis Roche con Av Francisco Miranda, Altamira, T0212-771 1000, www.caracaspalace.com.

A popular luxury hotel well-located at the heart of Chacao on the Plaza Francia. It boasts a crisp white marble lobby and sweeping staircase, 2 restaurants, pool, spa, gym and business centre.

$$$ Hotel Chacao and Suites

Av Francisco de Miranda y Av José Félix Sosa, T0212-956 6900, www.hotelchacaosuites.com.

A smart new luxury option with modern, stylish, minimalist decor, spacious carpeted rooms and well-equipped suites to suit executive travellers. Amenities include Wi-Fi and restaurant.

$$$ Pestana Caracas

1 Av Urb Santa Eduvigis, T0212-208 1900, www.pestana.com.

Luxury hotel near Miranda metro station and Parque del Este, business-oriented with all facilities, fitness-centre, pool, restaurant and penthouse bar.

$$$ Renaissance

Av Eugenio Mendoza con C Urdaneta, La Castellana, T0212-908 4222, www.marriott.com/ccsbr.

A well-located hotel with bright contemporary decor, tasteful and well-equipped rooms, Asian restaurant, lounge bar, pool and gym. Good reports.

$$ The VIP

3 Transversal con Av San Juan Bosco, Altamira, T0212-319 4300, www.thevipcaracas.com.

Young, stylish boutique hotel with good-sized, crisply attired rooms, some with balconies, as well as a fine gourmet restaurant and slick lounge bar.

$ La Floresta

Av Avila Sur, T0212-267 4477, www.hotelafloresta.com.

Simple, reasonable, generic rooms with cable TV, hot water and Wi-Fi. A bit dated and the remodelled rooms are better; some have a nice view over the park. Good location near Altamira metro and Plaza Francia. Parking.

$ Residencia Montserrat

Av Avila Sur, T0212-263 3533.

A good 3-star option with a range of reasonable rooms and apartments, but ask to see before accepting. Near Plaza Francia and Altamira metro. Pleasant, well run, helpful, parking. Wi-Fi in lobby.

Near airport
See Litoral Central, page 42.

Restaurants

Thanks to the creative input of generations of immigrants, Caracas' restaurant scene is extensive and diverse. There are more decent establishments than can be listed here, but an excellent online guide is www.miropopic.com.

Central area

There are lots of classic Spanish haunts in the downtown area, full of atmosphere and history. You should use taxis at night as it is unsafe. Call ahead for reservations.

$$ Bar Basque
Alcabala a Peligro, La Candelaria, T0212-572 4857.
Intimate and well-established, this is a renowned family-run Caracas favourite that has been serving fine home-cooked Basque cuisine for 3 generations. Just a handful of tables and an excellent menu of fresh seafood, poultry and meat dishes. One of the best.

$$ Café Casa Veroes
Veroes a Jesuitas, T0212-564 7457. Mon-Fri 0900-1600.
Sophisticated traditional Venezuelan food in a colonial house built in 1759 (www.casadelahistoriadevenezuela. com). A bastion of elegance in an otherwise shabby neighbourhood. Great ambiance and a changing menu.

$$ La Cita
Esq de Alcabala, La Candelaria, T0212-573 8819.
Serving traditional Spanish food for 56 years, including seafood, fish stews and paella. Bustling, festive and packed at lunchtime. Book ahead.

$$ La Cocina Criolla de Francy
Av Este 2 y Sur 11, La Candelaria, T0212-576 9849. Open 0900-1800, closed Sun.
Founded by Francy Moncada, his kitchen serves wholesome traditional Venezuelan cuisine, including rabbit, lamb, and arepitas. A good place to sample local flavours.

$$ La Tertulia
Alcabala a Urapal, La Candelaria, T0212-574 1476.
Family-run tapas restaurant with an extensive menu and daily specials. Famous for its lamb chops, octopus, tapas and Spanish-style fresh fish. Busy at noon.

Sabana Grande

This area has some cafés, bars (*tascas*) and restaurants. Places on the Blv Sabana Grande are good for people-watching. There is also an array of fast-food joints in CC El Recreo, most of them on the 6th floor.

$$ Da Guido
Av Fco Solano, T0212-763 0937.
A long-running Italian restaurant and Sabana Grande institution, as reliable as it was 50 years ago. It has a small menu of hearty home-cooked fare, simple, fresh, and authentic, the way good Italian food should be. Has a 2nd branch at 6 Av con 5 Transversal, Altamira, T266 9927, equally popular.

$$ La Huerta
Av Fco Solano con 1ra Av de Las Delicias, T0212-762 5228.
Spanish *tasca* with a dash of Venezuelan, including tapas, seafood paella, rabbit, goat, and lamb. Popular with locals watching Spanish football. A good stock of wine.

$ Jaime Vivas
C San Antonio, T0212-763 4761.
The place for hearty local Caracas food, especially *pabellón.* Simple, no frills, and a bit dated, but maintains loyal clientele.

Chuao/Las Mercedes
The area has a good selection of upmarket restaurants and US-style steakhouses and chains.

$$$ Astrid y Gaston
Londres entre Av Caroní y Nueva York, T0212-993 1119, Las Mercedes, www.astridygaston.com.ve.
High-end Peruvian restaurant, one of the finest in Caracas, serving traditionally flavoured seafood and specials like rabbit and kid.

$$ Coco Thai and Lounge
CC Tolón, piso 3, Las Mercedes.
Excellent Thai, Vietnamese, and Japanese cuisine, including tasty chicken in coconut curry, duck spring rolls and sashimi. Excellent presentation and flavours, great ambience, open-air terrace and striking eastern decor.

$$ La Castañuela
C Trinidad con C París.
Good paella and seafood in generous portions. Popular and festive at weekends with live music and dancing. Attentive service.

$$ La Montanara
C Caroní con Madrid, Las Mercedes, T0212-991 2812.
An authentic Italian trattoria (some say the best in the city) and one of the most popular restaurants in the district. Great atmosphere, often buzzing and full with diners, so be prepared to wait.

$$ Mokambo
C Madrid con Monterrey, Las Mercedes, T0212-991 2577.

A pleasant brunch, lunch and dinner spot frequented by well-to-do crowds. They serve creative Mediterranean cuisine.

Altamira, La Castellana

$$$ Aprile
4 Av con 5 Transversal, Altamira, T0212-264 5775.
Upscale and fashionable Italian restaurant serving ceviche, pastas, steak and fries. Smart interior, cosmopolitan vibe. Reservations a must.

$$ Chez Wong
Edif IASA, Plaza La Castellana, T0212-266 5015, www.chezwong.com.ve.
Creative and unconventional Chinese food, including good dim sum and Peking duck. Minimalist decor.

$$ El Alazán
Av Luis Roche, entre 5 y 6 Transversal, Altamira, T285 0275.
Carnivores should not miss this place, one of the best places in Caracas to enjoy a slab of prime beef. Big, noisy, popular and an institution for 3 decades. Good wines.

Los Palos Grandes

$$ Amapola
1 Av entre 1 y 2 Transversal, T0212-283 3680.
Creative Venezuelan dishes handed down by Grandmother and an imaginative use of local flavours. Bright, light decor and an outdoor terrace.

$$ Avila Burger
6 Transversal entre 3 y 4, Cuadra Gastronómica, www.avilaburger.com.
Buzzing gourmet burger joint with an enticing array of hearty options. Fun and casual.

$$ Catar
Cuadra Gastronómica, 6 Transversal, T0212-285 0649. Closed Mon.
Relaxed, stylish café/restaurant with an eclectic menu. Try the delicious thin crust pizzas and a melt-in-the-mouth chocolate pudding. Good selection for vegetarians. Several other good restaurants in this gastronomic block.

$$ Come a Casa
1 Av con 1 Transversal, T0212-283 1707.
Low-key Sicilian-style trattoria serving wholesome home-cooked pasta. Cosy atmosphere and outdoor terrace.

$ Arepa Factory Tradicional
2 Transversal entre Av Andrés Bello y 2 Av, T0212-285 1125.
Don't be put off by the name, this fast-food joint serves Venezuelan gourmet *arepas* with sophisticated fillings.

$ El Presidente
3 Av entre 1 y 2 Transversal.
An unpretentious local institution serving wholesome home-cooked fare. Ideal for a quick lunch.

Cafés and bakeries

Arabica Coffee Bar
Av Andrés Bello con 1 Transversal, T0212-283 7024.
Good Venezuelan coffee with great pastries, the best *empanadas* in the city. Small and cosy.

Miga's
Av Luis Roche con 1 Transversal, opposite Altamira Suites Hotel, www.migas.com.ve.
Busy café/bakery/deli chain with a dozen or so outlets selling fresh breads, cakes, salads, sandwiches and meat dishes, some vegetarian options, open late. OK, convenient, nothing special.

St Honoré
1 Transversal con Av Andrés Bello, T0212-286 7982, www.sthonore.com.ve.
Popular café and bakery with covered terrace, good for lunch. Some of the best bread in town, often recommended.

Bars and clubs

Caracas has a vibrant nightlife. Clubs don't usually come to life until after 2300, and then go on to the early hours. Las Mercedes district is full of busy, trendy bars. Always take care when leaving in the small hours.

Bars

360° Rooftop Bar
19th floor of Altamira Suites Hotel, 1 Av, Los Palos Grandes.
Hip, sophisticated wine bar with panaromic views of the city, snack on pizza or sushi and sip delicious cocktails. A must just for the views.

Centro Comercial San Ignacio
See Shopping, opposite.
Has many fashionable, though pricey bars and the occasional nightclubs, popular with wealthy young Venzuelans. Try **Whisky Bar** (Nivel Blandín), usually packed, trendy and friendly crowd, long bar with terrace area, open daily. Or **Suka** (Nivel Blandín) with giant hammock and good cocktails.

Clubs

El Maní es Así
Av Fco Solano y C El Cristo, Sabana Grande, T0212-763 6671, www.elmaniesasi.com. Tue-Sun till 0400/0500.
Famous for its live salsa and dancing, casual.

Juan Sebastián Bar
Av Venezuela entre C Sorocaima y C Mohedano, El Rosal, T0212-951 0595. Closed Sun.
Caracas' temple of jazz, live music.

Moulin Rouge
Av Fco Solano, Sabana Grande.
Club famous for its live rock music.

Entertainment

For details of cinemas and other events, see the newspapers, *El Universal* (the cinema page on www.el-universal.com has full listings) and *El Nacional.*

Ateneo de Caracas, *Av La Salle, Quinta La Colina, Colinas de Los Caobos.* Concerts, ballet, theatre and film festivals.
Centro de Acción Social para la Música, *Blv Amador Bendayán de Quebrada Honda, Los Caobos (metro Colegio de Ingenieros).* Concert hall built for the Youth and Children's Orchestras of Venezuela. See the web page of *El Sistema* (FundaMusical Bolívar) for forthcoming concerts and events www.fundamusical.org.ve.
Centro de Estudios Latinoamericanos Rómulo Gallegos (CELARG), *Av Luis Roche con 3ra Transversal, Altamira, T0212-285 2721, www.celarg.org.ve.* Cultural centre with cinema showing alternative films, theatre, exhibitions, talks.
Trasnocho Cultural, *Urb Las Mercedes, Centro Comercial Paseo Las Mercedes, Nivel Trasnocho, T0212-993 1910, www. trasnochocultural.com.* Theatre, cinemas, exhibitions, lounge bar with live DJs Thu-Sat, bookshop, café and yoga centre.

Shopping

Chocolate

Blue Moon, *C La Paz, Plaza de El Hatillo, T0212-963 3023, www. bluemoonchocolates.com.* Divine chocolatier with small café selling hot chocolate mixes.
La Praline Chocolatier, *Av Andrés Bello con 3ra Transversal, Los Palos Grandes, T0212-284 7986, www.lapraline.com. ve.* Ultimate heaven for chocaholics, delicious chocolates crafted from Venezuelan cacao. The packets of hot chocolate make great gifts.

Handicrafts

Good-quality Sun craft market between Museo de Bellas Artes and Museo de Historia Natural (metro Bellas Artes).
Hannsi, *C Bolívar, El Hatillo, T0212-963 5577, www.hannsi.com.ve.* A superstore of Venezulean crafts and products made up of numerous small rooms.

Malls

Most shopping takes place in Caracas' numerous malls, such as **Centro Sambil** (Av Libertador, 1 block south of Chacao Metro), one of the largest in South America; **CC El Recreo** (Av Casanova y El Recreo, Sabana Grande); **CC Tolon** and **Paseo Las Mercedes** (both on Av Principal de Las Mercedes), and the exclusive **San Ignacio** (several blocks north of Chacao Metro).

Markets

Mercado de Chacao, *Av Avila, 3 blocks north of Chacao metro. Daily except Sun 0800-1200.* Good food, fruit and veg market.
Mercado Peruano, *Colegio de Ingenieros metro, Blv Amador Bendayán. From 0900*

on Sun. Popular small Peruvian food market with ceviche stalls.

Mercado Quinta Crespo, *off Av Baralt, El Silencio metro. Daily.* One of the largest central food markets, shabby but vibrant.

What to do

Baseball

The popular baseball season is from late Sep to Jan. The capital's local team, Los Leones del Caracas, plays at the Estadio Universitario, Los Chaguaramos. Tickets can be bought at the stadium's box office, www.leones.com.

Tour operators

Akanan, *C Bolívar, Edf Grano de Oro, pb loc C, Chacao, T0212-264 2769, www. akanan.com.* Excellent and professionally managed ecotour operator with an emphasis on nature and adventure with riding, cycling, climbing, rafting, hiking and other outdoor activities outside Caracas. Small groups, personalized service and years of experience working with documentary film crews. Recommended.

Alborada Venezuela, *Plaza La Castellana, Torre IASA, oficina 101, T0212-263 1820, www.alboradavenezuela.com.* Tours focusing on nature conservation, also specialist interest, adventure trips and tours beyond Venezuela.

Alpiviajes, *Av Sucre, Centro Parque Boyacá, Torre Centro, Los Dos Caminos, T0212-285 0410, www.alpiviajes.com.* Tours throughout Venezuela, including fishing trips and adventure sports, English spoken, good for flights and advice. Flying safari tours in private plane. Recommended.

Ascanio Birding Tours, *Apartado Postal 78006, La Urbina 1074 Caracas, T0212-242 4949, www.abtbirds.com.* Specialists in birdwatching tours in Venezuela and neighbouring countries.

Candes Turismo, *Av Francisco de Miranda, Edif Roraima, p 3, of 3C, T0212-953 1632, www.candesturismo.com.* Well-established tour operator, range of destinations, helpful, efficient, English, Italian, German spoken.

Cóndor Verde, *Av Caura, Torre Humboldt, M 3, Prados del Este, T0212-655 0101, www.condorverdetravel.com.* Operate throughout the country, well-established, German-run.

Kayaman, *T0414-124 2725, www. kayaman.com.* Dedicated to kayaking, courses and construction. See related company, **Rafting Barinas**, page 94.

Natoura Travel & Adventure Tours, *T0274-252 4216 (in US T303-800 4639), www.natoura.com.* Tailor-made tours throughout Venezuela. Specialists in adventure tours and ecotourism. See also page 78.

Osprey Travel, *Av Casanova, Sabana Grande, 2 Av de Bello Monte, Edif La Paz, p 5, of 51, T0414-310 4491, www. ospreyexpeditions.com.* Tours in Venezuela (also Colombia and Panama), diving, language courses, advice from English speaking staff. Office opens by appointment. Recommended.

Tucaya, *Quinta Santa Marta, 1 Av Urb Campo Claro, Los Dos Caminos, T0212-234 9401, www.tucaya.com.* Small company with good reputation, popular with French speakers.

Venezuela X, *T0414-255 1591, www. venezuelax.com.* Adventure tours of all types, on land, water and in the air, for all levels. Have a base camp south of Barinas for rafting, trekking and mountain-biking trips, T0273-400 3625.

Transport

Air

The **airport** for international and domestic flights, Maiquetía (*www.aeropuerto-maiquetia.com.ve*) is 28 km from Caracas near the port of La Guaira, and has 2 terminals   Maiquetía (national) and Simón Bolívar (international), 5 mins apart via an a/c walkway from international to national, but an open-air sidewalk from national to international (less secure after dark). International passengers must check in at least 3 hrs before departure or they may lose their seat. National flights need 2 hrs check in. Always allow plenty of time to get to the airport as the route can be very congested (minimum 30 mins, up to 2-3 hrs in heavy traffic). It is unsafe to travel between Maiquetía and the city in the hours of darkness, so for evening or pre-dawn flights, it is recommended you stay in one of the hotels near the airport (see Litoral Central listings, below; taxi from the airport BsF 60-90).

Taxis are the safest form of transport to and from the airport. It is best not to arrive at the airport without having pre-arranged a pick up. There have been incidents of foreigners getting taken in what seem to be marked taxis, only to be driven off, robbed and left in the middle of nowhere. If the hotel does not have its own taxis, ask them to contact a driver. On no account go with one of the freelance or unlicensed drivers who crowd the terminal. Official taxis are all black with a yellow logo and from 4 companies   Astrala, Taxi Tours, Taxib and Utac. You buy tickets from official counters and will be accompanied to the taxi by a member of staff. Double check the driver's ID. The fare varies depending on time of day and district, BsF 270-330

Tip...
In both terminals, many people offer to change money on the black market. There is no way of knowing if they are trustworthy.

(US$1.40-1.70 at Simadi rate – fares given on *www.aeropuerto-maiquetia.com.ve*). There is also the private firm, **Taxi to Caracas**, *www.taxitocaracas.com*.

Airport **shuttle buses** are run by **Sitssa** (*T0212-242 0212/0800-748772, www.sitssa.gob.ve*) from national terminal, level 2, to the Alba Caracas Hotel, 0600-1900, BsF 40 (US$0.20). Also **UCAMC**, from the national terminal exit. If heading for a hotel in Chacao or Altamira on arrival, get off at Gato Negro metro station (same fare) and take metro from there (with luggage only at off-peak times). To get to the airport, catch the shuttle buses under the flyover at Bolívar and Av Sur 17, Parque Central, 250 m from Bellas Artes metro (poorly lit at night, not safe to wait here in the dark), or at metro stations such as Parque Central and Gato Negro. (Watch your belongings around Gato Negro.) The service runs 0500-2200, every 30 mins, 1-2 hrs, depending on traffic. An alternative is to take a bus to Catia La Mar (US$0.15) and get out at the airport. Taxis remain the best and safest option, however.

Bus

Local TransMetrópoli buses (*www.transmetropoli.com.ve*) run on 23 routes mostly from El Silencio or Chacaíto to the suburbs, 0500-2100; they have wheelchair access. Also being introduced is a mass transport system, **BusCaracas**, using magnetic cards, single journey BsF4. Regular buses are overcrowded in rush hour and charge extra after 2100. Bus tickets cost BsF4. Por puesto minibuses, known as *busetas*, *carmelitas* or *carritos* run on regular routes; fares depend on the distance travelled within the city.

Long distance Always take identification when booking a long-distance journey. Times and fares of buses are given under destinations. The Terminal Oriente at Guarenas for eastern destinations is clean, modern and relatively safe. It can be reached by numerous buses from the city centre and Petare. Take a taxi at night.

The La Bandera terminal for all western destinations is a 500 m, unsafe walk from La Bandera metro station on Line 3. City buses that pass are prominently marked 'La Bandera'. Give yourself plenty of time to find the bus you need although there are bus agents who will assist in finding a ticket for your destination. Tickets are sold in advance except for nearby destinations such as **Maracay** and **Valencia**. Those first on get the best seats so it is advisable to arrive an hour before departure. There is a left luggage office, cash machines, restaurant and many food and drink kiosks.

The more upscale **Aeroexpresos Ejecutivos** (*Av Principal De Bello Campo, Quinta Marluz, Bello Campo, Chacao, T0212-266 2321, www.aeroexpresos.com.ve*) (timetables and prices available online), a private bus company, runs regular services to Barquisimeto, Maracaibo, Maracay, Maturín and Valencia. Prices are more expensive than others, but worth it for the more comfortable and modern buses and for the extra security. Other good companies are **Peli Express**, *Corredor Vial Parque del Este, Los Dos Caminos* (to Puerto La Cruz, Barinas, El Vigia, Mérida, Coro, Punto Fijo and

Maracaibo); and **Rodovías**, 150-m walk from metro station *Colegio de Ingenieros, Galpon Terminal Rodovías, Local Pc 7-A, Urb Los Caobos, www.rodovias.com.ve* (to the east, Valencia and Maracaibo). **Sitssa**, see above, also runs nationwide bus services – see website for prices.

Buses to places near Caracas leave from the old Nuevo Circo bus station (eg **Los Teques** – US$0.15, **Higuerote** – US$0.25, **Catia La Mar**, **La Guaira**).

Car
Car hire Self-drive cars are available at both terminals of the airport (offices daily 0700-2100) and in town. Some companies also have counters at major hotels.

Metro
The metro (*www. metrodecaracas. com.ve*) operates 0530-2300. No smoking, no heavy luggage. The lines are **Line 1** (west–east) from Propatria to Palo Verde; **Line 2** (north–south), from El Silencio to Las Adjuntas, with connection to Caricuao and Zoológico and a continuation from Las Adjuntas to Los Teques (Alí Primera); **Line 3**, south from Plaza Venezuela via El Valle to La Rinconada; **Line 4**, extending Line 2 west–east from Capuchinos to Plaza Venezuela/ Zona Rental. **Line 5**, running east through Las Mercedes to Warairarepano, is being built. **Line 6**, from Zoológico to La Rinconada is planned. **Line 7** is a bus route from Las Flores via La Hoyada and La Bandera to Los Ilustres.

A single ticket costs BsF4, BsF8 return, whereas a 10-journey (*multi abono*) ticket is BsF54. Student discounts are

> **Tip...**
>
> There's a good selection of transport maps at shops in Altamira and La California stations.

available with ISIC card; apply at Parque del Este station. There are also *Metrotarjetas* (pre-paid cards) for 20, 30 and 40 trips. Metrobuses connect with the Metro system get transfer tickets (*boleto integrado*, BsF6) for services to southern districts, route maps displayed at stations; retain ticket after exit turnstile. Metrobuses are modern, comfortable, recommended but infrequent. Metrocable systems run from Parque Central (Line 4) to San Agustín barrio, from Petare to La Cruz del Morro and from Palo Verde to Mariche and to La Dolorita . Another cable will soon run from Petare to Warairarepano.

Taxi

Even though they are a legal requirement, meters are never used. Negotiate fares in advance; always offer 10% less than the driver's first quote and bargain hard. Taxi drivers are authorized to charge an extra 20% on night trips after 1800, on Sun and all holidays, and extra for answering telephone calls. After 1800 drivers are selective about destinations. Beware of taxi drivers trying to renegotiate fixed rates because your destination is in 'a difficult area'. See warning above under Air about pirate taxis from the airport. See also under Air (or in Yellow Pages) for radio taxis.

> **Tip...**
>
> Never tell a driver it's your first visit to Caracas.

Around Caracas

great escapes from the urban sprawl

Between the capital and the Caribbean coast is the national park of Waraira Repano, not only a popular recreational area for caraqueños, but also a refuge for wildlife within earshot of the city and a good place for birdwatching and hiking. The coast itself is also a favourite weekend escape, although it can get busy. Nor, at weekends, can you expect to have Colonia Tovar to yourself; it's a German immigrant town to which city folk flock for the local produce and mild climate.

Parque Nacional Waraira Repano and Monte Avila

Inparques, Av F de Miranda, Parque Generalísimo Francisco de Miranda (opposite Parking 2), Caracas, T0212-273 2807, www.inparques.gob.ve. Closed Mon and Tue morning.

The 85,192-ha **Parque Nacional Waraira Repano** (formerly **El Avila**) forms the northern boundary of Caracas. The green slopes rise steeply from both the city and from the central Caribbean coast. Despite being so close to the capital, fauna includes red howler monkeys, jaguar and puma. There are also several species of poisonous snake. Access is from Caracas, with several marked entrances along the Cota Mil (Avenida Boyacá), designed for hikers.

A **cable railway**, the Teleférico Warairarepano ① *Final Av Principal de Maripérez (Simón Rodríguez), T0212-901 5555 or 793 5960, www.ventel.gob.ve, Tue 1200-2100, Wed-Thu 1030-0200, Sat 0900-0200, Sun 0830-2100, foreigners US$1.10, Venezuelans US$1, students with card, children 4-12, over 60s and disabled US$0.30; take a taxi from Colegio de Ingenieros metro station*, runs up to Monte El Avila (2175 m).

The 20-minute ride offers fantastic views of Caracas on clear days and is highly recommended. Courting couples wander the restaurant, food stalls and skating rink at El Avila station on the summit. From here you can look down the other side of Monte Avila over the village of Galipán all the way to the Caribbean Sea. The **Humboldt Hotel** on the summit has been refurbished and is open for guided tours but not yet for sleeping.

If you're not taking the cable car, El Avila station can also be reached in 45 minutes by shared 4WD *carritos* that leave regularly from the entrance to the park at San Bernardino (on the edge of sketchy barrios, take care). Alternatively, trucks leave from the **Avila** hotel, about US$1 per person. A recommended trip is to ride up in a vehicle and hike back down (note that it is cold at the summit, around 13°C, take a sweater).

From El Avila station you can take a 4WD *carrito* to the village of Galipán, www.galipan.net, founded by Spanish immigrants from the Canary Islands and today a popular weekend excursion for *caraqueños*. The village has plenty of good restaurants serving excellent pork sandwiches and rich hot chocolate, as well as stone-built cabins and stalls selling strawberries and cream, jams and flowers. There are posadas for overnight stays. Also worth visiting is the old coffee hacienda **Los Venados** ⓘ *Senderos Aéreos, T0424-200 6169, www.senderosaereos. com, Thu-Sun 0900-1530 (Sat-Sun only in low season)*, where there are picnic areas and a **zip-wire** (known as 'canopy').

Hiking in the national park

Hikers should go in groups of at least three, for mountain and personal safety. If you want to camp, inform any Puesto de Guardaparques of your route, where you intend to stay and get their permission; also leave a mobile phone number with them. Always take water and something for the cold at altitude. The unfit should not attempt any of the hikes.

Pico Naiguatá (2765 m) This is a very strenuous hike. Take the metro to La California, then a bus going up Avenida Sanz, ask for the Centro Comercial El Marqués. From there walk up Avenida Sanz towards Cota Mil (Avenida Boyacá), about four blocks. At the end of Avenida Sanz, underneath the bridge, is the entrance to the Naiguatá trail. In about 40 minutes you reach La Julia *guardaparques* station.

Pico Oriental (2600 m) From the Altamira metro station take a bus to 'La entrada de Sabas Nieves', where the **Tarzilandia** restaurant is. From here a dirt road leads up to the **Sabas Nieves** *guardaparques* station, a steep 20- to 40-minute hike with good views of the city, popular with keep-fit *caraqueños*. The path to Pico Oriental starts at the back of Sabas Nieves and is extremely easy to follow. **Note** Paths beyond Sabas Nieves are shut in dry season (roughly February-June depending on the year) to prevent forest fires.

Hotel Humboldt (2150 m) This is a relatively easy route of three hours. Take the Metro bus from Bellas Artes station to El Avila stop; opposite is a grocery. Turn the

Black Forest Ghetto

Venezuela's devastating War of Independence left a chronic shortage of farm labour to work the land. In response to the problem, immigration laws were amended to attract farmers from Europe. So, with the financial backing of Don Martín Tovar, a wealthy creole landowner, 392 men, women and children from the Black Forest community of Kaiserstuhl set sail for Venezuela.

Instrumental in the settlement's success were Agustín Codazzi, an Italian geographer, and his map maker Alexander Benitz, a young engraver from Kaiserstuhl. They had already visited Venezuela to scout for possible sites, returning to France to sign up the land-hungry peasants and craftsmen. They also hired the emigrants' ship and bought food and equipment – including a printing press and sawmill. On 11 January 1843, Codazzi and Benitz set sail from Le Havre with the 392 hopeful emigrants.

Things soon went badly wrong. Over 100 lives were lost to smallpox during the long voyage and when the vessel finally reached Venezuelan shores, it was quarantined for three weeks, after which it was allowed to land near Choroní. From there, the intrepid settlers dragged all their gear up the mountains and down to Maracay, where they were greeted by the then president, General José Antonio Páez. Then began the long, arduous trek up to present-day Tovar, where they finally arrived, depleted and exhausted, on 8 April.

The colony was self-sufficient, with its own typesetters, carpenters, blacksmith, shoemaker, baker, tailor, barrel-maker, teacher, priest and brewer (who produced the first beer in Venezuela). They set about recreating their Black Forest community in complete isolation, eating traditional food, drinking their own beer, keeping up their customs and traditions and marrying off their blond-haired children to one another. The colonists themselves worsened their isolation by banishing members who married Venezuelans. This led to inbreeding, cultural poverty and an increase in illiteracy.

For almost exactly a century, they survived in their remote mountain home, untouched by the outside world. Then, in 1942, Colonia Tovar became a township, Spanish became the official language and residents were free to marry whom they pleased. Finally, with the opening of a paved road to Caracas in 1963, Tovar's stubborn isolation ended. Curious caraqueños came on weekend trips and Tovar's residents travelled to Caracas to sell their local fruits and beer. With the outside contact, the German language began slowly to disappear. There is still a preponderance of fair-haired, light-skinned residents but their grandchildren have dark hair and Spanish names. The once-traditional costumes are now worn for the benefit of tourists rather than through a determination to preserve local customs.

Colonia Tovar is said to have been the inspiration for Isabel Allende's fictional backwater, Agua Santa, in her best-selling novel Eva Luna, which she corner and walk two blocks up towards the mountain. At the top of the street turn left; almost immediately on your right is the park entrance. **Note** This area is not safe before 0800 or after dark. Plenty of people take this route, starting 0830-0900, giving enough time to get up and down safely and in comfort.

Litoral Central

The Litoral Central is the name given to the stretch of Caribbean Coast directly north of Caracas. A paved road runs east from Catia La Mar, past the airport and then through the towns of Maiquetía, **La Guaira**, Venezuela's main port, dating back to 1567, and Macuto. This became the state of Vargas in January 1999 and in December that year was the focus of Venezuela's worst natural disaster of the 20th century. Prolonged heavy rains on deforested hillsides caused flash floods and landslides, killing an estimated 30,000 people, many of whose bodies were never recovered, and leaving 400,000 homeless. From La Guaira a panoramic road runs to the beaches at Chichiriviche de la Costa, Puerto Cruz (nice beach, no shade, bars) and Puerto Maya (very nice beach with shade and services).

Colonia Tovar
1½ hrs from Caracas on Ruta 4, www.colonia-tovar.com.

This picturesque mountain town was founded in 1843 by German immigrants from Kaiserstuhl in the Black Forest; a small **museum** ⓘ *Sat, Sun and hols 0800-1800*, tells the history of the founding pioneers. They retained their customs and isolation until a paved road reached the settlement in 1963. It is now very touristy, attracting hordes of weekend visitors, but the blond hair, blue eyes and Schwartzwald-accented German of the inhabitants remain, as do many traditions and dances. Local produce includes breads, blackberry jam, bratwurst and beer. Colonia Tovar offers delightful landscapes, a mild climate, old architecture and dignified hospitality in its many restaurants, cafés and hotels. However, the winding drive up from Caracas on Ruta 4, through La Yaguara, El Junquito and the Parque Nacional Macarao, is murder (up to four hours) at weekends, with long traffic jams, few picnic spots and little accommodation.

Listings Around Caracas

Where to stay

Litoral Central
If you're arriving or leaving the airport at odd times, there are some good choices in Catia La Mar and Macuto as an alternative to Caracas. These places often provide free transfers, or a taxi costs about US$4, 5-20 mins depending on traffic.

$$$ Express Maiquetía
Av La Armada, T0212-700 0781, www. hoteleuro.com.
Useful business hotel with pool, tennis, airport transfer.

$$$-$$ Olé Caribe
Final Av Intercomunal, El Playón, 1160, Macuto, T0212-620 2000, www.hotelolecaribe.com.
A good, if expensive bet near the airport, safe in room, breakfast, pool.

$ Buena Vista Inn
Av el Hotel y C 4, Qta Buenavista Inn, Urb Playa Grande, Catia la Mar, T0212- 352 9163, http://buenavistainn.com.ve.
Convenient for airport, pick-up extra.

$ Catimar
Urb Puerto Viejo Av Principal, Catia La Mar, T0212-351 7906, www.hotelcatimar.com.
Price includes transfers to and from airport (you may have to phone them from Asistencia al usuario desk), nice bar, restaurant, basic rooms, expensive for what's offered. Near small Puerto Viejo beach, said to be safe, with a few restaurants (**Brisas del Mar, Puerto Mar**), snack bar.

$ Posada Doña Alcinda
Av Principal La Atlántida C 7, T0212-619 1605, www.posadaalcinda.com.
Suites and standard rooms, bar, airport transfer, diving courses and other activities can be arranged.

$ Posada Il Prezzano
Av Principal de Playa Grande c/c 5, Catia La Mar, T0212-351 2626, www.ilprezzano.com.
Italian-run, spotless, pleasant, good value, restaurant.

$ Santiago
Av La Playa, Urb Alamo, Macuto, T0212-213 3500, www.hotelsantiago.com.ve.
Comfortable, restaurant with live music, pool, secure parking, 15 mins' drive to airport.

Restaurants

Parque Nacional Waraira Repano

$$$ Casa Pakea
Ctra San Antonio de Galipán, Sector Manzanares (a la derecha de la Rosa Mística), T0212-415 5353.
Special transport from **Hotel Avila**, San Bernardino, or from the cable car station in Galipán. Fabulous restaurant in a wonderful location at the top of Monte Avila, traditional Basque food.

$$$ La Galipanier
Galipán, T0414-249 1978, www.legalipanier.com.
Hot soups and Swiss-style fondues. A bit classy and a very romantic setting overlooking the valley.

Transport

Colonia Tovar
Travelling to Colonia Tovar is definitely not recommended at weekends, although it is generally easy to get a lift if there are no buses.

Bus Take the metro to **La Yaguara** and from there take a *por puesto* to **El Junquito** (1 hr if no traffic, US$0.50), then change for **Colonia Tovar** (1 hr, US$0.50). Last public transport back to Caracas 1800, later at weekends.

West from
Caracas

The Central Highlands run through this varied region. North of the highlands is the Caribbean, with secluded coves and popular resorts, such as Puerto Colombia. Straddling the mountains is the birders' paradise of Parque Nacional Henri Pittier. Two coastal national parks, Morrocoy, which lies offshore, and Los Médanos, around the old city of Coro, are further highlights of this area. West of Coro is the city and lake of Maracaibo; for most Venezuelans this region is summed up in three letters – oil. For others, it can be summed up in four letters – heat. Both are certainly true. To the south, though, are the eastern extremities of the Andean mountain chain, with quaint villages, lakes and high passes on the way to the Sierra Nevada de Mérida.

Best for
Beaches ▪ Birdwatching ▪ Colonial towns

Maracay is a hot, thriving industrial city and is the gateway to Henri Pittier National Park. The city has some pleasant leafy residential neighbourhoods and is the centre of an important agricultural area.

Maracay

In its heyday Maracay was the favourite city of Gen Juan Vicente Gómez (dictator, 1909-1935) and some of his most fantastic whims are still there. **Jardín Las Delicias** ① Av Las Delicias, en route to Choroní; take an Ocumare bus from terminal, with its beautiful zoological garden (closed Monday), park and fountain, was built for his revels. The heart of the city is **Plaza Girardot**, on which stands the attractive, white **Cathedral**, dating back almost to the city's foundation in 1701. There is an interesting collection of prehispanic artefacts in the **Museo de Antropología e Historia** ① South side of the plaza, T0243-447 2521, Tue-Sun 0800-1200, 1400-1800, free. The opposite end of the same building has rooms dedicated to Gómez and Bolívar. **Plaza Bolívar**, said to be the largest such-named plaza in Latin America, is 500 m east. The **Museo Aeronáutico de las Fuerzas Aéreas Venezolanas** ① Av Las Delicias con Av 19 de Abril, 1 block from Plaza Bolívar, T0243-233 3812, Sat-Sun 0900-1700, has an interesting collection of aircraft and memorabilia. The **San José festival** is on 16-25 March.

★Parque Nacional Henri Pittier

A land of steep, lush, rugged hills and tumbling mountain streams, the 107,800-ha park rises from sea-level in the north to 2430 m at Pico Cenizo, descending to 450 m towards the Lago de Valencia. Named after Swiss conservationist and engineer Henri Pittier, the park was established in 1937 and is the oldest in the country. Estimates of bird species range from 20 to 50 (about 42% of all species in Venezuela), including seven different eagles and eight kites. The park extends from the north of Maracay to the Caribbean and south to the valleys of Aragua. The dry season is December to March and the rainy season (although still

Parque Nacional Henri Pittier

agreeable) is April to November. The variation in altitude produces a great range of vegetation, including impressive lower and upper cloud forests and bamboo.

Two paved roads cut through the Park. The Ocumare (western) road climbs to the 1128-m-high Portachuelo pass, guarded by twin peaks (38 km from Maracay). At the pass is Rancho Grande, the uncompleted palace/hotel Gómez was building when he died (in a state of disrepair) and the **Estación Biológica Alberto F Yépez** ⓘ *bioestacion@gmail.com*. It is close to the bird migratory routes; September and October are the best months. There are many trails in the vicinity. Permits to visit the park, walk the trails or stay at the station are available from the offices at the Facultad de Agronomía, Universidad Central de Venezuela, Maracay campus.

Aragua Coast

To Cata and Cuyagua The road to the coast from Rancho Grande goes through **Ocumare de la Costa** (population 10,405, 48 km from Maracay), to **La Boca de Ocumare** and **El Playón** (hotels and restaurants at both places). The road is very busy at weekends. Some 20 minutes west by boat is **La Ciénaga**, a pretty place that has little shade. A few kilometres east is **Bahía de Cata**, now overdeveloped, particularly at the west end. The smaller beach at **Catita** is reached by fishing boat ferries (10 minutes, US$0.50), or a 20-minute walk, tricky over rocks at the start. In Cata town (5 km inland) is the small colonial church of San Francisco; devil dancers here fulfil an ancient vow by dancing non-stop through the morning of 27 July each year. **Cuyagua** beach, unspoilt, is 23 km further on at the end of the road. It has good surfing but dangerous rips for swimmers. There are devil dancers here too, on movable date in July/August.

To Choroní

The second twisty and narrow (eastern) road through the Parque Nacional Henri Pittier is spectacular and goes over a more easterly pass (1830 m), to **Santa Clara de Choroní**, a small colonial town with attractive, pastel single-storey houses. The **Fiesta de San Juan** on 31 May is worth seeing. Choroní is a good base for walking, with many opportunities for exploring the unmarked trails, some originating in picturesque spots such as the river pools (*pozos*) of El Lajao (beware of the dangerous whirlpool) and Los Colores, 6 km above Choroní. Other recommended *pozos* are La Virgen, 10 km from Choroní, and La Nevera, 11 km away.

> **Tip...**
>
> There are no ATMs in Choroní or Puerto Colombia and credit cards are accepted by very few places. Take enough cash. The nearest banks and Italcambio (www.italcambio. com) are in Maracay.

☆Puerto Colombia and around

Just beyond Choroní is the popular fishing village of **Puerto Colombia**, a laid-back place with several narrow streets lined with colonial buildings. During high season, its small main bay attracts arts and crafts sellers. It is a good place to stay and spend a couple of days beach-hopping with boat rides to different bays. Five minutes' walk across the river lies Puerto Colombia's main attraction; the dazzling long stretch

Chocolate money

The Aragua coast was developed by the Spanish as a major centre of cacao production. The indigenous cacao plant thrived in the warm coastal valleys and the unusually sweet Venezuelan cacao enjoyed an enviable reputation. Trade at first was mostly with the protected market of Mexico but Dutch traders were soon willing to pay even higher prices as they sought to establish their reputation as producers of superior chocolate.

The cacao boom which began in the mid-17th century not only boosted the economic importance of Caracas but also reinforced the wealth and power of a tiny landowning oligarchy. This elite, known as the *gran cacao*, spent lavishly on imported luxury goods from Europe and enjoyed a hectic social whirl of cultural events. At the same time, the black slaves, on whose backs the prosperity of the gran cacao was built, lived in grinding poverty.

The independence wars and the instability which followed ended the cacao boom as the plantations fell into neglect. At the same time, tastes were changing in Europe, where coffee was replacing cocoa as the favourite drink.

of white beach known as Playa Grande, lined with palm trees beneath mountains. There is a row of good fish restaurants at the beach entrance. At weekends drummers drum and dancers gyrate and the beach gets crowded with campers and families. At other times it's more peaceful, with brightly painted fishing boats (available for hire) and frigate birds wheeling overhead. If swimming, beware the strong undertow. There are public showers at the entrance.

A very bumpy, 30-minute boat ride east goes to **Cepe**, another beautiful long beach with good swimming, popular with campers. Boats usually take six to 10 people. From the beach, there is a delightful 25-minute walk to **Pueblo de Cepe** through the Henri Pittier park. Several places on the beach serve fish, salad and *tostones*. Most locals bring their own supplies in the obligatory beer cooler. From the beautiful unspoiled beach there are fishing and scuba diving trips. The latter, with guide and equipment, explore the only bit of coral on this stretch of the coast. At Cepe's west end, you can climb the hill and descend to **Playa Escondida**, a deserted but more rocky beach.

Other beaches include to the east, before Cepe, Valle Seco (some shade, natural pool protected by reef) and **Chuao**. To the west are Diario (small, no shade), Aroa (lovely, with river and palms, rough sea but one safe bathing area, no services, take everything with you, three hours' hike from Choroní, go early) and Uricao (also isolated).

Tourist information

Tourist information for the state is provided by **latur** (*Hotel Golf Maracay, Urb Las Delicias, Final Urb Cantarrana, T0243-242 2420*). The municipal website is *www.aragua.gob.ve.*

Where to stay

Maracay
Budget hotels are in streets around Plaza Girardot.

$ Caroní
Ayacucho Norte 197, Bolívar, T0243-554 4465.
Hot showers, comfortable, cheap. Recommended.

$ Mar del Plata
Av Santos Michelena 23, T0243-246 4313, mardelplatahotel@gmail.com.
Central, with hot water, excellent.

$ Posada El Limón
C El Piñal 64, El Limón suburb, near Parque Nacional Henri Pittier, T0243-283 4925, www.posadaellimon.com.
Dutch owned, some way from centre, Caracas airport transfers in good car with English-speaking driver, relaxed and pleasant, family atmosphere, spacious rooms, dorm, laundry, pool, good restaurant, parking, trips to Parque with guide.

$ Princesa Plaza
Av Miranda Este entre Fuerzas Aéreas y Av Bermúdez, T0243-232 0177, www. hotelprincesaplaza.com.ve.
Large commercial hotel, 1 block east of Plaza Bolívar, convenient, inexpensive restaurant.

Aragua Coast
Ocumare de la Costa
Most posadas are in El Playón; websites like www.turismodeplaya. com give a selection. Expect to pay $$-$. Recommendations change annually, but see **Posada Angel** (*www. posadaangelencostadeoro. blogspot. com*) or **Posada La Estancia** (*www. posadalaestancia.com*).

$$-$ De La Costa Eco-Lodge
California 23, T0243-993 1986, www.ecovenezuela.com.
Comfortable, upmarket lodge near beach, with outdoor bar serving food, restaurant, roof terraces with good sea views, pool, landscaped gardens, excursions, equipment hire, specialist bilingual guides. Includes breakfast.

La Ciénaga

$$$ pp Coral Lagoon Lodge
La Ciénaga, T0243-217 7966, www.ecovenezuela.com.
An all-inclusive dive resort accessible only by boat. Beautiful location on waterfront with view of mountains. 6 rooms in 2 cabins sleeping 2-4 people, fans, solar power with back-up generator, rainwater and seawater used. Hammocks, deckchairs, kayaks and snorkelling. Diving with PADI and SSI instructors to underwater grottos, canyons, reefs and wrecks.

Choroní
See **www.choroni.info** for listings and locations of many hotels and posadas.

$$ Hacienda El Portete
C El Cementerio, T0243-219 8861, www.elportetechoroni.com.

Restored cocoa plantation, colonial-style large grounds, pool, restaurant, many children's facilities, excursions.

$$ Hacienda La Aljorra
1 km south in La Loma, T0243-218 8841, laaljorra@hotmail.com.
On roadside, out of town, $ on weekdays, breakfast included, hot water, 300-year-old cacao hacienda in 62 ha of wooded hillside. Large rooms, relaxing and peaceful.

$ Posada Colonial El Picure
C Miranda No 34-A, T0243-991 1296, www.hosteltrail.com/posadaelpicure.
Colonial house in village centre, backs onto river. Popular with travellers, welcoming, 4 dorms and a private room, restaurant with vegetarian options.

Puerto Colombia and around
There are dozens of posadas for all budgets in town, but most are fully booked during high season when prices rise by around 40%.

$$ Hostal Casa Grande 1
Morillo 33, T0243-991 1251, www.hostalcasagrande.com.ve.
One of the best in town, attractive colonial decor, pool, gardens, parking, spa at weekends. Excellent. Also has newer **Casa Grande 2**, same street, with restaurant.

$ Casa Luna
Next to Hostal Colonial, Morillo 35, no obvious sign, T0243-951 5318, www.jungletrip.de.
Colonial house, 4 basic rooms and 1 dorm, fan, shared bath, German and English spoken, tourist information. Ask here for **Casa Nova** and **Posada Alfonso**, both $$-$, most rooms with bath. Tours to Pittier park, diving trips and airport transfers.

$ Costa Brava
Murillo 9, near Malecón, T0243-991 1057, suarezjf@cantv.net.
Cheaper in low season. Basic, cheaper without bath, fans, laundry, good food, parking, English spoken, family run. Recommended.

$ Hostal Vista Mar
C Colón at western end, T0243-991 1250, http://hostalvistamar.net.
On seafront, pleasant, terraces with hammocks, some rooms with sea view, some with a/c, helpful, secure parking.

$ La Posada de Choroní
C Principal, 2 blocks from Malecón, T0243-991 1191, www.laposadadechoroni.3a2.com.
Rooms are cheaper without TV and in low season, hot water, colonial with rooms off central garden, parking.

$ Posada Alonso
Near checkpoint, T0416-546 1412, alons0243@hotmail.com.
Quiet, hammocks, laundry. Recommended.

$ Posada Doña Enriqueta
Color 3, T0243-991 1158, just off the seafront, www.hosteltrail. com/posadadonaenriqueta. 40% discount Mon-Thu
Basic rooms, books tours, helpful.

$ Posada Pittier
On road to Choroní, 10-min walk from Puerto Colombia, T0243-991 1028, www.posadapittier.com.
Small, immaculate rooms, more expensive at weekends, cheaper without breakfast, good meals, helpful, garden. Recommended.

$ Posada Turpial
José Maitin 3, T0243-991 1123,
www.posadaturpial.com.
Colonial house, well-organized, cosy,
attractive, nice atmosphere, good
restaurant, rooms around patio, safety
deposit box, German and English
spoken. Book in advance. Owners run
travel agency www.turpialtravel.com
and organize local tours, dive trips.
Recommended.

$ Hostal Colonial
on Morillo, opposite bus stop,
T0243-431 8757, http://choroni.net.
Popular hostel, good value, with fan,
laundry, German owner. Also good tours
in the Pittier park.
   Camping is possible on Playa Grande,
no permission needed and there are
showers on beach; beware of theft.
Crowded during high season.

Cepe and Chuao
Several posadas in Chuao, but they are
some distance from the beach (those
listed are closer). Camping is permitted
on Chuao and Cepe beaches.

$ El Gran Cacao
200 m up the hill from the port at Chuao,
T0243-872 4680.
Comfortable, with a/c or fan.
Recommended.

$ La Luzonera
On the plaza, T0243-242 1284.
The best of the cheaper options, with
restaurant ($$ half board), also has
2 houses for rent.

$ La Terraza del Morocho
Av Principal Las Tejerías 44, Chuao,
T0414-450 3341.
Helpful, ask about guides for excursions.

Restaurants

Maracay
Many excellent restaurants in the Av
Las Delicias area and a variety of cheap
restaurants in streets around Plazas
Girardot and Bolívar.

Puerto Colombia
Several places in town serve fish
and seafood.

$$-$ Mango
Trino Rangel.
Informal setting in patio, delicious catch
of the day, pastas, vegetarian options,
generous portions. Recommended.

$$-$ Willy
Vía Playa Grande 1, just after bridge
along the river. In low season only opens
Fri-Sun.
Very popular, good seafood and
meat dishes.

What to do

Puerto Colombia
Jungle Trip Choroní, *see Casa Luna,*
Where to stay, above. Good trips in the
national park.
Posada Puerto Escondido, *Cepe, T0243-*
241 2114, www.puertoescondido.com.ve.
Offers courses and trips to a variety of
dive sites.

Transport

Maracay
Bus The bus station is 2 km southeast
of the centre, taxi US$1.50. It has two
sections Terminal Oriente for long
distance and Terminal Nacional for
regional buses. *Por puestos* are marked
'Terminal' for the bus station and
'Centro' for the centre (Plaza Girardot).

To **Maracaibo**, AeroExpresos, US$4.50 (US$2.25 regular). To **Valencia**, US$0.75, 1 hr, and **Caracas**, US$0.65-1.25 by *autobus*, US$2 by *microbus*, 1½-2 hrs. **Mérida** US$2.45-5, 12 hrs; **Ciudad Bolívar**, US$2.65-5, 10 hrs. To **Coro**, US$1.50-4, 7¾ hrs.

Parque Nacional Henri Pittier
Bus Depart from Maracay Terminal; pay full fare to **Ocumare** or hitch from the alcabala at El Limón.

Aragua Coast
Bus From **Maracay** to El Playón, 2-2½ hrs, US$0.50. To **Cata** from El Playón US$0.50 from plaza, from **Ocumare de la Costa** to El Playón, US$0.50.

Choroní
Bus There is a single, new bus station between Choroní and Puerto Colombia, serving both towns. **Maracay–Choroní**, beautiful journey through Henri Pittier park, every 2 hrs from 0630-1700, more at the weekend, US$0.50, 2½-3 hrs. Road congested at holidays and weekends.

Puerto Colombia
Bus From **Maracay** terminal buses leave from platform 5. Buses to Maracay depart every hour 0500-1700, US$2.50, 2-3 hrs.

Taxi From **Maracay** US$3.50 pp, 1-1½ hrs.

Valencia and around

oranges, petroglyphs and beautiful beaches

The great basin in which lie the Lago de Valencia and the industrial town of Valencia is 100 km west of Caracas. The basin, which is only 450 m above sea-level, receives plenty of rain and is one of the most important agricultural areas in the country. Near the city are several groups of petroglyphs while the coast has some very popular beach areas. Best known of these is the Morrocoy national park, but you have to seek out the quiet spots.

Valencia

A road through low hills thickly planted with citrus, coffee and sugar runs 50 km west from Maracay to the valley in which Valencia lies. It is hot and humid with annual rainfall of 914 mm. Like its Spanish namesake, Valencia is famous for its oranges.

Founded in 1555, Valencia is the capital of Carabobo State and Venezuela's third largest city. It's the centre of its most developed agricultural region and the most industrialized. The **Cathedral**, first built in 1580, is on the east side of **Plaza Bolívar**. The statue of the Virgen del Socorro (1550) in the left transept is the most valued treasure; on the second Sunday in November (during the Valencia Fair) it is paraded with a richly jewelled crown. The city's handsome **Plaza de Toros** ① *South end of Av Constitución beyond the ring road*, is the second largest in Latin America after Mexico City (it is also used for shows). The magnificent former **residence of General Páez** ① *Páez y Boyacá, open Tue-Sun at 0900, closed for lunch Tue-Fri and at 1400 Sat-Sun, free*, is now a museum. Páez was the hero of the **Carabobo** battle, the site of which is 30 km southwest of Valencia on the highway to San Carlos (bus from Avenida Bolívar Sur y Calle 75 or Avenida 5 de Julio). The monument surrounded by splendid gardens and the view over the field from the mirador where the Liberator directed the battle in 1814 is impressive. Other attractive buildings are the **Casa de los Celis** (1766) ⓘ *Av Soublette y C Comercio, T617 6867, Tue-Sun 0900-1600*, a well-restored colonial house and National Monument which also houses the **Museo de Arte e Historia**, and the **Casa Estrella** (1766) ⓘ *Av Soublette y C Colombia, Tue-Fri 0900-1700, Sat-Sun from 1000*, now a historical museum and cultural centre. **Tourist office** ⓘ *Sector San José, Centro Comercial y Profesional, Av Bolívar Norte, p 4, of 30 y 32.*

Around Valencia

Most important of the region's petroglyphs can be found at the **Parque Arqueológico Piedra Pintada** (part of Parque Nacional San Esteban), where lines of prehispanic stone slabs, many bearing swirling glyphs, march up the ridges of Cerro Pintado. At the foot of Cerro Las Rosas is the **Museo Parque Arqueológico Piedra Pintada** ⓘ *Sector Tronconero, vía Vigirmia, Guacara, T0416-446 5059, Tue-Sun 0900-1600, free*, has 165 examples of rock art and menhirs (tours, parking, café).

Other extensive ancient petroglyphs have been discovered at **La Taimata** near Güigüe, 34 km east of Valencia on the lake's southern shore. There are more sites on rocks by the Río Chirgua, reached by a 10 km paved road from Highway 11, 50 km west of Valencia. About 5 km past Chirgua, at the **Hacienda Cariaprima**, is a remarkable 35-m-tall geoglyph, a humanoid figure carved into a steep mountain slope at the head of the valley.

Coast north of Valencia

Puerto Cabello, 55 km from Valencia, was one of the most important ports in the colonial Americas, from which produce was transported to the Dutch possessions. Puerto Cabello has retained its maritime importance and is Venezuela's key port. Plaza Bolívar and the colonial part of town are by the waterfront promenade at Calle 24 de Julio.

To the east is **Bahía de Patanemo**, a beautiful, tranquil horseshoe-shaped beach shaded by palms. It has three main sectors, Santa Rita, Los Caneyes and Patanemo itself, with the village proper, further from the beach than the other two. All three have lodging, but it may be difficult to find meals midweek (try at posadas). Offshore is the lovely **Isla Larga** (no shade or facilities), best reached by boat from Quizandal, 15 minutes. There are several cafés along the beachfront. Nearby are two sunken wrecks that attract divers. From Puerto Cabello, take a *por puesto* from the terminal, 20 minutes, US$0.50, a taxi US$2.

Parque Nacional Morrocoy

Palm-studded islets and larger islands (*cayos*) with secluded beaches make up Parque Nacional Morrocoy. The largest and most popular of the islands within the park is **Cayo Sombrero**, with two over-priced fish restaurants. No alcohol is sold on this or other islands; be aware of hidden extra costs and take your own supplies. It is very busy at weekends and during holidays and is generally dirty and noisy. But there are some deserted beaches, with trees on which to sling a hammock. For peace and quiet, take boats to the farthest cayos. **Playuela** is beautiful and is considered to have one of the nicest beaches of all. It has a small restaurant at weekends and there's a nice walk to Playuelita. **Boca Seca** is also pleasant, with shade and calm water suitable for children, but it can be windy. **Cayo Borracho**, one of the nicest islands, has become a turtle-nesting reserve, closed to visitors. **Playa Azul**, a nice small cayo, has shallow water. The water at **Pescadores** is very shallow. **Los Muertos** has two beaches with shade, mangroves and palms. **Mero**'s beach is beautiful, with palms, but is windy. With appropriate footwear it is possible to walk between some of the islands. Calm waters here are ideal for waterskiing while scuba diving is best suited to beginners. Only by diving to deeper waters will you see coral, although in all locations there are still fish to watch. Take insect repellent against *puri puri* (tiny, vicious mosquitoes) and flies.

Adjoining the park to the north is a vast nesting area for scarlet ibis, flamingos and herons, the **Cuare Wildlife Sanctuary**, a Ramsar site. Most of the flamingos are in and around the estuary next to Chichiriviche, which is too shallow for boats but you can walk there or take a taxi. Birds are best watched early morning or late afternoon.

Tucacas and Chichiriviche

Tucacas is a hot, busy, dirty town, where bananas and other fruit are loaded for Curaçao and Aruba. Popular and expensive as a beach resort, it has garish high-rise blocks and casinos. A few kilometres beyond Tucacas, towards Coro, is **Chichiriviche**, smaller, more relaxed, but lined with tacky shops, also dirty and not that attractive. Both provide access to Parque Nacional Morrocoy, each town serving separate *cayos*, but only as far as Cayo Sombrero. Apart from this and the diving options, few have a good word to say about Tucacas or Chichiriviche.

Listings Valencia and around

Where to stay

Valencia

There are several business hotels, also ones for all budgets along the very long Av Bolívar.

$$ Dinastía
Av Urdaneteo y Av Cedeño,
T0241-858 8139, www.dinastiahotel.com.
Central, just off Av Bolívar, all services, restaurant.

$ Marconi
Av Bolívar 141-65, T0241-823 4843.

Small, modern hotel, simple rooms, helpful, safe, laundry, recommended, take bus or colectivo from bus station to stop after 'El Elevado' bridge.

Coast north of Valencia

At **Patanemo** there are hotels and posadas in the village (eg **Chachita** C Bolívar 99, and **María Lucía**).

$$-$ Posada Edén
Final Av Principal Los Caneyes,
T0416-442 4955.
The best posada in the region, small, comfortable, hot water, restaurant and pool.

$ Posada Natal Mar
At entrance to Caneyes sector, 100 m
from turn-off to Bahía de Patanemo,
T0412-536 7961.
Small but clean rooms, but no windows,
restaurant upstairs.

$ Posada Santa Margarita
Bolívar 4-36, Puerto Cabello,
T0242-361 4112,
www.posadasantamargarita.com.ve.
Converted colonial house in historic
district, 2 blocks from waterfront
promenade, day trips, attractive
rooms, cheaper with fan, roof terrace,
restaurant, small pool. Book in advance.

Parque Nacional Morrocoy
Camping is allowed at **Cayo Paiclá**
and **Cayo Sol** but not year round and
you must first make a reservation
with **Inparques** (National Parks),
Av Libertador, Tucacas, T0259-812
0053 (Falcón office Intercomunal
Coro-La Vela, sector Sabana Larga,
Jardín Botánico Dr León Croizat, Coro,
Estado Falcón, T0268-277 8451); reserve
at least 8 working days in advance;
7 nights max, pay in full in advance
(very complicated procedure). Very few
facilities and no fresh water at **Paiclá**.
Playa Azul and **Paiclá** have ecological
toilets. At weekends and holidays
it is very crowded and litter-strewn
(beware rats).

$$$-$$ Villa Mangrovia
On Lizardo Spit between Tucacas and
Chichiriviche, T0414-581 7207.
One of few places in the park itself.
6 rooms, superb food and service,
charming owner, good birdwatching.
Book via www.turismodeplaya.com, or
Last Frontiers, in UK, T01296-653000,
www.lastfrontiers.com.

Tucacas
Chichiriviche has a wider choice
of budget places. Most hotels and
restaurants in Tucacas are on the long
Av Libertador, the main street.

$$ Aparto Posada del Mar
Av Silva, T0259-812 0524, www.
apartoposadadelmar.com.
Variety of rooms with a/c, pool,
restaurant, Wi-Fi, private jetty and
windsurfing centre.

$ Manaure
Av Silva (opposite Posada del Mar),
T0259-812 1011/818 6121, www.
paradormanaure.com.
Modern, low-rise hotel, a/c, hot water,
pool, good.

Chichiriviche
There are plenty of reasonably priced
posadas, eg **Casa Manantial**, Playa
Sur, 50 m from beach, T0259-818 6248,
www.posadacasamanantial.com.ve
($), **La Riviera**, Playa Norte, T0259-815
0369, http://posadalariviera.com.ve, and
Morokkue, Playa Norte, T0259-818 6492,
www.morokkue.com.ve ($).

$ Morena's Place
Sector Playa Norte, 10 mins walk
from bus stop, T0259-815 0936,
posadamorenas@hotmail.com.
Beautifully decorated house, fan,
hammocks, helpful hosts, English
spoken.

$ Posada Alemania
Av Cuare, T0259-881 1283, www.karibik-
pur-venezuela.de.
German-run, runs tours, rents snorkel
gear, 200 m from Playa Sur, nice garden.

$ Posada El Profe
2 C Playa Norte, T0259-416 1166, www.
posadaelprofe.com.

Welcoming B&B, several languages spoken, tours and information, contact Aminta in advance for best deals.

$ Posada Sol Mar y Arena
Mariño y Partida, T0259-815 0306.
Small rooms, welcoming, upstairs terrace with a grill, 1 block from sea, tours and all-inclusive packages offered.

$ Posada Villa Gregoria
C Mariño y R Yáñez, 1 block north of bus stop behind the large water tank, T0259-818 6359, http://posadavillagregoria. blogspot.co.uk.
Helpful, relaxing, good value, fan or a/c, laundry, small rooms, hammocks, garden, secure parking. Tours are available, English spoken.

What to do

Tucacas
Diving
Frogman Dive Center, *C Bolívar, Plaza Bolívar, T0414-340 1824, www. frogmandive.com.* Introductory, Open Water and Advanced courses, dive trips to Morrocoy, shop.
Submatur, *C Ayacucho 6, near Plaza Bolívar, T0259-812 0082, morrocoysubmatur1@cantv.net.*
Experienced owner, runs 4-day PADI courses and day trips with 2 dives; also rents rooms, $, fan and kitchen.

Transport

Valencia
Air The airport is 6 km southeast of centre. Taxi airport-bus terminal US$3.50. Daily flights to **Maracaibo**, **Porlamar**, **Caracas, Puerto Ordaz** and other cities (often via Caracas). **Dutch Antilles Express**, www.flydae.com, flies to **Curaçao** 6 days a week.

Bus Terminal is 4 km east of centre, part of shopping mall **Big-Low** (24-hr restaurants). Entry to platforms by *ficha* (token), US$1. Left luggage. Minibus to centre, frequent and cheap, but slow and confusing route at peak times; taxi from bus station to centre, US$5 (official drivers wear ID badges). To **Caracas**, frequent buses with **Aeroexpresos Ejecutivos** and others, 2½ hrs, US$1-1.35. Likewise to **Maracaibo**, US$2.25-4, 8 hrs. **Mérida**, 10-12 hrs, US$5.25 (regular bus US$2.75). **Puerto Cabello**, US$0.55, 1 hr. To **Coro**, US$1.50-4, 4½ hrs. To **Ciudad Bolívar**, US$3-5.25, 10 hrs.

Around Valencia
Bus To **Vigírima** 20 km northeast of Valencia at regular intervals (US$0.50), ask to get off at the 'Cerro Pintado' turn-off.

Parque Nacional Morrocoy
Ferry **From Tucacas** prices per boat from US$8 return to **Paiclá** to US$18 return to **Cayo Sombrero** (max 7 per boat). The ticket office is on the left of the car entrance to the Park. Boats to Boca Seca and Playuelita only leave from Tucacas. **From Chichiriviche** tickets are per boat and vary according to distance, around US$8-18. Prices are set for each cayo and there are long and short trips. There are 2 ports one in the centre, one at Playa Sur. Ask for the ticket system to fix the price and to ensure you're picked up on time for return trip.

Tucacas
Bus Frequent *por puesto* from **Valencia**, US$2, bus US$0.50. To **Coro**, US$1, 3 hrs.

Chichiriviche
Bus To **Coro**, take a bus from the station on Av Zamora to **Sanare**, US$0.50, every 20 mins, then another to Coro, US$1.30, 3 hrs.

The relaxed colonial city of Coro, with its sand-dune surroundings, sits at the foot of the arid, windswept Paranaguá Peninsula. Inland from Coro, the Sierra de San Luis is good walking country in fresher surroundings.

Coro

Coro, the capital of the Falcón state and former capital of the country, is a UNESCO World Heritage Site. Founded in 1527, it became an important religious centre for Christians and Jews alike. The city, 177 km from Tucacas, is relatively clean and well-kept and its small colonial part has several shaded plazas and beautiful buildings, many of which date from the 18th century. Recently, efforts have been made to preserve and restore its colonial heritage. In the rainy season the centre may flood. **Corfaltur tourist office** ⓘ *Paseo Alameda entre Falcón y Palmasola, T0268-253 0260, http://corfaltur.blogspot.co.uk*, English spoken, helpful. **State tourist office** Fondo Mixto de Turismo ⓘ *C Bolívar, CC Don Salim, of 3 y 4, T0268-251 3698.*

The **Cathedral**, a National Monument, was begun in 1583. **San Clemente church** ⓘ *Mass Mon-Sat 1930*, has a wooden cross in the plaza in front, which is said to mark the site of the first Mass said in Venezuela; it is believed to be the country's oldest such monument. There are several interesting colonial houses, such as **Los Arcaya** ⓘ *Zamora y Federación*, one of the best examples of 18th-century architecture, with the **Museo de Cerámica**, small but interesting, with a beautiful garden. **Los Senior** ⓘ *Talavera y Hernández*, where Bolívar stayed in 1827, houses the **Museo de Arte de Coro** ⓘ *T0268-251 5265, www.fmn.gob.ve/museos/museo-arte-coro, Mon-Sat 0900-1900, Sun 0900-1700, free*, exhibiting some interesting modern artwork. Opposite is the **Museo Alberto Henríquez** ⓘ *T0268-252 5299*, which has the oldest synagogue in Venezuela (1853), if not South America. Built 1764-1765, **Las Ventanas de Hierro** ⓘ *Zamora y Colón, Tue-Sat 0900-1200, 1500-1800, Sun 0900-1300, US$0.20*, is now the **Museo de Tradición Familiar**. Just beyond is the **Casa del Tesoro** (or del Obispo) ⓘ *C Zamora, T0268-252 8701, free*, an art gallery showing local artists' work. There are other handicraft galleries in the centre, such as **Centro Artesanal Generalísimo Francisco de Miranda** ⓘ *C Zamora, near Plaza San Clemente*. The **Jewish cemetery** ⓘ *C 23 de Enero esq C Zamora, visit by prior arrangement only, enquire at the Museo Alberto Henríquez or your hotel*, is the oldest on the continent, founded by Jews who arrived from Curaçao in the early 19th century. It has suffered rain damage and is being restored.

The **Museo de Coro 'Lucas Guillermo Castillo'** ⓘ *C Zamora by San Francisco, T0268-251 5645, Tue-Sat 0900-1230, 1500-1830, Sun 0900-1400*, is in an old monastery, and has a good collection of church relics.

Coro is surrounded by sand dunes, **Los Médanos de Coro**, which form an impressive **national park** ⓘ *0800-1700; outside town on the main road to Punto Fijo take bus marked 'Carabobo' from C35 Falcón y Av Miranda, or up Av Los Médanos and get off at the end, just after Plaza Concordia, from there walk 500 m to entrance,* *or take a taxi*. The place is guarded by police and is generally safe, but stay close to the entrance and on no account wander off across the dunes. Kiosk at entrance sells drinks and snacks.

The historic part of the town's port, **La Vela de Coro** (population 40,000), is included in the UNESCO World Heritage Site, with some impressive colonial buildings, lovely sea front, wooden traditional fishing boats and historic church. It has an unmistakable Caribbean feel, but it is in urgent need of facelift (taxi from Coro US$4). On the road to La Vela, near the turning, is the interesting **Jardín Botánico Xerofito Dr León Croizat** ① *Sector Sabana Larga, T0268-277 8451, drfalcon@inparques. gov.ve, Tue-Fri 0800-1200, 1300-1600, Sat and Sun 0900-1700, free, getting there take Vela bus from corner of C Falcón, opposite Banco Coro, and ask to be let off at Pasarela del Jardín Botánico – the bridge over the road.* It is backed by UNESCO and has plants from Africa, Australia, etc. Tours in Spanish.

Paraguaná Peninsula

Punto Fijo and around This area is a must for windsurfers and is a great place for walking and flamingo spotting. The western side of the peninsula is industrialized, with oil refineries at Cardón and Amuay connected by pipeline to the Lago de Maracaibo oilfields. The main town is **Punto Fijo**, a busy, unappealing place, whose duty-free zone attracts shoppers with cheap electrical goods and alcohol. It has a range of hotels and posadas, but the residential area of **Judibana**, about 5 km away, is better, with shopping centre, cinema and restaurants.

Adícora A quiet if run-down little resort on the east side of the peninsula. The beaches are very windswept and not great but they are popular with wind- and kite-

Coro

200 metres
200 yards

Where to stay
1 El Gallo
2 Intercaribe
3 Miranda Cumberland
4 Posada Casa Tun Tun
5 Posada Don Antonio
6 Posada La Casa de los Pájaros
7 Villa Antigua

Restaurants
1 Barra del Jacal
4 Mersi
5 Panadería Costa Nova

surfers. There are three windsurfing schools in town. Adícora is also a good base for exploring the beautiful, barren and wild peninsula where goats and wild donkeys roam.

Cerro Santa Ana (830 m) is the only hill on the peninsula and commands spectacular views. The entrance is at El Moruy; take bus to Pueblo Nuevo (0730-0800), then take one to Punto Fijo and ask to be dropped off at the entrance to Santa Ana. From the plaza walk back to the signpost for Pueblo Nuevo and take the dirt road going past a white building; 20 m to the left is **Restaurant La Hija**. Walk 1 km through scrubby vegetation (watch out for dogs) to the **Inparques** office (closed Monday to Friday but busy at weekends). Register here before attempting the steep three-hour climb. It's safer to go on Saturday or Sunday. Some posadas in Coro arrange trips to the Peninsula.

Laguna Boca de Caño (also called Laguna Tiraya) is a nature reserve north of Adícora, inland from Supi, along a dirt track that is usually fit for all vehicles. There is abundant bird life, particularly flamingos. It is the only mangrove zone on the east of the peninsula.

Sierra de San Luis

South of Coro, on the road to Barquisimeto, the Sierra includes the **Parque Nacional Juan C Falcón**, with tropical forest, caves and waterfalls. Visit it from the picturesque village of **Curimagua**; jeeps leave from Coro terminal, US$2, one hour. The lovely colonial town of **Cabure** is the capital of the Sierra. Jeeps leave from Coro terminal, 58 km, 1¼ hours, US$2. As well as hotels, Cabure has restaurants, bars, a bakery, supermarket and pharmacy. A few kilometres up the road is a series of beautiful waterfalls, called the Cataratas de Hueque. **The Spanish Road** is a fantastic three-hour walk through orange groves and tropical forest from Curimagua to Cabure. You will see many butterflies along the way. The path is not well marked, so it is best to hire a guide. Take water. It's very muddy in rains; take insect repellent and good shoes and be prepared to get wet. Ask at any of the hotels listed below. To walk the Spanish Road from Coro in one day, take transport to Cabure, ask to be dropped at the turn-off for the **Posada El Duende** (see below) and walk uphill 1 km to the Posada, where you begin the trek. The path eventually comes out to the Curimagua–Coro paved road, where you can take transport back to Coro.

Listings Coro and around *map p57*

Where to stay

Coro
Coro has several excellent posadas catering for travellers; book well in advance, especially in Dec.

$ El Gallo
Federación 26, T0268-252 9481,
www.hosteltrail.com/posadaelgallo.
In colonial part, French/Venezuelan owned, relaxed, spacious, shared baths, courtyard with hammocks, dorms and private rooms, some English spoken,

sandboarding, see Eric for tours to Sierra San Luis, a 1-day tour includes lunch.

$ Intercaribe
Av Manaure entre Zamora y Urdaneta, T0268- 251 1955, http://hotelintercaribe.jimdo.com.
Bland, modern, pool, a/c, small rooms.

$ Miranda Cumberland
Av Josefa Camejo, opposite old airport, T0268- 252 2111, www.hotelescumberland.com.
Large modern hotel, good value, restaurant, good pool area, travel agency.

$ Posada Casa Tun Tun
Zamora 92, entre Toledo y Hernández, T0268- 404 4260, http://casatuntun.vefblog.net.
Run by knowledgeable and welcoming Belgian couple. Restored colonial house with 3 attractive patios, kitchen facilities, laundry, relaxing hammock areas and dipping pool, dorms and rooms with and without bath and lovely decor. Good value, nice atmosphere, free morning coffee, changes US$. Highly recommended.

$ Posada Don Antonio
Paseo Talavera 11, T0268-253 9578.
Central, small rooms, parking.

$ Posada La Casa de los Pájaros
Monzón 74 entre Ampies y Comercio, T0268-252 8215.
Colonial house 6 blocks from centre, restored by the owners with local art and antiques, rooms with and without bath, hammock space, meals available, use of kitchen for small fee, laundry service, trips to local sights. Recommended.

$ Villa Antigua
C 58 Comercio 46, T0268-252 7499/0414-682 2924.

Colonial style, fountain in courtyard, restaurant.

Camping

About 30 km east of Coro at **La Cumara**, nice, good beach and dunes.

Adícora

$$$-$$ Archie's Surf Posada
Playa Sur, T0269-988 8285, www.kitesurfing-venezuela.com.
At entrance to Adícora, 5 mins' walk to centre. German-run, well established, organizes wind and kite surfing lessons. Also trips, horse riding and airport pick-ups. Furnished bungalows for 4-12, apartments for 2-4, hammocks. Prices in euros/dollars. Good reports.

$ Hacienda La Pancha
Vía Pueblo Nuevo, 5 km from Adícora in the hills, T0414-969 2649, http://haciendalapancha.tripod.com.
Beautiful, old, colonial-style house set in countryside, nice owners, restaurant, pool, no children.

$ Posada La Casa Rosada
C Comercio de Adícora, on Malecón, T0269-988 8004, www.posadala casarosada.com.
Pleasant, cosy, rooms for 2-8 people, garden and hammocks, breakfast extra, good restaurant. Recommended.

Sierra de San Luis
Curimagua

$ Finca El Monte
Vía La Soledad, 5 km from the village, T0268-404 0564, www.hosteltrail.com/fincaelmonte/.
Run by a Swiss couple on an eco-friendly basis. Peaceful, beautiful views, colonial style, hot water, meals, hammocks. Tours round the park include birdwatching

and cave tours. English, German and French spoken. Highly recommended.

Cabure

In town are several budget options.

$ Hotel El Duende
20 mins uphill from village, T0268-661 1079.
A beautiful 19th-century posada and garden, price depends on size of room, fan, cold water, good restaurant, horse riding, walking, peaceful. Recommended.

Restaurants

Coro

$ Barra del Jacal
Av Manaure y C 29 Unión.
Outdoors, pizza and pasta.

$ Mersi
C 56 Toledo y Zamora.
Good pizzas and *empanadas*.

Cafés

Panadería Costa Nova
Av Manaure, opposite Hotel Intercaribe.
Good bread, sandwiches and pastries, open late.

Festivals

Coro
26 Jul Coro Week.
Oct Cine en la Calle, programme of open-air films on Paseo Talavera.
Nov-Dec Tambor Coriano in many places.
28 Dec Los Locos de La Vela (La Vela).

What to do

Coro
Contact posadas in town for tours, eg **La Casa de los Párajos**.

Transport

Coro
Air Airport open for domestic flights; see also Las Piedras, below, for flights.

Bus Terminal is on Av Los Médanos, entre Maparari y Libertad, buses go up C 35 Falcón, US$0.15, taxi US$1.20. To/from **Caracas** US$1.75-3.50, 6-8 hrs; **Mérida**, US$2 (regular bus); **Maracaibo**, US$1.10-2.25, 4 hrs, *por puesto* US$3.50; **Tucacas**, every 20 mins, US$1, 3-4 hrs; **Punto Fijo**, *por puesto* US$1.

Punto Fijo
Air Airport at **Las Piedras** *por puestos* from C Garcés y Av Bolívar (don't believe taxis who say there are no *por puestos* from airport to town); taxi from Punto Fijo US$2, from bus terminal US$1. Daily flights to **Curaçao** with **Insel Air** (*www.fly-inselair.com*).

Bus Terminal is in Cariarubana district; *por puestos* to **Pueblo Nuevo, Adícora, Coro, Valencia** and **Maracaibo**. To **Maracay, Barquisimeto, Maracaibo** (US$2.50) and **Caracas** (US$4). **Expresos Occidente** has a terminal on C Comercio entre Ecuador y Bolivia.

Adícora
Bus Several daily to and from **Coro**, 0630-1700, US$0.50, 1 hr; to and from **Pueblo Nuevo** and **Punto Fijo**, several daily from 0600-1730.

Not many tourists find their way to the heart of Venezuela's oil business on the shores of Lake Maracaibo. Those that do are usually on their way to Colombia via the border crossing on the Guajira Peninsula to the north. If you've got the time to stop and can handle the heat, Maracaibo is the only town in Venezuela where occasionally you'll see indigenous people in traditional dress going about their business and nearby are reminders of prehispanic and oil-free customs.

Maracaibo

Maracaibo, capital of the State of Zulia, is Venezuela's second largest city and oil capital, with a population of over two million. The region is the economic powerhouse of the country with over 50% of the nation's oil production coming from the Lago de Maracaibo area and Zulia state. The lake is reputedly the largest fresh water reserve in South America. A long cement and steel bridge, Puente General Rafael Urdaneta, crosses Lago de Maracaibo, connecting the city with the rest of the country. Maracaibo is a sprawling modern city with wide streets. Some parts are pleasant to walk around, apart from the intense heat (or when it is flooded in the rainy season), but as in the rest of the country, security is becoming an issue. The hottest months are July to September, but there is usually a sea breeze from 1500 until morning.

Sights The traditional city centre is **Plaza Bolívar**, on which stand the **Cathedral** (at east end), the **Casa de Gobierno**, the **Asamblea Legislativa** and the **Casa de la Capitulación** (or **Casa Morales**) ① *Mon-Fri 0800-1600, free,* a colonial building and national monument. The Casa houses libraries, a gallery of work by the Venezuelan painter, Carmelo Fernández (1809-1887), several exhibition halls and a stunning interior patio dedicated to modern art. Next door is the 19th-century **Teatro Baralt**, hosting frequent subsidized concerts and performances.

Running west of Plaza Bolívar is the **Paseo de las Ciencias**, a 1970s development which levelled all the old buildings in the area. Only the **Iglesia de Santa Bárbara** stands in the Paseo. The Paseo de La Chinita continues west from Santa Bárbara to the Basílica de Nuestra Señora de Chiquinquirá. **Calle Carabobo** (one block north of the Paseo de las Ciencias) is a very good example of a colourful, colonial Maracaibo street. One block south of the Paseo is **Plaza Baralt** ① *Av 6,* stretching to Calle 100 and the old waterfront market (**Mercado de Pulgas**). The impressive **Centro de Arte de Maracaibo Lía Bermúdez** ① *Mon-Fri 0800-1200, 1400-1600, Sat-Sun 0930-1700,* in the 19th-century Mercado de Pulgas building, displays the work of national and international artists. It is a/c, a good place to escape the midday heat and for starting a walking tour of the city centre. Its walls are decorated with beautiful photographs of Maracaibo. The Centro holds frequent cultural events, including the **Feria Internacional de Arte y Antigüedades de Maracaibo (FIAAM)**. The new part of the city round **Bella Vista** and towards the university is in vivid contrast with the small **old town** near the docks. The latter, with narrow streets and brightly painted, colonial style adobe houses, has hardly changed from the 19th century, although many buildings are in an advanced state of decay. The buildings facing **Parque Urdaneta** (three blocks north of Paseo de las Ciencias) have been well-restored and are home to several artists. Also well preserved are the church of **Santa Lucía** and the streets around. This old residential area is a short ride (or long walk) north from the old centre. **Parque La Marina**, on the shores of the lake, contains sculptures by the Venezuelan artist, Jesús Soto (1923-2005).

Paseo de Maracaibo, or Vereda del Lago, 25 minutes' walk from Plaza Bolívar, is a lakeside park near the **Hotel del Lago**. It offers walks along the shores of the lake, stunning views of the Rafael Urdaneta bridge and of oil tankers sailing to the Caribbean. The park attracts a wide variety of birds. To get there take a 'Milagro' *por puesto* or a 'Norte' bus northbound and ask the driver to let you off at the entrance. Opposite is the **Mercado de los Indios Guajiros** (see Shopping).

Maracaibo to Colombia

About one hour north is the Río Limón. Take a bus (US$0.50, from terminal or Avenida 15 entre Calle 76 y 77) to **El Moján**, riding with the indigenous Guajira as they return to their homes on the peninsula. From El Moján, *por puestos* go to **Sinamaica** (US$1; taxi US$2.50).

Sinamaica is the entry point to the territory of Añu people (also known as Paraujanos) who live in stilt houses on Sinamaica lagoon (these houses inspired the invading Spaniards to christen the place 'Little Venice'). Some 15,000 Añu live in the area, although official numbers say there are only 4000. Their language is practically extinct (UNICEF has supported a project to revive it). The Añu use fibres to make handicrafts. To get to the lagoon, take a truck (US$0.50) from Sinamaica's main plaza on the paved road to Puerto Cuervito (five minutes), where the road ends at the lagoon. You can hitch a ride on a shared boat to one of the settlements for a few bolívares, or you can hire a boat by the hour (ask for Víctor Márquez, recommended). Main settlements on the lagoon are El Barro, La Bocita and Nuevo Mundo. **Parador Turístico de la Laguna de Sinamaica** has decent food, clean bathrooms and an excellent handicraft shop with local produce.

Beyond Sinamaica, the paved road past the Lagoon leads to the border with Colombia. Along the way you see Guajira people, the men with bare legs, on horseback; the women with long, black, tent-shaped dresses and painted faces, wearing the sandals with big wool pom-poms which they make and sell, more cheaply than in tourist shops. The men do nothing women do all the work, tending animals, selling slippers and raising very little on the dry, hot, scrubby Guajira Peninsula.

Border with Colombia *Colombia is 1 hr behind Venezuela.*

If you travel on the road between Maracaibo and the border, even if you are planning to visit just Sinamaica and its lagoon, carry your passport with you. Police and army checkpoints are numerous. They are friendly but can get tough if you don't have your documents, or don't cooperate. The border is closed to traffic between 1800 and 0500 and from 2200 for pedestrians. You need an exit card and stamp to leave Venezuela, payable in bolívares only. Ask for 90 days on entering

ON THE ROAD
☆The Lighthouse of Maracaibo

In the south and southwest of the Lago de Maracaibo is the Catatumbo delta, a huge swamp with fast-flowing, navigable rivers, luxurious vegetation and plentiful wildlife, making it one of the most fascinating destinations in the whole country. It is most famous, however, for the nightly displays of lightning over the lake, which are best seen from May to November or December. The phenomenon is yet to be explained. Indigenous people thought that it was produced by millions of fireflies meeting to pay the homage to the creator gods. Early scientific thought was that the constant silent flashing at three- to 10-second intervals was caused by friction between hot air moving south from Zulia and Falcón and cold currents from the Andes. Latest theories suggest it is the result of clashes between the methane particles from the marsh and the lake system between the Catatumbo and Bravo rivers. It has been proved that this phenomenon is a regenerator of the planet's ozone layer.

Whatever its origin, the spectacle is truly unique. It's best observed from Congo Mirador on the edge of the **Parque Nacional Ciénagas del Catatumbo**, at the southwestern end of the lake, right after nightfall. Several operators run tours from Mérida with boat transport (see page 77) and bilingual nature guides, who have information about birds, butterflies and flora.

To get to the Mirador independently is a real tropical adventure involving three to four hours on a motorboat from the port of **Encontrados**, a small town with basic services. It is not fully safe because of illegal immigration and contraband coming from Colombia. Travel should be arranged in a group, and security can be hired in town. If staying overnight on the boat, take plenty of water and food, mosquito repellent and antiseptics.

Encontrados lies at the entrance to the **Parque Nacional Ciénagas de Juan Manuel de Aguas Blancas y Aguas Negras** (daily 0700-1600), known for its impressive vegetation and migrating birds. If you're not going on a tour, you must get a permit from Inparques to enter the park. The Catatumbo lightning can be seen from some parts of the park and even from Encontrados itself. In town basic accommodation ($) is available at Hostería Juancho (Calle Piar 74, T0275-615 0448) and at the central Hotel La Nona Magdalena (Avenida Principal, near Plaza Bolívar, T0275-414 2951). Restaurants close around 1600.

To get to Encontrados takes about four hours by car from Maracaibo, or three to four hours from San Cristóbal. Drive south from Maracaibo on the Machiques–Colón road then, at El Manguito, take a road to Encontrados, over 70 km from the intersection.

Colombia and make sure you get an entry stamp from the Colombian authorities. From the frontier to Maicao, it's a 15-minute drive. Also see Colombia chapter.

Tourist information

Maracaibo

The **tourist office** is **Corzutur** (Av 18, entre C 78 y 79, CC Salto Angel, p 3, T0261-783 4928). All banks shut at 1530 and exchange money in the morning only. Best for dollars is **Casa de Cambio de Maracaibo** (C 78 con Av 9B). **Italcambio** has branches at the Lago Mall (by Hotel Venetur Maracaibo), Centro Sambil (Av Guajira, Zl Norte), CC Aventura (Av 12 y 13 con C 74 y 75) and the airport.

Where to stay

Maracaibo

It is best to reserve well in advance.

$$$ Kristoff
Av 8 Santa Rita con C 68 No 68-48, T0261-796 1000, www.hotelkristoff.com.
In the north of the city some distance from centre. Large hotel, with all services, fully refurbished, nice pool open to non-residents, disco, laundry service, restaurant.

$$ Hotel El Paseo
Av 1B y C 74, Sector Cotorrera, T0261-400 0000, www.hotelelpaseo.com.ve.
All rooms with breathtaking view of the lake, good, top of the range. **Girasol**, revolving restaurant on top floor with great view, international dishes.

$$ Venetur Maracaibo
Av 2 (El Milagro), near Club Náutico, T0261-794 4222, www.venetur.gob.ve.
With 360 rooms, some overlooking the lake. It was the Intercontinental, but is now part of Venetur.

$ Acuario
C 78 (also known as Dr Portillo) No 9-43, Bella Vista, T0261-797 1123, https://twitter.com/HotelAcuario.
Safe, small rooms, safe parking.

$ Doral
C 75 y Av 14A, T0261-797 8385, www.hoteldoral.com.
North of the city. Safe, decent rooms, helpful. Recommended.

$ Posada Oleary
Av Padilla, C 93 No 2A-12, Santa Lucía, T0261-723 2390, www.posadaoleary.com.
Small posada across from Hospital Central, convenient location, bright, safe.

$ Trece 27
C 79 (Dr Quintero) entre Av 13 y Av 13A, T0261-935 5544, www.hotelmaracaibotrece27.com.
New hotel north of the centre with modern facilities, parking, near services on Av Delicias and 5 de Julio.

Restaurants

Maracaibo

A range of US chains and Chinese restaurants (mostly on Av 8 Santa Rita) and pizzerias in the north of town. There are many good restaurants around the Plaza de la República, C77/5 de Julio and Av 31, in Bella Vista. Many places to eat and bars on C 72 and 5 de Julio. Most restaurants are closed on Sun. Many restaurants on *palafitos* (stilts) in Santa Rosa de Agua district, good for fish (*por puesto* US$0.25 to get there); best to go at lunchtime.

$$ El Zaguán
On C Carabobo (see above).
Serves traditional regional cooking, friendly service, good menu and food, pleasant bar.

$$-$ Koto Sushi
Av 11 entre C 75 y 76, Tierra Negra, T0261-798 8954.
Japanese food.

$$-$ Mi Vaquita
Av 3H con C 76.
Texan steakhouse, popular with wealthy locals, bar area for dancing, pricey drinks. No sandals allowed.

$$-$ Peruano Marisquería
Av 15 (Delicias) y C 69, T0261-798 1513.
Authentic Peruvian seafood dishes and international cuisine.

$ Bambi
Av 4, 78-70.
Italian-run with good cappuccino and pastries. Recommended. Has other branches.

$ Pizzería Napolitana
C 77 near Av 4. Closed Tue.
Excellent food but poor service.

$ Yal-la
Av 8 C 68, opposite Hotel Kristoff, T0261-797 8863.
Excellent, authentic Lebanese/Middle Eastern restaurant at very reasonable prices. Great vegetarian food.

Festivals

Maracaibo
5 Oct **Virgen del Rosario.**
18 Nov **NS de Chiquimquira** (La Chinita), processions, bullfights – the main regional religious festival.

Shopping

Maracaibo
There are several modern malls with all services and amenities, including multiplex cinemas. The most luxurious is **Centro Lago Mall.**

Handicrafts and markets
El Mercado de los Indios Guajiros, *C 96 y Av 2, El Milagro.* Open market, a few crafts, some pottery, hammocks, etc.
Las Pulgas, *south side of C 100 entre Av 10 y 14.* The outdoor market, enormous, mostly clothes, shoes, and household goods.

Most of the shops on **C Carabobo** sell regional crafts, eg **La Salita. El Turista** (C 72 y Av 3H, in front of Centro Comercial Las Tinajitas, T0261-792 3495).

Transport

Maracaibo
Air La Chinita airport is 25 km southwest of city centre (taxis US$5, no *por puestos*). Good bookshop in arrivals sells city map; several good but overpriced eateries; **Italcambio** for exchange, daily 0600-1800, no commission; car hire outside. Frequent flights to **Caracas, Valencia, Barquisimeto, San Antonio,** and **Porlamar.** International flights to **Miami.**

Bus The bus station (*Av 15 Las Delicias/ Av 17 Los Haticos*) is 1 km south of the old town. It is old and chaotic, unsafe at night. *Cambio* at bus terminal will change Colombian pesos into bolívares at a poor rate. Taxi to the city US$3. Ask for buses into town, local services are confusing. Several fast and comfortable buses daily to **Valencia**, US$2.25-4, 8 hrs. **San Cristóbal**, US$2-4.50, 6-8 hrs. **Barquisimeto**, 4 hrs, US$1.25-3. **Coro**, US$1.10-2.25, 4 hrs. **Caracas**, US$5, 10-13 hrs (**Aeroexpresos Ejecutivos**, *Av 15 con C 90 – Distribuidor las Delicias, T0261-783 0620*); regular bus US$2.50. **Mérida**, from US$1.75-4, 5-7 hrs.

Local *Por puestos* go up and down Av 4 from the old centre to Bella Vista. Ruta 6 goes up and down C 67 (Cecilia Acosta). The San Jacinto bus goes along Av 15 (Las Delicias). Buses from Las Delicias also go to the centre and terminal. From C 76 to the centre *por puestos* marked 'Las Veritas' and buses marked 'Ziruma'. Look for the name of the route on the roof, or the windscreen, passenger's side. Downtown to Av 5 de Julio in a 'Bella Vista' *por puesto* costs US$0.45-0.75, depending on distance. Taxis minimum US$1.50; from north to centre US$2 (beware overcharging, meters are not used). Public transport is being completely overhauled, but it will take years to complete. New large and small red public buses (government-owned) connect the north, centre and other parts of the city at US$0.15. Old private buses charge US$0.20.

Metro An elegant light-rail system is being developed, www.metrodemaracaibo.gob.ve. 6 stations of the first line are in operation, from Altos de la Vanega, southwest of the centre, to Libertador, via Sabaneta and Urdaneta Mon-Fri 0600-2000, Sat-Sun 0800-1800. Basic fare US$0.10. An extension to Línea 1 and Línea 2 are planned.

Border with Colombia
Maracaibo-Maicao
Bus **Busven** direct at 0400. Other buses operate during the morning, US$4. Or take a *colectivo* from Maracaibo bus terminal (5 passengers), US$5 pp; shop around, plus US$1 road toll, 2-3 hrs. Some drivers are unwilling to stop for formalities; make sure the driver takes you all the way to Maicao and arrive before the last bus to Santa Marta or Cartagena (1630).

The arid, fruit-growing area around the city of Barquisimeto leads to the lush Andean foothills of Trujillo state.

Barquisimeto

There are good air and road connections buses from Caracas take 5½ hrs, from Coro 7 hrs and from Barinas in the Llanos, 5 hrs.

The heart of old Barquisimeto is **Plaza Bolívar**, with a statue of the Liberator, the white-painted **Iglesia Concepción** and the **Palacio Municipal** ⓘ *Cra 17 y C 25*, an attractive modern building. It is now Venezuela's fourth largest city and capital of Lara state. For information contact **Corporación de Turismo de Lara** ⓘ *Cra 19 esq C 25, Palacio de Gobierno, T0251-231 4089, www.cortulara.com.ve*. On 28 December (morning) is the fiesta of **La Zaragoza**, when colourfully clad people are accompanied by music and dancing in the street. Huge crowds watch **La Divina Pastora** procession in early January, when an image of the Virgin Mary is carried from the shrine at Santa Rosa village into the city.

Barquisimeto to Mérida

Buses to Mérida (eight hours) take the Panamericana, which runs at the foot of the Andes near the border with Zulia state, via Agua Viva and El Vigía. More scenic routes take roads which climb towards the mountains, passing colonial towns and entering an increasingly rugged landscape. One such passes is the busy agricultural centre of **Quíbor**, 24 km southwest of Barquisimeto. Festivals on 18 January (**NS de Altagracia**) and 12 June (**San Antonio de Padua**).

Some 165 km southwest of Quíbor is **Boconó** (population 95,750), built on steep mountain sides and famed for its crafts. The **Centro de Acopio Artesanal Tiscachic** is highly recommended for *artesanía* (turn left just before bridge at entrance to town and walk 350 m). From Boconó there is a high, winding, spectacular paved road to Trujillo (see below).

Niquitao, a small town one hour southwest of Boconó, is still relatively unspoilt. Excursions can be made to the Teta de Niquitao (4007 m), two hours by jeep, the waterfalls and pools known as Las Pailas, and a nearby lake. Southwest of Niquitao, by partly paved road is **Las Mesitas**; continue up towards **Tuñame**, turn left on a good gravel road (no signs), cross pass and descend to **Pueblo Llano** (one basic hotel and restaurant), from where you can climb to the Parque Nacional Sierra Nevada at 3600 m, passing Santo Domingo (see also below). Good hiking in the area.

Valera

From the Panamericana in the lowlands, a road goes to the most important town in Trujillo state, Valera. Here, you can choose between two roads over the Sierra, either via Boconó and down to the Llanos at Guanare and Barinas, or via Timotes and Mucuchíes to Mérida. There are several upmarket business hotels, few decent budget ones, and lots of good Italian restaurants on the main street.

Trujillo

From Valera a road runs via the restored colonial village of **La Plazuela** to the state capital, Trujillo. This beautiful historic town consists of two streets running uphill from the Plaza Bolívar. It's a friendly place with a warm, subtropical climate. The **Centro de Historia de Trujillo**, on Avenida Independencia, is a restored colonial house, now a museum. Bolívar lived there and signed the 'proclamation of war to the death' in the house. A 47-m-high monument to the **Virgen de la Paz** ① *0900-1700, US$0.50*, with lift, was built in 1983; it stands at 1608 m, 2½ hours walk from town and gives good views to Lake Maracaibo but go early. Jeeps leave when full from opposite **Hotel Trujillo** (20 minutes, US$0.75 per person). For tourist information, visit the **Corporación Trujillana de Turismo** ① *Av Principal La Plazuela, Trujillito, T0272-236 1455, www.trujillotierramagica.gob.ve.*

Road to the high Andes

After **Timotes** the road climbs through increasingly wild, barren and rugged country and through the windy pass of **Pico El Aguila** (4118 m) in the Sierra de la Culata, best seen early morning, otherwise frequently in the clouds. This is the way Bolívar went when crossing the Andes to liberate Colombia, and on the peak is the statue of a condor. At the pass is the tourist restaurant **Páramo Aguila**, reasonably priced with open fire. People stop for a hot chocolate or a *calentado*, a herb liquor drunk hot. There are also food and souvenir stalls, and horses for hire (high season and weekends). Across from the monument is a small chapel with fine views. A paved road leads from here 2 km to a CANTV microwave tower (4318 m). Here are tall *frailejones* plants. Continuing north as a lonely track the road goes to the **Piñango lakes** (45 km) and the traditional village of **Piñango** (2480 m), 1½ hours. Great views for miles before the road reaches the Panamericana and Lago de Maracaibo.

Santo Domingo (altitude 2178 m), with good handicraft shops and fishing, is on the spectacular road up from Barinas to Mérida, before the Parque Nacional Sierra Nevada. Festival 30 September, **San Gerónimo**. The tourist office is on the right leaving town, 10 minutes from the centre.

Listings From the lowlands to Mérida

Where to stay

Barquisimeto to Merida

Boconó

$ Estancia de Mosquey
Mosquey, 10 km from Boconó towards Biscucuy, T0272-414 8322, T0414-723 4246, estanciamosquey@hotmail.com.

Family run, great views, rooms and cabañas, good beds, good restaurant, pool, recommended. There are other hotels and posadas in town, some on or near Plaza Bolívar, 1 opposite the bus station.

Niquitao

$ Posada Turística de Niquitao
T0414-727 8217/0416-771 7860, www.
ciberexpo.com/posadaniquitao/.
Rooms around a patio in a restored old
house, some with bunks, restaurant,
tours arranged with guide, also has
small museum.

Trujillo

$ Los Gallegos
Av Independencia 5-65, T0272-236 3193.
With hot water, a/c or fan,
with or without TV. As well as
several other places.

Road to the high Andes

Timotes

$ Caribay
Av Bolívar 41, T0271-828 9126.
With bar and restaurant.

$ Las Truchas
North entrance to town, T0271-808 0500,
www.andes.net/lastruchas.
44 cabins, with and without kitchen.
Also has a restaurant.

Santo Domingo

$$$-$$ La Trucha Azul
East end of town, T0274-898 8111, www.
latruchaazul.com.
Rooms with open fireplace, also suites
and cabins.

$$-$ Los Frailes
Between Santo Domingo and Laguna
Mucubají at 3700 m. T0274-417 3440, or
T0212-976 0530, reservacioneshlf@gmail.
com, www.hotellosfrailes.blogspot.com.

Cheaper in low season, includes
breakfast. Beautiful former monastery,
specializes in honeymoon packages,
rooms are simple, international menu
and wines.

$$-$ Moruco
T0274-898 8155/8070, out of town.
Good value, beautiful, also cabins, good
food, bar.

$ Paso Real
On the other side of the river from Los
Frailes, T0212-287 0517, 0414-974 7486.
A good place to stay, heating, restaurant.

Transport

Valera
Bus The terminal is on the edge of
town. To **Boconó**, US$0.50, 3 hrs; to
Trujillo, *por puestos*, 30 mins, US$0.25;
to **Caracas**, 9 hrs, US$2.25-4.50 (direct
at 2230 with **Expresos Mérida**); to
Mérida, 4 daily with **Trans Barinas**,
US$1.30, 4½ hrs; *por puestos* to **Mérida**,
3 hrs, US$2.25, leave when full (travel
by day for views and, especially in the
rainy season, safety); to **Maracaibo**,
micros every 30 mins till 1730, 4 hrs, US$2
(bus US$1).

Road to the high Andes

Santo Domingo

Bus Buses or *busetas* pass in both
directions every 2 hrs all day. **Mérida**
2 hrs, US$1 *por puesto*; **Barinas**
1½ hrs, US$1.50.

Mérida
& around

Venezuela's high Andes offer hiking and mountaineering, and fishing in lakes and rivers. The main tourist centre is Mérida (674 km from Caracas), but there are many interesting rural villages. The Transandean Highway runs through the Sierra to the border with Colombia, while the Pan-American Highway runs along the foot of the Andes through El Vigía and La Fría to join the Transandean at San Cristóbal.

The Sierra Nevada de Mérida, running from south of Maracaibo to the Colombian frontier, is the only range in Venezuela where snow lies permanently on the higher peaks. Several basins lying between the mountains are actively cultivated; the inhabitants are concentrated mainly in valleys and basins at between 800 m and 1300 m above sea level. The towns of Mérida and San Cristóbal are in this zone.

Best for
Climbing ■ Highland journeys ■ Hiking ■ Views

Mérida stands on an alluvial terrace – a kind of giant shelf – 15 km long, 2.5 km wide, within sight of Pico Bolívar, the highest mountain in Venezuela. The mountain is part of the Five White Eagles group. The summits are at times covered in snow, but the glaciers and snow are retreating. Founded in 1558, the capital of Mérida State retains some colonial buildings but is mainly known for its 33 parks and many statues. For tourists, its claims to fame are the great opportunities for adventure sports and the buzz from a massive student population.

Sights

In the city centre is the attractive **Plaza Bolívar**, on which stands the **cathedral**, dark and heavy inside, with **Museo Arquidiocesano** beside it, and **Plaza de Milla**, or **Sucre** ① *C 14 entre Avs 2 y 3*, always a hive of activity. The **Parque de las Cinco Repúblicas** ① *C 13, entre Avs 4 y 5, beside the barracks*, is renowned for having the first monument in the world to Bolívar (1842, replaced in 1988) and contains soil from each of the five countries he liberated (photography strictly prohibited). Three of the peaks known as the Five White Eagles (Bolívar, 5007 m, La Silla del Toro, 4755 m, and León 4740 m) can be clearly seen from here.

Plaza Las Heroínas, by the lowest station of the *teleférico* (see below) is busy till 2300, a recently renovated outdoor party zone, with artists exhibiting their work. Many cheap hotels, restaurants and tour operators are also located here.

Less central parks include **Plaza Beethoven** ① *Santa María Norte*, a different melody from Beethoven's works chimes every hour, but the site is now very neglected and run-down; *por puestos/busetas*, run along Avenida 5, marked 'Santa María' or 'Chorro de Milla', US$0.45. The **Jardín Botánico** ① *located on the way to La Hechicera, www.ciens.ula.ve/jardinbotanico, daily, 360 days a year, US$1.50*, has been recently remodelled and contains the largest collection of bromeliads in South America, sculptures, a canopy walkway, and botanical specimens from a range of ecosystems. The **Jardín Acuario** ① *beside the aquarium, high season daily 0800-1800, low season closed Mon, US$0.25; (busetas leave from Av 4 y C 25, US$0.25, passing airport)*, is an exhibition centre, mainly devoted to the way of life and the crafts of the Andean *campesinos*.

Essential Mérida

Getting around

Mérida's **airport** is on the main highway, 5 km southwest of the centre. The **bus terminal** is 3 km from the centre of town on the west side of the valley, linked by a frequent minibus service to Calle 25 entre Avenidas 2 y 3, US$0.25. City bus fares rise at weekends. A trolley bus system from the southern suburb of Ejido to La Hechicera in the north has been opened as far as Calle 40 (currently free), but as yet does not connect the downtown area. Mérida may seem safe, but theft does occur. Avoid the Pueblo Nuevo area by the river at the stairs leading down from Avenida 2, as well as Avenida 2 itself.

Mérida has several museums the small **Museo Arqueológico** ⓘ *Av 3, Edif del Rectorado de la Universidad de los Andes, just off Plaza Bolívar, T0274-240 2344, http://vereda.ula.ve/museo_arqueologico, Tue-Sat 0800-1200, 1400-1800, Sun 1400-1800, US$0.50,* with ethnographic and pre-Columbian exhibits from the Andes.

Mérida

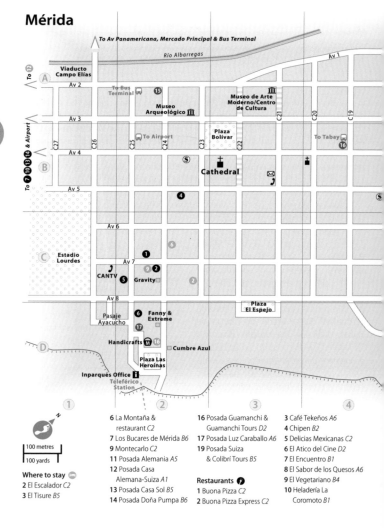

Where to stay 🛌
2 El Escalador *C2*
3 El Tisure *B5*

6 La Montaña &
  restaurant *C2*
7 Los Bucares de Mérida *B6*
9 Montecarlo *C2*
11 Posada Alemania *A5*
12 Posada Casa
  Alemana-Suiza *A1*
13 Posada Casa Sol *B5*
14 Posada Doña Pumpa *B6*

16 Posada Guamanchi &
  Guamanchi Tours *D2*
17 Posada Luz Caraballo *A6*
19 Posada Suiza
  & Colibrí Tours *B5*

Restaurants 🍴
1 Buona Pizza *C2*
2 Buona Pizza Express *C2*

3 Café Tekeños *A6*
4 Chipen *B2*
5 Delicias Mexicanas *C2*
6 El Atico del Cine *D2*
7 El Encuentro *B1*
8 El Sabor de los Quesos *A6*
9 El Vegetariano *B4*
10 Heladería La
  Coromoto *B1*

Museo de Arte Moderno ⓘ *Av 2 y C 21, T0274-252 4380, Mon-Fri 0800-1600, Sat-Sun 0800-1300, free*, is in the Centro Cultural Don Tulio Febres Cordero, which is a run-down but still impressive concrete building with political murals in front of its main entrance, and has several galleries and theatres.

11 La Abadía *B5*
12 La Astilla *A6*
13 La Ciboulette *B1*
14 T-Café *B1*

Bars & clubs 🍸
15 Birosca Carioca *A2*
16 El Hoyo del Queque *B4*
17 La Botana *D2*

Tourist information

Corporación Merideña de Turismo
Av Urdaneta beside the airport, T0800-637 4300, http://cormetur.merida.gob.ve. Mon-Sat low season 0800-1200 and 1400-1800, high season 0800-1800.
They supply a useful map of the state and town. Also in the bus terminal, same hours, have a map of the city (free), at Parque Las Heroínas, at the zoo in Chorros de Milla park and at the Mercado Principal, low season 0800-1200, 1400-1800, high season 0830-1830.

Inparques
National Parks, Sector Fondur, Parcelamiento Albarrega, C 02, paralela a Av Las Américas, T0274-262 1529.
Map of Parque Nacional Sierra Nevada (mediocre) US$1; also, and easier, at Teleférico for permits.

Useful addresses

If you need to register a theft for insurance purposes, ask at the tourist office first. The **CICPC** will provide a *constancia* reporting the crime and listing the losses. Their office is on Av Las Américas, at Viaducto Miranda, T0274-262 1952. Open daily but they won't issue a *constancia* on Sun. To get there, take any bus marked 'Terminal Sur' or 'Mercado' leaving from C 25. You can also get a *constancia* from the **Prefectura Civil del Municipio Libertador**, but it can take all day and is only valid for a limited period; at *Av 4 No 21-69, just off Plaza Bolívar*; opening hours variable. **Immigration office SAIME** (*Av 4 y C 16, quinta San Isidro N0 4-11, Parroquia Sagrario, T251 8588, Mon-Sat 0800-1700*). For those heading to Colombia, the Colombian consulate is at *Final Av Universidad Quinta Noevia, Casa No 80, Sector Vuelta de Lola, T0274-245 9724, http://merida.consulado. gov.co*, open 0730-1330.

Where to stay

Book ahead in school holidays and Feria del Sol. High season is mid-Jul to mid-Jan.

$ El Escalador
C 23 entre Avs 7 y 8, T0274-252 2563, el_escalador@hotmail.com.
A very simple little guesthouse run by a kindly old lady. Doubles or rooms with bed and bunks, hot water, Wi-Fi, free coffee, tourist information.

$ El Tisure
Av 4 entre C 17 y 18, T0274-252 6061, www.venaventours.com/hoteltisure.
A well-maintained colonial-style option, centrally located with 28 simple, calm, attractive rooms, including one enormous Presidential suite with a jacuzzi. Helpful and hospitable.

$ La Montaña
C 24 No 6-47 entre Av 6 y 7, T0274-252 5977, www.posadalamontana.com.
A friendly little *posada* with 19 rooms set around a courtyard, all with hot water, safe, fan, fridge, and Wi-Fi. Very helpful, English spoken, excellent restaurant. Mountain views from the sun terrace. Recommended.

$ Los Bucares de Mérida
Av 4 No 15-5, T0274-252 2841, www.losbucares.com.
Colonial-style with tranquil inner courtyards, attractive wood beams and red tile roofs. Simple whitewashed rooms with hot water, cheaper (and noisier) at the front. Amenities include parking and *cafetín*.

$ Montecarlo
Av 7 entre C 24 y C 25, T0274-252 5981, www.andes.net/hotelmontecarlo.
Simple rooms painted a calming sky blue. Ask for back one with view of mountain, safe, parking, hot water, restaurant.

$ Posada Alemania
Av 2 entre C 17 y 18, No 17-76, T0274-252 4067, www.posadaalemania.com.
Relaxed family atmosphere, cosy rooms with and without bath, leafy patio, laundry service, kitchen, communal areas, book exchange, and a good tourist information and ecotourism office. Popular with backpackers, discounts for long stays, breakfast included. English and German spoken, German owner. Recommended.

$ Posada Casa Alemana-Suiza
El Encanto, Av 2 No 38-130, T0274-263 6503, www.casa-alemana.com.
Stylish guesthouse with a nice family atmosphere. Rooms are spacious, including a suite overlooking Pico Bolívar. Amenities include breakfast salon, kitchen, living room and bar, billiard room, chimney room, and roof top-terrace overlooking the Andes. Bus station pick-up available, parking, discount in low season and for long stays, laundry service, English and German spoken. Also runs good tours and activities.

$ Posada Casa Sol
Av 4 entre C15 y C16, T0274-252 4164,
www.posadacasasol.com.
Renovated colonial-era house with
lovely rooms in distinctive, tasteful
style, modern art on walls, hot water,
Wi-Fi, beautiful garden, large breakfast
included. Very helpful, English, German
and Italian spoken. Limited parking. The
best in town, highly recommended.

$ Posada Doña Pumpa
Av 5 y C 14, T0274-252 7286,
www.donapumpa.com.
16 simple, spacious, well-maintained
rooms with good showers at this
quiet guesthouse. English-speaking
owner, parking.

$ Posada Guamanchi
C 24, No 8-86, T0274-252 2080,
www.guamanchi.com.
Owned by tour operator of same
name; if on a tour you are will receive
a discount. Rooms and dorms of
varying size, including 6 matrimonials
with private terrace and hammock
and Wi-Fi. Good communal areas,
including terraces overlooking
the plaza, shared fridges, kitchens,
TV room. Recommended.

$ Posada Luz Caraballo
Av 2 No 13-80, on Plaza de Milla,
T0274-252 5441.
Colonial-style building with antique
typewriters in the lobby, hot water,
superb cheap restaurant, good bar,
parking, secure.

$ Posada Suiza
Av 3 entre C 17 y 18, No 17-59,
T0274-252 4961, www.posada-suiza.net.
A 19th-century colonial home converted
to a guesthouse. Private rooms for
2 to 6 people, Wi-Fi in communal
areas, internal patios. Adventure tours

(trekking, rafting, riding, expeditions)
with **Colibrí Tours**, same phone,
www.colibri-tours.com.

Restaurants

Good restaurants in Centro Comercial
La Hechicera, Av Alberto Carnevalli,
northeast of the centre.

$$ El Chipen
Av 5, No 23-67, T0274-252 5015.
Established 50 years ago, El Chipen is the
oldest restaurant in Mérida and often
recommended by locals. They serve
Spanish and Venezuelan food, excellent
trout and cordon bleu. Lots of character
and old-world style.

$$ El Encuentro
*Av 4 y C 29, at Hotel Chama, T0274-252
4851. Open 1200-2200 (till 2300 Fri-Sat,
Sun till 1800).*
Smart joint, moderately classy, serving
gourmet international and Venezuelan
cuisine, including seafood starters, fish,
meat, chicken, pasta and risotto, wines
and cocktails. Good presentation, the
place for an intimate evening meal.

$$ La Abadía
Av 3 entre C 17 y 18, T0274-251 0933,
www.abadiacafe.com.
Kitsch and atmospheric old restaurant
set in an early 20th-century abbey and
attended by waiters in habits. Good
varied menu of salads, soups, meat,
pasta, and chicken. Romantic and
recommended. Also here is **Abadía
Tours** travel agency.

$$-$ La Astilla
C 14, No 2-20, Plaza de Milla.
Colourful pizzeria filled with hanging
plants and nostalgic music, varied
menu, frequented by locals and groups.

Good ambience, reasonable food, average service.

$$-$ La Ciboulette
Av 4 y C 29, T0274-252 4851, next to Hotel Chama. Mon-Sat 1800-2300.
Formerly Café Mogambo, a sophisticated European-style bistro with eclectic gastronomic offerings, including tapas and fine wine. Occasional live music.

$ Buona Pizza
Av 7 entre C 24 y 25, T0274-251 1274. Daily 1200-2300.
Thick-crust pizzas, popular with the locals and often buzzing in the evening. Express branch opposite and 2 other branches.

$ Café Tekeños
C 14 y Av 3, just of Plaza Milla.
A casual, bohemian eatery in a lovely rustic colonial building, liberally adorned with interesting art and antiques. They serve hot chocolate, juices and *tequeños* – tasty fried dough sticks with a variety of fillings. Recommended.

$ Delicias Mexicanas
C 25, entre Av 7 y 8, next to Hotel Altamira. Closed Tue.
Authentic Mexican joint with colourful furniture and art work by Diego Rivera. They serve old favourites from the homeland including *burritos*, fajitas, tacos and *chilaquiles*. Not really gourmet, but servings are massive.

$ El Atico del Cine
C 25 near Plaza Las Heroínas.
Movie-themed restaurant, bar, and café set in a cosy upstairs attic. They serve pizza and other international fare. Casual place, sociable vibe. Recommended.

$ El Sabor de los Quesos
On Plaza de Milla.
Cheap and popular locals' pizzeria, very busy, painted green and white with an inner patio.

$ El Vegetariano
Av 4 y C 18.
Low-key little vegetarian café. Wholesome menu includes unpretentious pastas, paella, Carpaccio, good salads, pasties, cake and juices.

Ice cream parlours

Heladería La Coromoto
Av 3 y C 29, T0274-252 3525. Tue-Sun 1415-2100.
Proud Guinness record holder serving the most ice cream flavours in the world, over 800, at least 60 choices daily, eg trout, avocado.

Bars and clubs

There is no cover charge for nightclubs but always take your passport or a copy. Use taxis to get back as the streets are deserted.

Birosca Carioca
Av 2 y C 24.
Popular alternative hang-out, with live music, grunge, rock, metal, Indie music. Take care outside.

El Hoyo del Queque
Av 4 across the road from Alfredo's. Open 1200-2400.
Usually packed, good meeting place, youthful student crowd. The best local bands play here, some nights free. Recommended.

La Botana
Plaza las Heroínas.
Raucous reggae bar that's packed with

drinkers on a Fri and Sat night. Live music and DJs. They also serve pizza.

Los Cibeles
Av 3 y C 25. Mon-Sat 1200-0100.
A popular salsa bar with an alternative vibe and a mixed crowd of young and old.

Festivals

For 2 weeks leading up to Christmas there are daily song contests between local students on Plaza Bolívar, 1700-2200. **Feria del Sol**, held on the week preceding Ash Wednesday. This is also the peak bullfighting season. **1-2 Jan, Paradura del Niño; 15 May, San Isidro Labrador,** a popular festival nationwide, but especially in Mérida.

Shopping

Camping shops
5007, *Av 5 entre C 19 y 20, CC Mediterráneo, T0274-252 6806, http://5007. freeservers.com.* Recommended.
Eco Bike, *Av 7 No 16-34, www.ecobike. com.ve.* For mountain bikes and equipment. Many tour operators rent equipment.

Handicrafts
Handicraft market on La Plaza de Las Heroínas, opposite *teleférico.*
Mercado Principal, *Av las Américas (buses for bus station pass by).* Has many small shops, top floor restaurant has regional *comida típica,* bargaining possible.

What to do

Language schools
Iowa Institute, *Av 3 y C 18, Edif 17-71, T0274-935-9775, Ilinguainstitute@gmail. com. Open 0800-1200, 1430-1800.*

Competitive prices, fully qualified teachers, homestays arranged. Recommended.
Latinoamericano de Idiomas, *CC Mamayeya, p 4, of C-5-38, T0274-244 7808.*

Parapenting
All agencies offer jumps. Conditions in Mérida are suitable for flying almost all year round. It takes on average 50 mins to get to a launch site and tandem jumps last 25-40 mins. There are 7 main sites. You can take your own equipment and hire a guide.
Xtreme Adventours, *Av 8, C24, Plaza Las Heroínas, T0274-252 7241, xatours@ hotmail.com.* Specializes in parapenting (latest equipment, safety) and many other adventure options, plus tours in the region. Also offers tours from Mérida to Canaima, Margarita and Los Roques.

Tour operators
Arassari Trek, *C 24 No 8-301 (beside the teleférico), T0414-746 3569, www.arassari. com.* Run by Tom and Raquel Evenou (based in Switzerland), mostly for rafting tours, but also Roraima, Los Llanos, canyoning, and horse-trekking.
Catatumbo Tour, *T0414-756 2575, www. catatumbotour.com.* Alan Highton and his team specialize in 2-day trips to Catatumbo to see the lightning, visit the communities of the region and experience the variety of habitats between the Andes and the delta. They have a camp at Ologa lagoon. Naturalist tours to other parts of the country offered. Very experienced, several languages spoken.
Fanny Tours, *C 24, No 8-31, T0274-252 2952, T0414-747 1349, www.fanny-tours. com.* Patrizia Rossi, José Albarrán for parapenting (the first to do it), reliable.

Apart from parapenting, specializes in mountain biking, with and without jeep support, bike hire, rafting; Llanos, Catatumbo, canyoning, trekking to mountains and some climbing; also tours combining all types of sport. Recommended.

Gravity Tours, *C 24 entre Av 7 y 8, 1 block from cable car, T0274-251 1279, T0424-760 8327, www.gravity-tours.com*. Bilingual guides, natural history and adventure tours, some extreme, including rock climbing, rafting, biking, Llanos trips and Gran Sabana.

Guamanchi Tours, *C 24, No 8-86, T0274-252 2080, www.guamanchi.com*. Owned by John and Joëlle Peña. Specializes in mountaineering and safari tours to Los Llanos, with 22 years' experience, including working with documentary crews. Good service, ethical ethos

and constantly updated equipment. They also offer rafting and kayaking from beginner to extreme, biking, birdwatching, paragliding, pendulum jumping and tours of Amazonas. They have a posada in town (see page 80) and at Los Nevados (see below). German, French, Italian and English spoken. Recommended.

Natoura Travel & Adventure Tours, *C 31 entre Av Don Tulio y prol Av 6 No 5-27, T0274-252 4216, T303-800 4639 (in US), www.natoura.com. Daily 0830-1800.* Friendly, award-winning company organizing tours throughout Venezuela, run by José Luis Troconis and Renate Reiners, English, French, German and Italian spoken, climbing, trekking, rafting, horse riding, mountain biking, birdwatching and equipment hire. Their self-drive option allows you to rent a car

and they will reserve accommodation for your route. Repeatedly recommended.

Transport

Air Scheduled flights to Mérida were suspended in 2014. However, there are frequent flights between Caracas and airports at **San Antonio** (3-5 hrs by road), or **El Vigía** (1½-2½ hrs away, shared taxi US$5.50 per car, an official will direct you to a taxi and set the price); both are served by several airlines.

Bus The terminal has 2 levels, the upper one for small buses, minivans and cars to nearby places, the lower for interstate buses. Taxis line up outside the main entrance; you will be shown to a taxi. A small exit tax is charged for journeys in the state and for long distance, payable at one of 2 kiosks leading to buses. Make sure you pay, officials check buses before departure. On interstate buses, it is essential to book in advance; for buses within the state you pay on board. The terminal has a tourist office, phones, toilets, luggage store and places to eat. Fares **Caracas**, US$2.55 (regular buses, several companies); **Maracay**, US$2.45-5; **Valencia**, US$2.75-5.25; **Maracaibo**, US$1.60-4; **Coro**, US$2-5.

Transportes Barinas (T0274-263 4651), to **Barinas** (US$1) via **Apartaderos** (US$0.35), to **Guanare** (US$1) and **Valera** (US$1.10). From upper level of terminal **Táchira Mérida**, T0414-712 5913, to **San Cristóbal** (US$1.50, 6 hrs) and **San Antonio**. Also to Jaji, Chiguará, Apartaderos, Barinas, El Vigía. **Líneas Unidas**, T0274-263 8472, *por puesto* microbus with TV, and car, to **Maracaibo**, every 2 hrs, US$2.60-4. If heading for **Ciudad Bolívar**, change buses in Valencia or Maracay.

Taxi In town US$1.

Sierra Nevada de Mérida

climb the peaks or take the cable car

The Sierra is a mixture of the wild and isolated and the very touristy. In the latter group fall the cable car up Pico Espejo and villages designed to lure the shopper, but it is not difficult to escape the tour groups. There are routes from the mountains to the llanos and to Colombia. This area is the heart of Venezuelan mountaineering and trekking. There are several important peaks and some superb hikes. Bear in mind that high altitudes will be reached and acclimatization is essential. Suitable equipment is necessary; you may consider bringing your own. Other activities in the Sierra Nevada include mountain biking, whitewater rafting, parapenting and horse riding. See What to do, page 77.

★Parque Nacional Sierra Nevada (South)

Close to Mérida is the popular hiking area around Los Nevados, with the added attraction of the highest cable car in the world (if it's running). The further you go from Mérida, the greater the off-the-beaten-track possibilities for hiking and exploration.

Since this is a national park, you need a permit from the Inparques (National Parks) offices in Mérida (see above) to hike and camp overnight. Permits are not given to single hikers (except to Los Nevados), a minimum of two people is needed. Have your passport ready. Return permit after your hike; park guards will radio the start of trek to say you've reached the end. If camping, remember that the area is 3500-4200 m so acclimatization is necessary. The night temperatures can fall below freezing so a -12°C sleeping bag is necessary, plus good waterproofs. Conditions are much more severe than you'd think after balmy Mérida. Don't leave litter. Some treks are very difficult so check with the tourist office before leaving. Water purification is also recommended. See Mérida Tour operators and Parque Nacional Sierra Nevada (North) below.

Pico Espejo The world's highest and longest aerial cableway (built by the French in 1957-1960) runs to **Pico Espejo** (4765 m) in four stages. It is called **Teleférico de Mérida Mukumbarí**. The teleférico was closed in late 2008 and a new system was due to open, along with improved hiking trails, in 2015 (www.telefericodemerida.travel). When operating, its final station is at Pico Espejo, with a change of car at every station, all of which have cafés, toilets and advice. Beware altitude sickness there is oxygen and a nursing station at higher points. **Barinas** is the ground level station, Plaza de las Heroínas; you can hire, or buy, hats, gloves and scarves here, the Venezuelans all do. **La Montaña** (2442 m) is the second station with a small Museo del Montañismo. You pass over various levels of forest. Next is **La Aguada** (3452 m), then **Loma Redonda** (4045 m). From here you can start the trek to Los Nevados (see below); you must inform Inparques if trekking to Los Nevados. Pause for 10 minutes at Loma Redonda before the last stage to Pico Espejo, where there is a statue of Nuestra Señora de las Nieves. Next door to Pico Espejo is **Pico Bolívar** (Mukumbarí, where the sun sleeps) with Humboldt behind. It has remnants of a glacier. In the other direction, closest is **La Silla del Toro** and you can see a statue of Francisco Miranda with the Venezuelan flag on an outcrop. On a clear day you can see the blue haze of the Llanos to the east and, west, as far as Sierra de Cocuy and Guicán in Colombia. Across Río Chama you can see Sierra de la Culata. It is advisable to spend only 30 minutes at Pico Espejo. Apart from Los Nevados trek, the only safe part to walk down is Loma Redonda to La Aguada; a rough but clear trail, two hours; wear boots, not for children or the elderly, take water.

Tip...

Do not attempt Pico Espejo alone; go with a guide, it is easy to get lost.

It is possible to hike from Pico Espejo to the cloud forest at **La Mucuy** (see below), two to three days walking at over 4000 m altitude, passing spectacular snow peaks and Lagos Verde and Coromoto. A tent and a warm sleeping bag are essential, as is a good map. If you start at Pico Espejo you will be at the highest point first, so although you will be descending, you may have altitude sickness from the word go.

Los Nevados Los Nevados (altitude 2711 m) is a colonial town with cobbled streets, an ancient chapel and a famous fiesta on 2 May. From here, it is a very testing two-day trek to **Pico Espejo**, with a strong chance of altitude sickness as the ascent is more than 1600 m. It is best done November-June early in the morning (before 0830 ideally), before the clouds spoil the view. In summer the summit is clouded and covered with snow and there is no view. Reputable trekking companies provide suitable clothing; temperatures can be 0° C. August is the coldest month.

From Los Nevados to **Loma Redonda** takes five to seven hours, four hours with mules (14 km). The hike is not too difficult; breathtaking views; be prepared for cold rain in the afternoon, start very early. The walk from Los Nevados to the village of **El Morro** (24 km) takes seven to nine hours (very steep in parts). (It's 47 km to Mérida; jeeps do the trip daily.) Sr Oviller Ruiz provides information on the history of the church of San Jacinto (the patron saint, whose fiesta is on 16 August) and the indigenous cemetery. The town, with its red tiled roofs, is an interesting blend of the colonial and the indigenous.

★**Parque Nacional Sierra Nevada (North) and Sierra de La Culata**
The Transandean highway snakes its way through the rugged mountain landscape, past neat, little towns of red-tiled roofs, steep fields and terraces of maize and potatoes. Just outside Mérida a side road goes to **El Valle**, known for *pasteles de trucha*, *vino de mora* and handicraft shops. The snow-tipped peaks of the high sierras watch over this bucolic scene, with Pico Bolívar lording it over them all. Throughout the park you will see a plant with felt-like leaves of pale grey-green, the *frailejón* (or great friar, *espeletia*), which blooms with yellow flowers from September to December. There are more than 130 species; tall ones grow at less than 1 cm a year.

Tabay and around At 12 km from Mérida, Tabay (30 minutes, altitude 1708 m) is named after an indigenous tribe. Its Plaza Bolívar has an attractive church, trees and plants. Around it are mini mercados, **Pizzería Valentina** (best in town), **Pastelitos** (at bus stop from Mérida, for *empanadas* in morning), and other transport stops. Jeeps run a regular service to **La Mucuy** cloud forest, 0600-2200, they are labelled (US$1 one way if five passengers). They drop you at the Guardaparques. There is nothing to pay for a day visit, but you pay per night if making the Travesía to Pico Espejo and the Teleférico (or alternative route) down to Mérida. When going back to Tabay, you may have to wait for a jeep; the driver will charge extra for backpacks. Jeeps also go to the **Aguas Termales** (from a different stop, just off Plaza Bolívar, US$0.50). It is possible to walk and there are signs. The man-made pool has 38°C water. The area is also good for walking and horse riding (see **Mano Poderosa**, Where to stay), all Mérida agencies go here.

Beyond Tabay the road goes through **Mucurubá** (2400 m) with a pleasant Plaza Bolívar and blue and white church, colonial buildings and handicrafts, and passes the **Monumento al Perro Nevado**. It depicts Simón Bolívar; the Indian boy, Tinjaca; the Mucuchíes dog, Snowy, and the father and son who gave Bolívar the dog in 1813. According to legend, both Tinjaca and Nevado were devoted to Bolívar until their death on the same day at the Battle of Carabobo, 1821. At **Mucuchíes** (altitude 2983 m) the statue of the Liberator on Plaza Bolívar also features Tinjaca and Snowy. Also on the Plaza is a wooden statue of San Isidro, patron saint of farmers;

Park life

The high *páramos* of the Venezuelan Andes are characterized more than anything else by the legendary *frailejón*, so named by the Spanish who thought they looked like a procession of friars (*fraile* means friar). This prolific plant, easily recognized by its curious felt-like leaves of pale grey-green, blooms with yellow flowers from September to December. It can grow up to 2 m tall on thick, wood-like stems. The *frailejón* not only adorns the *páramo* with its yellow blooms, but some of the 45 species found in Venezuela give off a delicate fragrance. And it doesn't just look and smell good. The leaves can be used for anything from wrapping butter to stuffing mattresses.

all rural communities honour him on 15 May. The patron saint of Mucuchíes is San Benito; this festival (and several others) on 27-30 December is celebrated by participants wearing flower-decorated hats and firing blunderbusses. **Tourist office** on Calle 9 as you enter from Mérida; internet at Calle 9 Independencia.

The road leads up from Mucuchíes to **San Rafael de Mucuchíes** (altitude 3140 m, fiesta 24 October). You should visit the remarkable church, pieced together from thousands of stones, by the late Juan Félix Sánchez (born 1900), nationally renowned as a sculptor, philosopher and clown. The chapel is dedicated to the Virgen de Coromoto; it was blessed by Pope John Paul II. The tombs of Sánchez and his companion of 50 years, Epifania Gil, are inside. Next door is his house, now a museum with photos, weavings and sculptures. Opposite is the library given by him to the community. He built a similar chapel at El Tisure. The picturesque road continues to **Apartaderos** (two hours from Mérida, see below). It follows the Río Chama valley in the heart of the cultivated highlands and the fields extend up to the edge of the *páramo*, clinging to the steep slopes. Main crops are potatoes (four harvests a year) onions, garlic and carrots. East of the Río Chama is the Sierra Nevada; to the west is the Sierra de La Culata. There are handicrafts, posadas and eateries.

Apartaderos (altitude 3342 m) is at the junction of Route 7 and the road over the Sierra Nevada to Barinas. About 3 km above Apartaderos, a narrow paved road (signposted) turns west off the highway at Escuela Estatal 121 and winds its way to **Llano del Hato** (3510 m) and on to the **Centro de Investigaciones de Astronomía** (3600 m) ① *T0274-245 0106, www.cida.ve, the 4 telescopes and modern facilities are open Wed-Sat 1500-1900, Apr-Jan subject to weather conditions (check website for details), US$0.50 for adults, US$0.25 under-18s and students with card, seniors and under-8s free.* At least two viewpoints on the way in give great views of the Lake Mucubají plateau. A good paved road descends 7 km from Llano del Hato to the Mérida highway at La Toma, just above Mucuchíes. Many prehispanic terraces and irrigation systems, adobe houses and ox-ploughed fields (*poyos*) are visible from the road.

Three kilometres beyond the junction of the roads from Barinas and Valera is the entrance to the **Parque Nacional Sierra Nevada** (Línea Cultura bus from

Mérida ends at the junction, two hours; taxis run from bus stop to park, US$2). At the turn-off to the park is a motel and restaurant. Near the entrance is **Laguna Mucubají**, at 3600 m, with free campsite; visitors' centre, bookshop, good maps, interesting museum. A two- to 2½-hour walk takes you to **Laguna Negra** and back (1½ hours on horseback, US$3 to hire a horse, guide US$1.50). A further 1½-hour walk from Laguna Negra is the beautiful **Laguna Los Patos**. There are many *frailejón* plants here. Guides (not always necessary) are at Laguna Mucubají or the hotels in Santo Domingo. *Páramo* tours to this area usually include Pico El Aguila (see Road to the high Andes, page 68).

From Mérida to the Panamericana
There are three routes from Mérida to the Panamericana which runs at the foot of the Andes near the border with Zulia state. The most northerly of them is the most interesting.

Via La Azulita This beautiful journey, starting in the highlands from Mérida, heads west. It passes La Chorrera waterfall on the way to **La Encrucijada** (restaurant and service station), where a side road leads to **Jají**, a pretty, restored colonial village with whitewashed houses, cobbled streets, arches on the exits to the plaza and a white and blue church. Most houses are given over to handicrafts shops. There are a few hotels and others in the hills, where there is good walking. A *buseta* from Mérida bus terminal, hourly, takes 50 minutes, US$0.50.

From La Encrujidada the road passes dairy farms before its descent through cloud forest. Towns passed on the way are San Eusebio and Mirabel. This is prime birdwatching territory as the road, paved but rough in parts, twists down through several habitats. **La Azulita**, 73 km, four hours from Mérida, is the base for birdwatching tours, with several lodges nearby. A modern cathedral stands on the Plaza. From La Azulita, the road meets the Panamericana at **Caño Zancudo**, passing en route the Cascada Palmita. Turn south for El Vigía, one of the hottest zones in South America, and routes to Lago de Maracaibo and Catatumbo.

Via El Ejido El Vigía is where the second route from Mérida meets the Panamericana. Transandean Route 7 leaves Mérida and passes through **El Ejido**, originally known as Las Guayabas, or 'the city of honey and flowers'. El Ejido and surrounding villages in the sugar cane zone are known for handicrafts and ceramics. One such historic town is **Mesa de los Indios** (www.andes.net/mesadelosindios), where sugarcane is produced, 5 km from El Ejido towards Jají, 1¼ hours from Mérida. It is famous for its musical traditions and for its artists. Every Saturday *La Retreta de Antonio Valero*, a youth group band, plays wind and percussion instruments in the plaza at 2000. Travellers may donate a wind instrument to the youngsters. Buses to La Mesa leave the plaza in El Ejido.

The main road follows the Chama valley, to Lagunillas and Tovar. **Lagunillas** was founded in the 16th century by Spaniard Juan Rodríguez Suárez on the site of a prehispanic ceremonial centre. Its elaborately choreographed dances honouring a beautiful indigenous princess can be seen at festivities taking place on 15 May.

More can be learned at **Museo Arqueológico Julio César Salas**, on Parque Sucre. **San Juan de Lagunillas**, 2 km away, is where Mérida was originally supposed to be built. Locals (and allegedly doctors) say that the climate is one of the healthiest in the world. There are botanical gardens and a colourful fiesta on 24 June.

Near **Estanques**, a winding road leads towards **Chiguará**, one of the best-preserved coffee towns in Venezuela. Bizarrely, it contains a theme park La Montaña de los Sueños ⓘ *www.montanadelossuenos.com, 1300-2100, daily, ticket office open 1300-1700, US$3.55, children US$3 and senior citizens US$2.50, food available*, devoted to the history of the Venezuelan film industry (1950s to 1970s), complete with sets, old aeroplanes, limousines, cameras and posters. There are also displays of local television, commercial music and theatre. Chiguará is 45 km from Mérida take bus or por puesto towards El Vigía and ask to be dropped at junction for Chiguará, from where you have to hitch or wait for infrequent bus or por puesto.

Beyond Estanques the main highway for bus and heavy traffic turns off Route 7. Near the intersection on the right is 19th-century **Hacienda La Victoria** with an interesting coffee museum. The highway descends from the grey, scarred mountains before the thickly wooded tropical hillsides above the plains. Buses between Mérida and San Crístobal then belt along the Panamericana to **La Fría** from where a four-lane motorway goes to San Cristóbal.

Via Tovar and La Grita The third route leaves the Transandean road at **Tovar** (96 km from Mérida), passing through Zea, a pleasant town in the foothills. From Tovar the road continues to **Bailadores** (fiesta from Christmas to Candlemas, 2 February), and **La Grita**, a pleasant town in Táchira state (Sunday market, fiesta 6 August). Near Bailadores is the pleasant **Parque La Cascada India Carú**, named after a legendary princess whose tears at the death of her warrior lover created the waterfall. This route takes the wild and beautiful old mountain road over Páramo de La Negra to San Cristóbal. Mérida–San Cristóbal buses go via La Fría, not this road; by public transport change in Tovar and La Grita.

San Cristóbal

The capital of Táchira State was founded in 1561. Today it's a large, busy, but friendly place built over hills and ravines, although a few blocks in historic centre, around the cathedral, retain a colonial air. You need to know which district you are in for orientation, eg La Concordia for the bus station. The **Fiesta de San Sebastián** in second half of January is a major international event, with parades, trade shows, and much more; book ahead, prices rise.

On Sunday, take a taxi to **Peribeca** (US$9 one way), a tiny colonial village with handicraft shops, restaurants and sellers of dairy products, fruit desserts and bewildering variety of liqueurs and infusions. The pretty handicraft alley is next to the modern church. There are four posadas and many restaurants open for Sunday lunch (the best is El Solar de Juancho). Alternatively, on Monday, go to the wholesale vegetable market of **Táriba**, just off highway going north. The town's huge white Basílica de la Virgen de la Consolación (1959) can be seen from the highway.

San Cristóbal to San Antonio

The border town of San Antonio is 55 km from San Cristóbal by a paved, congested road. At **Capacho** (25 km from San Antonio) is an interesting old Municipal Market building, with lions at the four corners.

San Antonio is connected by international bridge with Cúcuta on the Colombian side (16 km); continue by road or air to Bogotá. San Antonio has a colonial cathedral and some parks, but is not tourist-oriented. Avenida Venezuela leads to Venezuelan customs. You can catch most transport here, to Cúcuta, San Cristóbal, even to Caracas, but the bus terminal is off the road to the airport at the roundabout at end of Avenida Venezuela, turn left (Calle 11), take a Circunvalación combi marked Terminal (US$0.25). Also buses to airport. There is a festival on 13-20 May.

Border with Colombia This is the main crossing point between the two countries and the border formalities are geared towards locals. Few foreigners travel overland here. Make sure you get a Venezuelan exit stamp at **SAIME** ⓘ *Cra 9 entre 6 y 7, Antiguo Hospital San Vicente, T0276-771 2282.* You will have to fill out a departure card and pay departure tax across the street. **Colombian consulate** ⓘ *Cra 20 entre C 3 y 4, T0276-771 5890, open 0800-1400;* better to get a visa in Mérida. The border is open 0500-1800 for vehicles, till 2200 for pedestrians. Colombian formalities are taken care of right after the bridge immigration procedures are straightforward with only a passport check and stamp. Colombian and Venezuelan citizens do not need any immigration formalities. Foreigners can arrange exit and entry stamps 0800-1800, often much later. If you only travel

> **Tip...**
>
> Venezuelan time is 30 minutes ahead of Colombian.

to Cúcuta (even to spend the night), no immigration formalities are needed. Just cross the bridge by bus, taxi or por puesto and return the same way. If you plan to travel further to Colombia, however, you will need both Venezuelan exit stamp and Colombian entry stamp. Many *casas de cambio* on Avenida Venezuela near the international bridge will change Colombian pesos, but not all change cheques or even US dollars cash. The exchange rate for bolívares to pesos is the same in San Antonio as in Cúcuta.

Entering Venezuela, get your passport stamp at immigration and take bus, por puesto or taxi across the bridge. Ask the driver to take you to Venezuelan immigration, otherwise you will be taken to the centre of San Antonio and will have to backtrack. You can also cross the bridge on foot. Information centre is at the end of the bridge on Venezuelan side. Go to SAIME for entry formalities then look for a bus or *por puesto* to San Cristóbal on Av Venezuela, or go to the bus station (taxi from SAIME US$1). If Venezuelan customs is closed at weekends, it is not possible to cross from Cúcuta. There is a customs and Guardia Nacional post at Peracal outside San Antonio; be prepared for luggage and strip searches. There may be more searches en route.

If crossing by private vehicle, car documents must be stamped at the SENIAT office at the Puente Internacional, just before San Antonio. Two different stamps are needed at separate **SENIAT buildings** ⓘ *Mon-Fri 0800-1200, 1330-1700, Sat 0800-*

1200, final Av Venezuela, Edif Nacional San Antonio de Táchira, T0276-771 1145/1620, www.seniat.gob.ve. It's essential to have proof of car/motorbike ownership. You must check in advance if you need a visa and a *carnet de passages* (see box, page 173). See Cúcuta, Colombia chapter, for details on exit formalities. Once in Venezuela, you may find police are ignorant of requirements for foreign cars.

Listings Sierra Nevada de Mérida

Tourist information

Cotatur
Complejo Ferial de Pueblo Nuevo, Antigua Sede de Radio Club, T0276-611 0954/357 9578, www.cotatur.gob.ve; see also www.traveltachira.com.ve.

Inparques
Parque Metropolitano, Av 19 de Abril, T0276-346 6544.

Where to stay

Los Nevados

$ pp El Buen Jesús
T0274-252 5696.
Hot water, meals available.

$ pp Posada Bella Vista
Behind church.
Hot water, hammocks, great views, restaurant.

$ pp Posada Guamanchi
T0274-252 2080, www.guamanchi.com.
Solar power, great views, with and without bath, 2 meals included. Recommended.

El Morro

$ Posada run by Doña Chepa
As you enter from Los Nevados.
Warm. Recommended.

$ pp Posada El Orégano
Including meals, basic, good food. Recommended.

Tabay

$$ Casa Vieja
Transandina via Páramo, San Rafael de Tabay, inside the Parador Turístico El Paramito, T0273-611 6634, www.casa-vieja-merida.com.
Plant-filled colonial house, German and Peruvian owners, good doubles, hot water, breakfast and dinner available, good food, relaxing, very helpful, information on independent trips from Tabay and transport, English, French and German spoken. Travel agency, **Caiman Tours**, for Llanos, wildlife and adventure tours, see also www.birds-venezuela.de and www.nature-travel.net. From the bus terminal in Mérida take a bus via Mucuchíes or Apartaderos, 30 mins to Tabay, get off exactly 1.5 km after the gas station in Tabay village (just after you pass Plaza Bolívar); the bus stop is called El Paramito. There is a sign on the road pointing left. Free pick-up from the airport or terminal with reservation. They also have a second posada in the village of Altamira de Cáceres. Warmly recommended.

$ La Casona de Tabay
On the Mérida road 1.5 km from the plaza, T0274-283 0089, posadalacasona@cantv.net.

A beautiful colonial-style hotel, surrounded by mountains, comfortable, home cooking, family-run. Take *por puesto*, 2 signposts.

$ pp Posada de la Mano Poderosa
Beyond San Rafael de Tabay on road to Mucuchíes, T0412-950 9000, www.lamanopoderosa.com.
Dorms, lovely, quiet, hot showers, good food, great value, get off at La Plazuela then walk 15 mins towards Vivero Fruti Flor.

Mucuchíes

$ Los Conquistadores
Av Carabobo 14, T0274-872 0350, www.losconquistadoreshotelresort.com.
Nice decor, modern, heating, lots of facilities like pool tables and other games, garden, parking, restaurant 0800-2200, *tasca*, and bike hire. Arranges transport for tours, ATM.

$ Posada Los Andes
Independencia 25, T0274-872 0151, T0414-717 2313.
Old house on street above plaza, run by Las Hermanas Pironi Belli, 5 cosy rooms, hot water, shared bathrooms, TV in living room, excellent restaurant (breakfast extra, criollo and Italian food, 0800-2030). Highly recommended.

San Rafael de Mucuchíes

$ Casa Sur
Independencia 72, T0274-657 7698, njespindola@yahoo.com.
Hot water, heating, breakfast extra, other meals on request.

$ El Rosal
Bolívar 37, T0274-872 0331, T0426-574 1130, www.posadaelrosal.com.

Hot water, good, also cabins with kitchenette, no breakfast, café nearby, restaurant for groups, *tasca* at weekends.

$ Posada San Rafael del Páramo
Just outside San Rafael, 500 m from the Capilla de Piedra, on road to Apartaderos, T0274-872 0938.
Charming converted house with lots of interesting sculpture and paintings, hot water, heating, also cabin with kitchenette, walking and riding tours (guide extra). Recommended.

Apartaderos

$$ Hotel Parque Turístico
Main road, T888 0094.
Cheaper in low season. Attractive modern chalet-style building, heating, very hot showers, helpful owner, expensive restaurant. Recommended.

$ Hotel y Restaurante Mifafí
On main road, T0274888 0131, www.refugiomifafi.com.
Cheaper without heating, pleasant rooms and cabins, hot water, good food. A welcoming, reliable choice.

$ Posada Viejo Apartaderos
Outside town, coming from Mucuchíes, T0274-888 0003.
Next to *bomba*, with **La Matica de Rosa** restaurant, Sra Marbeles. Open only in high season. Good value, good restaurant with reasonable prices.

From Mérida to the Panamericana

Jají

$$ Estancia La Bravera
18 km from Jají towards La Azulita, T0212-978 2627, 0426-520 7310, www.estancialabravera.com.
Cabins in beautiful flower gardens in the cloud forest, great for birdwatching

and for relaxing, hot water, includes breakfast and dinner, lunch extra, uses home produce, holds an annual Estancia Musical (Aug). Recommended.

$$ Hacienda El Carmen
Aldea La Playa, 2 km from Jají (there is public transport), T0414-639 2701, T0414-630 9562, www.haciendaelcarmen.com.ve.
On a working dairy and coffee-processing farm, built 1863, fascinating buildings, lovely rooms, one with jacuzzi, some simpler rooms, breakfast included, coffee tours, owner Andrés Monzón.

$$-$ Posada Restaurant Aldea Vieja
C Principal, just off Plaza, T0426-926 0367, http://aldeavieja.com.
Colonial-style main building, also cabins for 4-8, lovely views, simple rooms, hot water, meals extra, playground.

$ Posada Turística Jají
Beside the Prefectura, on the plaza, T0274-416 6333.
4 rooms with hot water, no TV, historic, 2 fountains, restaurant 0800-2100, breakfast included if staying a few days.

La Azulita

$ El Tao
On a side road beyond Remanso, 4-5 km, 6 mins in car from La Azulita, T0274-511 3088, T0416-175 0011, www.eltaomerida.com.
Taoist owners and oriental-style spa with saunas, and natural therapies, many birds, favoured by birders, lovely gardens, very safe and peaceful, nice public areas. Cabins for 2-4, restaurant, boxed lunches and early breakfast for birding groups.

$ Posada Turística La Azulita
On Plaza Bolívar.
Rooms around restaurant in courtyard, OK food. Some other lodgings in town.

$ Remanso del Quebradón
Close to junction, T0416-289 1081, www.remanso.com.ve.
4 rooms, on a small coffee farm with fruit trees in the gardens, restaurant, popular with birdwatchers.

San Cristóbal
Cheapest hotels around the bus station (eg **Río de Janeiro**, C 1, No 7-27, Urb Juan Maldonado, La Concordia, by bus station, and **Tropical**, Prol 5ta Av No 7472, opposite bus station, T0276-347 2932), $$ business hotels in the centre and more upmarket places in the northwestern suburbs.

$$ Del Rey
Av Ferrero Tamayo, Edif El Rey, T0276-343 0561.
Good showers, fridge, kitchenette, laundry, no breakfast but *panadería* in building, pizzas.

$$ Lidotel
Sambil San Cristóbal Mall, Autopista Antonio José de Sucre, Las Lomas, T0276-510 3333, www.lidotelhotelboutique.com.
Attached to an enormous, posh shopping mall, with all the luxuries of 4-star hotel, pool, very well run. Recommended.

$ Posada Rincón Tachirense
Av Ferrero Tamayo con C 3, N Ft-19, La Popita, T0276-341 8753, www.posadarincontachirense.com.
Not central, down hill from **Del Rey**, cheaper with shared bath, comfortable, breakfast and will ring out for pizza. Recommended.

$ Posada Turística Don Manuel
Cra 10 No 1-104, just off Av 19 de Abril,
Urb La Concordia, T0276-347 8082.
Rooms are across street; Sra Carmen
will direct you. Hot water, family run,
fridge, fan, limited kitchen facilities, no
breakfast, parking. Sleeps 8, always book
in advance, convenient.

San Cristóbal to San Antonio
Capacho

$ La Molinera
20 mins from San Cristóbal at Capacho,
municipalidad de Independencia,
T0276-788 3117.
Rooms and suites in a beautiful,
traditional posada with swimming
pool and handmade furniture. Good
Tachirense food in its restaurant.

San Antonio
Many hotels near town centre.

$ Adriático
C6 y Cra 6, T0276-771 5757.
Not far from Av Venezuela,
3-star, functional.

$ Neveri
C 3, No 3-13, esq Carrera 3,
T0276-771 5702.
Safe, parking nearby, 1 block from
Customs, opposite Guardia Nacional
barracks. No food, dated. Internet
next door.

Restaurants

San Cristóbal
El Barrio Obrero has the main
concentration of eateries, bars and discos.
Try **Rocamar**, Cra 20 y C 14, for seafood.
Also pizza places and *pastelerías*.

$$-$ La Olleta
Cra 21, no 10-171, just off plaza, Barrio
Obrero, T0276-356 6944.
Smart, simple decor, Venezuelan
and international with creative
touches, well presented.

Around town there are many *panaderías*
and *pastelerías* for snacks as well as
bread and cakes, coffee and other drinks,
eg **América**, Cra 8, Edif La Concordia, no
4-113, La Concordia (several on Cra 8 y C
4, La Concordia); also **Táchira** branches.

San Antonio

$ Rosmar
Cra 6 y C 6, opposite Hotel Adriático.
Very popular for lunch, several choices,
OK food.

Transport

Los Nevados
Jeep Los Nevados-**Mérida**, late
afternoon (depart 0700 from Plaza Las
Heroínas in Mérida), 5-6 hrs, US$2.50 pp,
US$10 per jeep, very rough and narrow
but spectacular.

Tabay
Regular bus service from **Mérida** C 19
entre Avs 3 y 4, every 10 mins, US$0.35;
taxi US$2 (more at night).

Apartaderos
Bus To **Mérida** from turn-off to Barinas;
bus to **Barinas** on the road over the
Sierra Nevada is unreliable, best to catch
it in Mérida.

San Cristóbal
Air Airport at Santo Domingo, 40 km
away. Helpful tourist kiosk with leaflets,
map of San Cristóbal US$0.50. Taxi to San
Cristóbal US$4, can take as little as 35 mins,
but normally much more, lots of traffic,

nice scenery (tourist office says no other option). Daily flights to/from **Caracas**. Alternatively fly to San Antonio (see below) for better public transport links.

Bus Local buses cost US$0.25. 'Intercomunal' goes from Av Ferrero Tamayo (northwest) to Bus Terminal. 'Tusca' from Av Ferrero Tamayo to centre. Taxis US$2 for a short run.

The bus station is in La Concordia, in the southeast. It is a bus terminal, shopping mall, market, phone exchange and food court all lumped together. Terminal tax US$0.10, paid on bus before departure. Company offices are grouped together, but **Expresos Occicente** have their own terminal nearby. To **Mérida**, US$1.50, 5 hrs, with **Táchira-Mérida** (buy ticket on bus); also **Expreso Unido**. Buses to Mérida go via the Panamericana, not over the Páramo. National Guard Control at La Jabonesa, just before San Juan de Colón, be prepared for luggage search. To **Maracaibo**, 6-8 hrs, US$2-4.50. To **Caracas**, US$3-8, 15 hrs; **Valencia**, US$2.75. To **Barinas**, US$1.25. To **San Fernando de Apure** via **Guasdualito**, US$3.50. To **San Antonio**, 1¼ hrs (but San Cristóbal rush hour can add lots of time), US$0.50, **Línea San Antonio**, T0276-347 0976 (San Antonio 0276-771 2966) and **Unión de Conductores**, T346 0691 (San Antonio 771 1364). To **Cúcuta**, **Línea Venezuela**, T0276-347 3086 (Cúcuta T0270-583 6413) and **Fronteras Unidas**, T0276-347 7446 (Cúcuta T0270 583 5445), US$1, Mon-Fri 0800-1200, 1400-1800.

Opposite terminal on Rugeles, **Coop de Conductores Fronterizos** cars, T0276-611 2256, to **San Antonio**.

San Antonio

Air The airport has exchange facilities (mainly for Colombian pesos). Taxis run to SAIME (immigration) in town, and on to Cúcuta airport. Flights to **Caracas**.

Bus From terminal several companies to **Caracas**, via the Llanos, Valencia and Maracay. Caracas US$3-8 (*bus-cama*). **Expresos San Cristóbal** have office on Av Venezuela, close to Customs, 1800 to Caracas, 13-14 hrs; **Expresos Mérida**, Av Venezuela, No 6-17, at 1900. **Táchira-Mérida** to **Mérida** and **Barquisimeto**; **Expresos Unidos** to Mérida. To **San Cristóbal**, catch a bus on Av Venezuela.

Border with Colombia

Air It is cheaper, but slower, to fly **Caracas**–San Antonio, take a taxi to Cúcuta, then take an internal Colombian flight, than to fly direct Caracas–Colombia. The airport transfer at San Antonio is well organized and taxi drivers make the 25-min trip with all stops.

Bus On Av Venezuela *por puestos/colectivos* to **Cúcuta** charge US$0.50, and buses US$0.25 payable in bolívares or pesos, 30 mins. Some say to terminal, others to centre. Taxi to Cúcuta, US$4. On any transport that crosses the border, make sure the driver knows you need to stop to obtain stamps. *Por puesto* drivers may refuse to wait. Taxi drivers will stop at all the offices.

Los Llanos
& Amazonas

A spectacular route descends from the Sierra Nevada to the flat Llanos, one of the best places in the world to see birds and animals. This vast, sparsely populated wilderness of 300,000 sq km – one-third of the country's area – lies between the Andes to the west and the Orinoco to the south and east.

Southwest of the Guayana region, on the banks of the Orinoco, Puerto Ayacucho is the gateway to the jungles of Venezuela. Although it takes up about a fifth of the country, Amazonas and its tropical forests is for the most part unexplored and unspoilt.

Best for
Birdwatching ▪ Ranches ▪ Wilderness ▪ Wildlife

wildlife abounds on these extensive flood plains

★The Llanos are veined by numerous slow-running rivers, forested along their banks. The flat plain is only varied here and there by mesas, or slight upthrusts of the land. About five million of the country's 6.4 million cattle are in the Llanos, but only around 10% of the human population. When the whole plain is periodically under water, the *llaneros* drive their cattle into the hills or through the flood from one mesa to another. When the plain is parched by the sun and the savanna grasses become inedible they herd the cattle down to the damper region of the Apure and Orinoco. Finally they drive them into the valley of Valencia to be fattened.

In October and November, when the vast plains are still partially flooded, wildlife abounds. Animals include capybara, caiman, monkeys, anacondas, river dolphins, pumas and many bird species. Though you can explore independently, towns are few and distances are great. It's better to visit on a tour from Mérida (page 70), or stay at one of the ecotourism *hatos* (see below).

> ## Tip...
>
> Motorists travelling east to Ciudad Bolívar can either go across the Llanos or via San Carlos, Tinaco, El Sombrero, Chaguaramas, Valle de la Pascua (see below) and El Tigre. The latter route requires no ferry crossings and has more places with accommodation.

Valencia to Barinas

A good road goes to the western Llanos of Barinas from Valencia. It goes through **San Carlos**, **Acarigua** (an agricultural centre and the largest city in Portuguesa state) and **Guanare**, a national place of pilgrimage with a cathedral containing the much venerated relic of the Virgin of Coromoto. The **Santuario Nacional Nuestra Señora de Coromoto** ⓘ *25 km form Guanare on road to Barinas, open 0800-1700*, is on the spot where the Virgin appeared to Cacique Coromoto in 1652. An imposing modern basilica dedicated to the Virgin, it was inaugurated by Pope John Paul II in 1996. Buses run from Calle 20 y Carrera 9, Guanare, every 15 minutes (US$0.20). Pilgrimages to Coromoto are 2 January and 11 September and Candlemas is 2 February.

The road continues to **Barinas**, the capital of the cattle-raising and oil-rich state of Barinas. A few colonial buildings remain on the plaza the **Palacio del Marqués** and the **Casa de la Cultura**. Also here is the beautifully restored, 19th-century **Escuela de Música**; the cathedral is to the east. The shady Parque Universitario, just outside the city on Avenida 23 de Enero, has a botanical garden. **Tourist office (Corbatur)** ⓘ *C Arzobispo Méndez, edif Vifran, p 1, diagonal al Banco Exterior, T0273-552 7091.* Helpful, maps, no English spoken; kiosks at airport and bus station. From Barinas there is a beautifully scenic road to Apartaderos, in the Sierra Nevada de Mérida (see page 82).

ON THE ROAD

Capybara (Chigüire)

One of the most common sights in the lowlands is the capybara, or chigüire, a large aquatic rodent that looks like a cross between a guinea pig and a hippopotamus. It is the largest of all the rodents at over 1-m long and weighing over 50kg. They live in large groups along the riverbanks, where they graze on the lush grasses. It comes out onto dry land to rest and bask in the sun, but at the first hint of danger the whole troop dashes into the water. Its greatest enemies are the jaguar and puma. They are rather vocal for rodents often emitting a series of strange clicks, squeaks and grunts.

Towards San Fernando de Apure

At Lagua, 16 km east of Maracay, a good road leads south to San Fernando de Apure. It passes through **San Juan de los Morros**, with natural hot springs; **Ortiz**, near the crossroads with the San Carlos–El Tigre road; the Guárico lake and **Calabozo**. Some 132 km south of Calabozo, San Fernando is the hot and sticky capital of Apure state and a fast-growing trade and transport hub. From San Fernando travel east to Ciudad Bolívar (page 129) or south to Puerto Ayacucho (see below).

San Fernando to Barinas

From San Fernando a road heads west to Barinas (468 km). It's a beautiful journey, but the road can be in terrible condition, eg between Mantecal, La Ye junction and Bruzual, a town just south of the Puente Nutrias on the Río Apure. In the early morning, many animals and birds can be seen, and in the wet season caiman (alligators) cross the road. **Mantecal** is a friendly cattle-ranching town with hotels and restaurants. **Fiesta**, 23-26 February.

Listings Los Llanos

Where to stay

Barinas

$ El Palacio
Av Elías Cordero con C 5, T0273-552 6947.
Good value, parking, near bus terminal so front rooms are noisy.

$ Internacional
C Arzobispo Méndez on Plaza Zamora, T0273-552 2343, hotelinternacional_3@hotmail.com.
Safe, good restaurant.

$ Varyná
Av 23 de Enero, near the airport, T0273-533 2477.
Hot water, restaurant, parking. Recommended.

Staying at a tourist ranch

An alternative to travelling independently or arranging a tour from Mérida is to stay at a tourist ranch. Most are in Apure state and can be reached from Barinas or San Fernando de Apure.

$$ Hato El Cedral
About 30 mins by bus from Mantecal (see above). Address in Caracas Av La Salle, edif Pancho p 5, of 33, Los Caobos, T0212-781 8995, www.elcedral.com.
A 53,000-ha ranch, where hunting is banned. Fully inclusive price, tax extra (high season Nov-Apr), a/c, hot water, land and river safaris, guides, pool. The government has nationalized the ranch, see www.venetur.gob.ve for nationalized ranches.

$$ Hato La Fe
Km 51 between Calabozo and San Fernando de Apure at Corozopando in Guárico state, T0414-272 4205.
All-inclusive tours include animal-watching trips and horse riding. 8 bedrooms in a colonial-style house, pool, camping available.

$$ pp Hato Piñero
A safari-type lodge at a working ranch near El Baúl (turn off Tinaco–El Sombrero road at El Cantón), T0273-541 8900, www.venetur.gob.ve.
2-night, 3-day packages, including food, lodging, tours with local guides, but not return transport from Caracas. Bird- and animal-watching trips. Now government owned, but still accepts visitors and tour groups. Contact **Ascanio Birding Tours** in Caracas (www.abtbirds.com), well in advance to make a reservation. From Caracas, 6 hrs; from Ciudad Bolívar, 9 hrs.

$ pp Rancho Grande
Close to Mantecal, T0416-873 1192.
Run by very friendly and knowledgeable Ramón Guillermo González. All inclusive, good wildlife spotting and horse riding trips, 4-day packages.

San Fernando de Apure
Most hotels are within 1 block of the intersection of Paseo Libertador and Av Miranda.

$ El Río
Av María Nieves, near the bus terminal, T0247-341 1928.
Good value.

$ Gran Hotel Plaza
C Bolívar, T0247-342 1746, 2 blocks from the bus terminal, www.granhotelplaza.com.
Good, safe hotel with parking.

$ La Torraca
Av Boulevard y Paseo Libertador by Plaza Bolívar, T0247-342 2777.
Rooms have balcony overlooking centre of town. Recommended.

$ Trinacria
Av Miranda, near bus terminal, T0247-342 3578.
Huge rooms, fridge.

What to do

Barinas
Campamento Colibrí, *Plaza Bolívar Caño Grance, La Acequia, T0273-514 3022, T0414-748 0064, www.campamentocolibri. com.* Rafting trips in association with **Colibrí Tours** in Mérida.
Grados Alta Aventura, *Altamira de Cáceres, T0416-877 4540, www.grados. com.ve/2011.* For rafting trips, kayaking, birdwatching and other adventures, in a historic town.
Rafting Barinas, *T0273-311 0388, www. rafting barinas.com.* With Campamento Aguas Bravas, Carretera nacional vía San Cristóbal, La Acequia, Caño Grande, Km 4, for rafting excursions.

Transport

Barinas

Air Aeropuerto Nacional, Av 23 de Enero. Flights to **Caracas**.

Bus To **Mérida**, 6 a day with **Transportes Barinas**, US$1, spectacular ride through the mountains, 5-7 hrs (sit on right for best views); also to **Valera** at 0730, 1130, US$1.50, 7 hrs. To **Caracas**, US$2-5, 8 hrs, a few companies go direct or via **Maracay** and **Valencia**. To **San Cristóbal**, several daily, US$2, 5 hrs; to **San Fernando de Apure**, US$1.75, 9 hrs with **Expresos Los Llanos** at 0900, 2300; the same company also goes to **Maracaibo** (at 2000 and 2200, US$2.50-5, 8 hrs).

San Fernando de Apure

Air Aeropuerto Las Flecheras, Av 1 de Mayo, T0247-341 0139. Flights to **Caracas**.

Bus Terminal is modern and clean, not far from centre; US$1.50 taxi. To **Caracas**, US$1.65-4, 7 hrs; to **Maracay**, US$1.50; to **Puerto Ayacucho**, US$1.30, 8 hrs; to **Calabozo**, 1½ hrs, US$0.75.

San Fernando to Barinas

Bus San Fernando de Apure–Mantecal 3½ hrs, US$2; Mantecal–Barinas, 4 hrs, US$2.

Amazonas

a remote, riverine region for determined travellers

Much of Amazonas is stunningly beautiful and untouched, but access is only by river. The more easily accessible places lie on the course of the Orinoco and its tributaries. The best time to visit is October to December after the rains, but at any season, this is a remote part of the country.

San Fernando to Puerto Ayacucho

Route 2 runs south from San Fernando to Puerto Páez, crossing several major rivers. Between the Capanaparo and Cinaruco rivers is the **Parque Nacional Cinaruco-Capanaparo** (also called Santos Luzardo), reached only from this road. Puerto Páez lies at the confluence of the Meta and Orinoco rivers. On the opposite bank of the Meta is **Puerto Carreño** in Colombia. A ferry (US$0.50) crosses the Orinoco from Puerto Páez to **El Burro**, which lies just west of the paved Caicara–Puerto Ayacucho road. From the El Burro turn-off it is 88 km to Puerto Ayacucho; taxi two hours, US$2. If Route 2 is closed, the journey to Puerto Ayacucho from San Fernando involves a minimum 15-hour detour via the Caicara ferry.

Puerto Ayacucho

The capital of the State of Amazonas is 800 km via the Orinoco from Ciudad Bolívar, but no direct boats journey up river. At the end of the dry season (April), it is very hot and humid. It is deep in the wild, across the Orinoco from Casuarito in Colombia. **Museo Etnológico Monseñor Enzo Ceccarelli** ⓘ *Av Río Negro, Tue-Sat 0830-1200, 1430-1830, Sun 0900-1300, US$0.50,* has a library and collection of regional exhibits,

Tip...

Malaria is prevalent in this area; so make sure you take precautions.

recommended. In front of the museum is a market, Plaza de los Indios, open every day, where local *indígenas* sell handicrafts. One block away is the cathedral. Prices in Puerto Ayacucho are generally higher than north of the Orinoco. **Tourist office** ⓘ *Avenida Río Negro, T0248-521 0033*, is in the Gobernación building.

Excursions November to December is the best time, when rivers are high but the worst of the rains has passed. In the wettest season, May-June, it may be difficult to organize tours for only a few days. At any time of year, permission from the military may be required to travel independently on the rivers.

You can walk up **Cerro Perico** for good views of the town, or go to the Mirador, 1 km from centre, for good views of the Ature rapids. A recommended trip is to the village of Pintado (12 km south), where petroglyphs described by Humboldt can be seen on the huge rock **Cerro Pintado**. This is the most accessible petroglyph site of the many hundreds which are scattered throughout Amazonas.

Some 35 km south on the road to Samariapo is the **Parque Tobogán de la Selva**, a pleasant picnic area based around a steeply inclined, smooth rock over which the Río Maripures cascades. This waterslide is great fun in the wet season; crowded on Sunday, take swimsuit and food and drink. A small trail leads up from the slide to a natural jacuzzi after about 20 minutes. Enquire at agencies in town about tours.

The well-paved road from Puerto Ayacucho to **Samariapo** (63 km) was built to bypass the rapids which here interrupt the Orinoco, dividing it into 'Upper' and 'Lower'; the powerful Maripures Rapids are very impressive.

Listings Amazonas

Where to stay

Puerto Ayacucho

$$-$ Gran Hotel Amazonas
Av Evelio Roa y Amazonas, T0424-299 8553, www.amazonas.travel.
Refurbished, with a/c, fridge, pool, restaurant and bar.

$$-$ Orinoquia Lodge
On the Río Orinoco, 20 mins from airport, book through Wao Turismo, T0212-214 1027, www.waoturismo. com, Cacao Travel, www.cacaotravel. com, or through, T0212- 977 1234, www. casatropical.com.ve.
Nice setting, comfortable lodgings in thatched huts, full board.

$ Posada Manapiare
Urb Alto Parima, 2da entrada, casa 1, T0212-284 2015, www.amazonas.travel.
Pleasant, good services, lots of information, excellent choice, with restaurant, small pool, safe parking.

$ Residencial Internacional
Av Aguerrevere 18, T0248-521 0242.
A/c (cheaper without), comfortable, shower, locked parking, safe but basic, good place to find tour information and meet other travellers, if no room available you can sling up your hammock, bus drivers stay here and will drive you to the terminal for early starts.

ON THE ROAD

Killer fish

The much-maligned piranha has a fearsome reputation as a flesh-eating monster who will tear any unsuspecting tourist to shreds within seconds of setting foot in a tropical river. But is this infamous fish really so bad? Or is it merely the unfortunate victim of some bad publicity?

There are over 30 types of piranha in South America but only one or two types are flesh eaters. Some feed on other fish and some are even vegetarian. The red-bellied piranhas, though, are real flesh eaters. These 20-cm-long fish with razor-sharp teeth hunt in packs or schools in the many rivers that intersect the Llanos floodplains.

They breed early in the wet season, when both sexes turn a dark shade and the female is swollen with eggs. Then begins the courtship ritual, which can last several nights, as the female takes her time in deciding on her potential partner's suitability as a father. Once her mind is made up they mate and the female takes off, leaving the male to guard the eggs.

Although as many as 4000 come from a single batch of eggs, only a handful survive the first few months. Their greatest test comes in the dry season when there is a danger of becoming isolated from the main rivers and food becomes scarce. The weaker piranhas then become victims as they fall prey to the stronger ones in a frenzy of cannibalism. Birds also join in, feeding on the dying fish. The fabled killer now has no defence against the elements. Those that are too large to be swallowed by the storks are picked off by vultures. Caiman also feed on dying piranhas, attracted by the birds. Piranhas are their favourite snack.

But when the rains come the savannah is turned into a huge inland sea and the tables are turned. The piranhas prey on the great white egrets, which nest in the trees. In their desperate attempts to find more food than their parents can supply, the clumsy chicks leave the nest and fall in the rivers where they are grabbed by the piranhas.

Río Manapiare area

$$$ Campamento Camani
In a forest clearing on the banks of the Río Alto Ventuari, 2 hrs by launch from San Juan de Manapiare, T0248-521 4865, www.campamentocamani.com.
From Puerto Ayacucho daily aerotaxi takes 50 mins. Maximum 26 at any one time, mosquito nets, all amenities, excursions available. Has 2-, 3- and 4-night packages including transport, full board and jungle excursions.

What to do

It is strongly recommended to go on tours organized by tour agents or guides registered in the **Asocación de Guías**, in the Cámara de Turismo de Puerto Ayacucho, Casa de la Piedra, on the Arteria Vial de la Av Orinoco with Av Principal (the house on top of the large rock). Some independent guides may not have permission to visit Amazonas. Those listed below arrange permits and insurance, but shop around.

Coyote Expediciones, *Av Aguirrevere 75, T0248-521 4583, T0416-448 7125, coyotexpedition@cantv.net.* Helpful, professional, English spoken, organizes trips staying in indigenous villages.

Expediciones Aguas Bravas Venezuela, *Av Río Negro, No 32-2, in front of Plaza Rómulo Betancourt, T0248-521 4458/0541, aguasbravas@cantv.net.* Whitewater rafting, 2 daily 0900-1200 and 1500-1800, 3-13 people per boat, reservations required at peak times, take insect repellent, sun protector, light shoes and swimsuit. See also **Rafting Barinas**, page 94.

Transport

Puerto Ayacucho
Air Airport 7 km southeast along Av Orinoco.

Bus **Expresos del Valle** to **Ciudad Bolívar** (US$2.50, 10 hrs; take something to eat, bus stops once for early lunch), **Caicara, Puerto Ordaz** and **San Félix**; **Cooperativa Cacique** to **San Fernando de Apure**, US$1.30, 8 hrs; both companies in bus terminal. **Expresos La Prosperidad** to **Caracas** and **Maracay** from Urb Alto Parima. Bus from **Caracas**, daily, US$3.25, 12 hrs (but much longer in wet season).

Ferry Ferry service across the Orinoco to Casuarito, US$0.50.

East
coast

Beautiful sandy bays, islands, forested slopes and a strong colonial influence all contribute to make this one of the most visited parts of the country. The western part, which is relatively dry, has the two main cities, Puerto La Cruz and Cumaná; the latter is possibly the oldest Hispanic city on the South American mainland. As you go east, you find some splendid beaches.

Offshore are two of Venezuela's prime holiday attractions, Isla de Margarita, a mix of the overdeveloped and the quiet, and the island paradise of the Los Roques archipelago.

Best for
Beaches ▪ Diving ▪ Idyllic islands ▪ Marine life

Very much a holiday coastline, the first part takes its name from the sweeping Barlovento bay in Miranda state. Onshore trade winds give the seaboard a lusher aspect than the more arid landscape elsewhere.

Caracas to Higuerote

It is some five hours from Caracas to Puerto La Cruz through Caucagua, from which there is a 58 km road northeast to **Higuerote**; the best beaches are out of town. A coastal road from Los Caracas to Higuerote has many beaches and beautiful views.

Parque Nacional Laguna de Tacarigua

At 14 km before Higuerote on the road from Caucagua is Tacarigua de Mamporal, where you can turn off to the **Parque Nacional Laguna de Tacarigua**. The

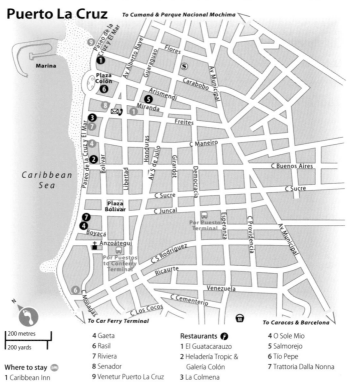

Puerto La Cruz

Where to stay 🛏	
1 Caribbean Inn	
4 Gaeta	
6 Rasil	
7 Riviera	
8 Senador	
9 Venetur Puerto La Cruz	

Restaurants 🍴	
1 El Guatacarauzo	4 O Sole Mio
2 Heladería Tropic & Galería Colón	5 Salmorejo
3 La Colmena	6 Tío Pepe
	7 Trattoria Dalla Nonna

39,100-ha national park is an important ecological reserve, with a lagoon separated from the sea by a landspit, mangroves, good fishing and many water birds, including flamingos (it usually takes a day-long boat trip to see them; the best time is 1700-1930; permit required from Inparques at the *muelle*, US$2.65, open 0500-1830). Around 20,700 ha of the park are offshore. Boat trips leave from the Inparques *muelle* and cost about US$18 per person in a group of four. The beaches beyond here are unspoilt and relaxing, but mosquitoes are a problem after sunset.

Puerto La Cruz and around

Originally a fishing village, Puerto La Cruz is now a major oil refining town and busy, modern holiday resort. Tourist facilities are above average, if expensive, and the sea is polluted.

The seafront avenue, Paseo de La Cruz y El Mar (formerly Paseo Colón), extends to the eastern extremity of a broad bay. To the west the bay ends at the prominent El Morro headland. Most hotels, restaurants, bars and clubs are along Paseo de La Cruz y El Mar, with excellent views of Bahía de Pozuelas and the islands of the Parque Nacional Mochima (see below). Vendors of paintings, jewellery, leather and hammocks are on Paseo de La Cruz y El Mar in the evening.

The **Santa Cruz** festival is on 3 May, while 8 September is the **Virgen del Valle**, when boats cruise the harbour clad in palms and balloons; afternoon party at El Faro, Chimana, lots of salsa and beer.

The main attractions of Puerto La Cruz lie offshore on the many islands of the beautiful Parque Nacional Mochima and in the surrounding waters. For details of how to get there, see below. The tourist office is **Fondoturismo** ① *C Bolívar, Ed Araya, local 3 PB, T0281-267 1632, Mon-Fri 0800-1300*, very helpful and friendly.

Listings Caracas to Puerto La Cruz *map opposite*

Where to stay

Puerto La Cruz
Newer, upmarket hotels are at Lechería and El Morro; cheaper hotels are concentrated in the centre, though it's not easy to find a cheap hotel.

$$$ Venetur Puerto La Cruz
Paseo de La Cruz y El Mar, east edge of the centre, T0281-500 3611, www.venetur.gob.ve.
5-star hotel with all facilities, including gym, spa, marina and beach access.

$$-$ Rasil
Paseo de La Cruz y El Mar y Monagas 6, T0281-262 3000, www.hotelrasil.com.ve.
Rooms, suites and bungalows, 3 restaurants, bar, pool, tour office, gym, money exchange, car rental, convenient for ferries and buses.

$$-$ Riviera
Paseo de La Cruz y El Mar 33, T0281-267 2111, www.hotelriviera.com.ve.
Seafront hotel, some rooms have balcony, bar, watersports, very good location, restaurant, poor breakfast.

$ Caribbean Inn
*Freites, T0281-267 4292, hotelcaribbean@
cantv.net.*
Big rooms, well-kept small pool, very
good service.

$ Gaeta
*Paseo de La Cruz y El Mar y Maneiro, T265
0411, www.hotelgaeta.com.ve.*
Modern, good location but very small
rooms, restaurant.

$ Senador
Miranda y Bolívar, T0281-267 3522.
Back rooms quieter, restaurant with
view, parking.

Restaurants

Puerto La Cruz
Many on Paseo de La Cruz y El Mar, eg
Tío Pepe, delicious seafood. **O Sole Mio**,
cheap, excellent, wide variety. **Trattoria
Dalla Nonna**, Italian food.

$ El Guatacarauzo
De La Cruz y El Marnear Pizza Hut.
Live music, salsa, good atmosphere
and value.

$ La Colmena
Next to Hotel Riviera.
Vegetarian.

$ Salmorejo
Miranda y Honduras.
For chicken and seafood, with a terrace.

Cafés

Heladería Tropic
*Galería Colón on Paseo de La Cruz y
El Mar.*
Good ice cream.

What to do

Puerto La Cruz
Several companies, mostly on Paseo
de La Cruz y El Mar, run **diving
courses**. They're a bit more pricey than
Santa Fe and Mochima. Hotels and
travel agents also organize trips. The
nearest recompression chamber is on
Isla Margarita.
Jakera, *www.jakera.com*. Sea kayaks
for rent from their lodge at Playa
Colorada (T0293-808 7057), trips to
whole country arranged (lodge in
Mérida too, office C 24, No 8-205, Plaza
Las Heroínas, Mérida, T0274-252 9577,
0416-887 2239), also Spanish lessons
and volunteering. Chris and Joanna are
helpful, English spoken.

Transport

Puerto La Cruz
Bus Bus terminal to the east of town;
por puesto terminal at Av Juncal y
Democracia, many buses also stop here.
To **Caracas** by regular bus, US$1.50.
To **Ciudad Bolívar** US$1.35; to **Ciudad
Guayana** US$7.50. To **Cumaná**, bus
US$0.35, 1½ hrs. To **Carúpano**, US$1,
5 hrs. *Por puesto* to **Playa Colorado**
US$0.50 and to **Santa Fe** US$1. Along
Av 5 de Julio runs a bus marked
'Intercomunal'. It links Puerto La Cruz
with the city of Barcelona (which has
the nearest airport) and intervening
points. Another Barcelona bus is marked
'Ruta Alternativa' and uses the inland
highway via the Puerto La Cruz Golf
and Country Club and Universidad de
Oriente, US$0.25.

Ferry For details of ferries to Isla de
Margarita, see page 124.

Parque Nacional Mochima

blissful beaches and offshore islands

★Beyond the cities of Barcelona and Puerto La Cruz, the main focus is the Mochima National Park, one of the country's most beautiful regions. Hundreds of tiny Caribbean islands, a seemingly endless series of beaches backed by some of Venezuela's most beautiful scenery and little coves tucked into bays, all offer excellent snorkelling, fishing and swimming.

Along the coast

Starting east from Puerto La Cruz is the **Costa Azul**, with the islands of the Parque Nacional Mochima offshore. Highway 9 follows the shore for much of the 85 km

Essential Parque Nacional Mochima

Getting there

The highway between Puerto La Cruz and Cumaná runs through the park with access to many beautiful beaches. Tour companies offer trips to the islands from Puerto La Cruz, but you can also go independently with the cooperative boatmen, *peñeros*. One dock, **Transtupaco**, is next to **Venetur Puerto La Cruz**. The other **Embarcadero de Peñeros**, is on the point at the southwest end of Paseo de La Cruz y El Mar, by Calle Anzoátegui. Departures from 0900-1000, return at 1600-1630; US$2 per person. If beaches are full, the authorities will stop boats leaving. Tourist office in Puerto La Cruz provides tour operators for day trips to various islands for swimming or snorkelling; six-hour trip to four islands costs US$20 per person, including drinks. The islands to the east (Isla de Plata, Monos, Picuda Grande and Chica and the beaches of Ña Cleta, Conoma and Conomita) are best reached from the ports at **Guanta**, called Barinita and Valle Seco, US$3.50 (taxi from town, or *por puesto* from C Freites between Avenida 5 de Julio and Calle Democracia, and ask to be dropped off at the Urbanización Pamatacualito). Boat trips to the islands can also be taken from **Santa Fe** or **Mochima** (see below).

When to go

At Christmas, Carnival and Easter this part of the coast becomes extremely congested so patience is needed as long queues of traffic can develop. Accommodation is very hard to find and prices increase by 20-30%. Try to visit at quieter times of year.

Advice and regulations

To prevent littering and pollution, especially on the islands, carry out all your rubbish (no alcohol in glass bottles may be taken). Camping on the islands in Parque Nacional Mochima is possible, but not advisable. To stay overnight you need a permit from Inparques, Parque Andrés Eloy Blanco, US$1.50. Only camping gas cookers allowed. On day trips, take your own food as the island restaurants are expensive. When hiring a parasol for the day, make sure exactly what is included in the price and beware 'extra services'.

to Cumaná, but a new highway is being built. The road is spectacular but if driving take great care between Playa Colorada and Cumaná. It passes the 'paradise-like' beaches of **Conoma** and **Conomita**. Further along is **Playa Arapito** (posada, $, restaurant, parking extra). Here boats can be hired to **La Piscina**, a beautiful coral reef near some small islands, for good snorkelling (with lots of dolphins); US$8 per boat.

Playa Colorada is a popular beach (Km 32) with beautiful red sands and palm trees (take a *por puesto* from corner of terminal in Puerto La Cruz, US$0.50). Nearby are **Playa Vallecito** (camping free, security guard, bar with good food and bottled water on sale, plenty of palm trees for slinging a hammock) and **Playa Santa Cruz**. At **Playa Los Hicacos** is a lovely coral reef.

In Sucre State 40 km from Puerto La Cruz is **Santa Fe**, larger and noisier than Mochima, but still a good place to relax. The attractive beach is cleaned daily. It has a market on Saturday. Jeep, boat or diving tours available. Fishermen offer boat trips, for around US$10 per person to Playas Colorada or Blanca; it's cheaper to hire your own boat, or hitch to Colorada.

The little village of **Mochima** beyond Santa Fe, is 4 km off the main road (hitching difficult). It's busy at weekends but almost deserted through the week. Boats take tourists to nearby beaches, such as **Playa Marita** and **Playa Blanca** (excellent snorkelling, take own equipment). Both have restaurants, but take food and water to be safe. Boats to the nearby beaches cost US$8 (up to six people), depending on distance. Arrange with the boatman what time he will collect you. There are also five- to six-island trips, US$10-16. Canoeing trips are available and walks on local trails and to caves (ask for information, eg from Carlos Hernández, or Rodolfo Plaza, see Diving, below).

Listings Parque Nacional Mochima

Where to stay

Along the coast
Playa Colorada

$$ Sunset Inn
Av Principal, T0416-887 8156.
Clean, comfortable, pool, hot water.

$ Quinta Jaly
C Marchán, T0293-808 3246/0416-681 8113.
Hot water, very quiet, also 1 bungalow sleeps 6, family atmosphere, English and French spoken, use of kitchen, laundry facilities, good breakfast extra, multilingual library. Recommended.

$ Villa Nirvana
6-min walk uphill from beach, opposite Jaly, run by Sra Rita who is Swiss, T808 7844.
Rooms with fan or a/c, also mini-apartments with kitchen for 2-6 people, hot water, kitchen facilities, English, French and German spoken, book exchange, laundry, breakfast extra.

Santa Fe

$$$-$$ Playa Santa Fe Resort and Dive Center
T0293-231 0051, www.santaferesort.com.
Renovated posada with rooms and suites, laundry service, owner Howard Rankell speaks English, can arrange transport to beaches, kitchen.

$ Bahía del Mar
T0293-231 0073/T0426-481 7242, www.posadabahiadelmar.com.
Pleasant rooms with a/c or fan, upstairs rooms have a cool breeze, owners María and Juan speak French and some English.

$ Café del Mar
first hotel on beach, T0293-231 0009.
A/c or cheaper with fan, good restaurant. Rogelio Alcaraz speaks English and Italian, arranges tours to islands.

$ Cochaima
On beach, T0293-642 07828.
Run by Margot, noisy, popular, a/c or fan, safe. Recommended.

$ La Sierra Inn
Near Café del Mar, T0293-231 0042.
Self-contained garden suite with fridge and cooker, run by Sr José Vivas, English spoken, helpful, tours to islands. Recommended.

$ Las Palmeras
T0293-231 0008, www. laspalmerassantafe.blogspot.com.
Behind Cochaima, fan, room for 5 with fridge and cooker. Price negotiable, ask about light work in exchange for longer stays. English, German, Italian and Portuguese spoken

$ Petit Jardin
Behind Cochaima, T0293-231 0036/T0416-387 5093, www.lepetitjardin-mochima.com.
A/c or fan, hot water, kitchen, pool, helpful.

Mochima

Various apartments are available for larger groups, look for signs.

$ Posada Doña Cruz
T0293-416 6114.
A/c, cable TV. Run by José Cruz, family also rents rooms at **Posada Mama Cruz** on the plaza with a/c and living room.

$ Posada El Embajador
Av W Larrazabal, T0293-416 3437, by the jetty.
Good value, comfortable, breakfast, boat trips arranged.

$ Posada Gaby
At end of road with its own pier next to sea, T0293-431 0842/0414-773 1104.
A/c or fan, breakfast available, lovely place.

$ Posada Mochimero
Omain street in front of Restaurant Mochimero, T0414-773 8782.
A/c or fan, rooms with bath.

$ Villa Vicenta
Av Principal, T0293-416 0916.
Basic rooms with cold water and larger rooms with balcony, also cold water, dining room, owner Otilio is helpful.

Restaurants

Along the coast
Santa Fe

$ Club Naútico
Open for lunch and dinner.
Fish and Venezuelan dishes.

$ Los Molinos (Julios)
Open from 0800.
Beach bar serves sandwiches, hamburgers and cocktails.

Mochima

$ El Mochimero
On waterfront 5 mins from jetty.
Highly recommended for lunch and dinner.

$ Il Forno de Mochima
Main street.
Run by Roberto Iorio, for those who would like a change from seafood, home-made pastas and pizza.

$ Puerto Viejo
On the plaza.
Good food, if a bit pricey, good views.

What to do

Mochima

Diving Rodolfo Plaza runs a diving lodge and school (**La Posada de los Buzos**, T0424-807 6470, 0414-180 6244, www.laposadadelosbuzos.com) and hires equipment, also walking, rafting (mochimarafting@hotmail.com), kayaking and canoeing trips.

Transport

Santa Fe
Getting there from **Cumaná**, take *por puesto* 1 block down from the Redonda del Indio, along Av Perimetral, US$1.
It may be difficult to get a bus from **Puerto La Cruz** to stop at Santa Fe, take a *por puesto* (depart from terminal, US$1, 1 hr), or taxi, US$3.50 including wait.

Mochima
Bus From **Cumaná** to Mochima take a bus from outside the terminal and ask to be let off at the street where the transport goes to Mochima, US$0.50; change here to crowded bus or jeep (US$0.25). No buses between Santa Fe and Mochima, take a *por puesto*, bargain hard on the price, US$5-8 is reasonable. Bus to Cumaná, 1400, US$0.50.

Cumaná

a charming riverside town

Cumaná was founded in 1521 to exploit the nearby pearl fisheries. It straddles both banks of the Río Manzanares. Because of a succession of devastating earthquakes (the last in 1997), only a few historic sites remain. Like any other city it is not safe at night, the port area (1.5 km from the centre) especially so. Main festivals are 22 January, Santa Inés, a pre-Lenten carnival throughout the state of Sucre and 2 November, the Santos y Fideles Difuntos festival at El Tacal.

Sights
A long public beach, **San Luis,** is a short bus ride from the centre of town; take the 'San Luis/Los Chaimas' bus. The least spoilt part is the end by the old **Hotel Los Bordones.**

The **Castillo de San Antonio de la Eminencia** (1686) has 16 mounted cannons, a drawbridge and dungeons from which there are said to be underground tunnels leading to the Santa Inés church. Restored in 1975, it is floodlit at night (but don't go there after dark, it's not safe). The **Castillo de Santa María de la Cabeza** (1669) is a rectangular fortress with a panoramic view of San Antonio and the elegant homes below. **Convento de San Francisco**, the original Capuchin mission of 1514, was the first school on the continent; its remains are on the Plaza Badaracco Bermúdez facing the beach. The **Church of Santa Inés** (1637) was the base of the Franciscan missionaries; earthquakes have caused it to be rebuilt five times. A tiny 400-year-old statue of the Virgen de Candelaria is in the garden. The **home of Andrés Eloy Blanco** (1896-1955) ① *0800-1200, 1430-1730, free*, one of Venezuela's greatest poets and politicians, on Plaza Bolívar, has been nicely restored to its turn-of-the-20th century elegance. On the opposite side of the plaza is **La Gobernación** around a courtyard lined by cannon from Santa María de la Cabeza; note the gargoyles and other colonial features. There are markets selling handicrafts and food on both sides of the river.

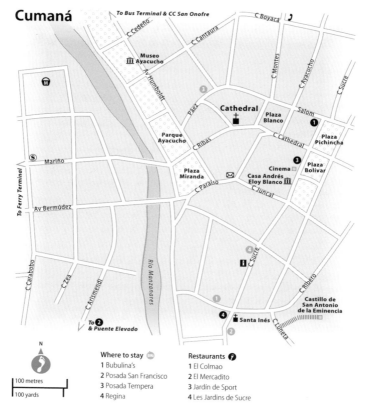

Cumaná

Where to stay 🛏
1 Bubulina's
2 Posada San Francisco
3 Posada Tempera
4 Regina

Restaurants 🍴
1 El Colmao
2 El Mercadito
3 Jardín de Sport
4 Les Jardins de Sucre

The **Museo Gran Mariscal de Ayacucho** ⓘ *Consejo Municipal in Parque Ayacucho, Tue-Fri 0845-1130, 1545-1830; free tours*, commemorates the battle of Ayacucho with portraits, relics and letters of Bolívar and José Antonio Sucre (Bolívar's first lieutenant). **Museo del Mar** ⓘ *Av Universidad with Av Industrial, Tue-Sun 0830-1130, 1500-1800, US$1*. To get there take San Luis minibus from the cathedral, has exhibits of tropical marine life, at the old airport.

Listings Cumaná *map p107*

Tourist information

Corsotur
C Sucre 49, T0293-441 0136, http://sucrecorsotur.blogspot.co.uk.
Mornings only.
This office is very helpful, English spoken.

Where to stay

$$ Nueva Toledo Suites
End of Av Universidad, close to San Luis beach, T0293-451 8118 ext 401, www.nuevatoledo.com.
Pool, beach bar, good value all-inclusive deals.

$ Bubulina's
C Santa Inés, ½ a block west of Santa Inés church, T0293-431 4025, bubulinas10@hotmail.com.
In the historic centre, beautifully restored colonial building, hot water, good service, German spoken.

$ Posada San Francisco
C Sucre 16, near Santa Inés, T0293-431 3926, posadafrancisco@cantv.net.
Renovated colonial house, courtyard, spacious rooms, hot water, cheaper rooms with fan, very helpful, bar, restaurant. Recommended.

$ Posada Tempera
C Páez 7, behind the cathedral, T0293-431 2178, www.tempera-posada.com.
Charming, comfortable small posada in historic centre, hot water, a/c, Wi-Fi, good breakfast extra, laundry service, parking outside or in nearby guarded parking lot. Also here is **Topaz** tour operator.

$ Regina
Arismendi y Av Bermúdez, T0293-431 1073.
Hot water, restaurant, helpful.

Restaurants

All central restaurants close Sun lunchtime. After dark take a taxi.

$$ Les Jardins de Sucre
Sucre 27, in front of the Santa Inés church.
French food, good service, outdoor seating. Recommended.

$ El Colmao on Plaza Pichincha
C Sucre.
Serves very good fish, with charming service, karaoke.

$ El Mercadito at Puente Elevado.
For excellent cheap lunches, fish and seafood.

$ Jardín de Sport
Plaza Bolívar.
Outdoor café, good food, noisy atmosphere. Recommended.

What to do

Posadas San Francisco, Tempera and **Bubulina's** can help arrange local tours, as well as sailing and diving trips.

Transport

Bus Terminal 3 km northwest of the centre on Av Las Palomas, just before the junction with the peripheral road. Local bus into centre US$0.25, taxi US$1-2. To **Puerto La Cruz**, US$0.40, 1½ hrs. To **Güiria**, US$1.35, **Expresos Los Llanos** once a day, *por puesto* US$3.50 (6-7 hrs), beware of overcharging, often stop in Irapa. To **Carúpano**, US$1, 2-3 hrs. To **Caripe**, you have to go to **Santa María**, south of Cariaco, and change to *por puesto* there. To **Caracas**, US$1.75 (7-8 hrs), frequent service; many daily to **Ciudad Guayana** and **Ciudad Bolívar**, US$2 and US$1.55 respectively.

Ferry For Ferries to **Araya Peninsula** and **Isla de Margarita**, see below and page 124.

Araya to Paria

don't miss the detour to the Cueva del Guácharo

This section is bounded by two peninsulas, Araya, which is an area of desert landscapes and pink salt lakes, and Paria, a finger of land stretching out to the most easterly point on Venezuela's Caribbean coast and a place of peaceful, coastal towns, beaches and forest. The eastern mountains, rising to 2000 m at their highest point, receive abundant rainfall in their tropical forest.

Araya Peninsula

The main settlement is Araya which has an airport and a ferry dock. The major sight is the **Fortaleza de Santiago de León**, built by Spain to protect the salt mines, but of which very little now remains. Construction began in 1622 and it took 47 years to complete. Entry is free, but the only facilities are a refreshment stand and a picnic area. Today the mines are exploited by a state-owned corporation, ENSAL. Windsurfing is excellent, but only for the experienced.

Carúpano

This is a colonial town dating back to 1647, from which 70% of Venezuela's cocoa is shipped. The area around Plaza Santa Rosa has been declared a national heritage site. Buildings include the **Museo Histórico**, containing a comprehensive database on the city, and the **Iglesia Santa Rosa**. The **Casa del Cable** ① *T0294-331 3847, www.fundacionthomasmerle.org.ve*, location of the first telecommunications link with Europe, is the headquarters of the Fundación Thomas Merle, run by Wilfried Merle, who has been instrumental in setting up ecotourism and economic development projects in the Paria Peninsula. Carúpano is famous throughout Venezuela as the last place still celebrating a traditional pre-Lenten Carnival days of dancing, rum drinking, with masked women in black (*negritas*). Book well ahead for places to stay at this time (February). Other local festivals are 3 May, **Velorios de la Cruz** (street dances); 15 August, **Asunción de la Virgen**. On the outskirts of Carúpano is **Playa**

Copey (ask the *por puesto*/bus to drop you at Playa Copey if arriving from Cumaná or other westerly points, or take a taxi from town, US$8). It is not easy to change foreign currency in Carúpano. See www.carupano.org.

Caripe and around

A paved road runs inland from Carúpano to Caripe via Cariaco and Santa María. Between Cariaco and Casanay, **Las Aguas de Moisés** ① *T0294-416 8184, www. lasaguasdemoises.com, open 0800-1600, US$2, US$1.55 for seniors and children, ask to be let off from bus or por puesto on Cariaco-Carúpano route*, is a tourist park containing 11 large thermal pools. The waters are said to be curative and there are lots of sporting and other activities. Camping ($) is available, or **Hotel Faraón** (T0294-555 1036).

    Caripe is an attractive town set in gorgeous mountain scenery. There is a lively daily market. It is 12 km from the famous Cueva del Guácharo and a good place to escape from the beaches. It's especially good for walking and biking. At San Francisco, on the Maturín–Cumaná road (212 km, all paved but twisty; beautiful tropical mountain scenery), is a branch road running 22.5 km northeast to Caripe. **Feria de las Flores** is on 2-12 August and **NS del Pilar** is 10-12 October. See http:// caripe.net. To get to Caripe from Caracas you must go to **Maturín** (the capital of Monagas state), offering relatively expensive accommodation), then take a *por puesto*. Alternatively go to Cumaná and then to Santa María for *por puesto* services.

Cueva del Guácharo

Open 0830-1600, US$2 with compulsory guide in Spanish, speak some English and German. Leave backpacks at the ticket office, photography is not allowed. To go further into the caves permits from Inparques in Caracas are needed.

This remarkable cave was discovered by Humboldt and has since been penetrated 10.5 km along a small, crystal-clear stream. In the first caves live around 18,000 *guácharos* (oil birds) with an in-built radar system for sightless flight. Their presence supports a variety of wildlife in the cave blind mice, fish and crabs in the stream, yellow-green plants, crickets and ants. For two hours at dusk (about 1900) the birds pour out of the cave's mouth. Through a very narrow entrance is the **Cueva del Silencio** (Cave of Silence). About 2 km in is the **Pozo del Viento** (Well of the Wind).

    Wear old clothes, stout shoes and be prepared to get wet. In the wet season it can be a bit slippery; tours in the cave may be closed in August-September because of rising water level. There is a caving museum with good cafeteria. Opposite the road is a paved path to **Salto Paila**, a 25-m waterfall, about 30 minutes' walk, guides available for US$3. A beautiful path, built by Inparqes, starts at the caving museum, with some nice shelters for picnics. Camping is allowed by the cave for US$1, or you can sleep without a tent under the roof by the café for free.

Paria Peninsula

Río Caribe This lovely fishing village (population 51,100, 20 km east of Carúpano) used to be a major cacao-exporting port. It is a good jumping-off point for the beautiful beaches of **Playa Medina** (in an old coconut plantation, 25 km east) and **Pui Puy**, both famous for their crystal-clear water and golden sands. Playa Medina is safe, has shade for rent and stalls selling food and drink; it is crowded at weekends and holidays. Cabins at the beach are expensive (**$$** per person). To get to Playa Medina, take a taxi, US$10 return trip per car, US$11 to Pui Puy, as *camionetas* do not go to the beaches, only to the entrance, from where it's two hours' walk or more (not safe). Surfing at Playas Pui Puy and Querepare; visit **Querepare** between May and August to watch sea turtles laying their eggs.

Further east is the delightful village of **San Juan de las Galdonas** and some great beaches. Near Chacaracual, 15 minutes' drive from Río Caribe is **Paria Shakti** ⓘ *T0294-611 8767/T0416-401 8098, paraishakti@gmail.com, see Facebook*, a 1.6-ha cacao plantation and holistic health centre that offers factory tours and massages. Next door, visit **Aguasana**, a hacienda with mineral-rich hot springs and mud pools (see Where to stay, below). Near Bohordal is **Campamento Hato Rio de Agua**, a buffalo ranch available for day visits and milk factory tours; many species of birds can be seen (also see Where to stay). Day trips are also available to **Caño de Ajíes** with a visit to a waterfall and the estuary which flows into the Golfo de Paria; you can see crocodiles, birds and snakes. It is part of the Parque Nacional Turuépano.

Güiria At Bohordal, the paved road from Río Caribe across the mountains meets Route 9, which continues to the pleasant town of **Irapa** (hotels, bus connections). The paved highway continues 42 km to **Güiria** (www.guiria.com.ve), a friendly, peaceful town and a badly littered beach. **Feria de la Pesca**, 14 July.

Macuro A quiet town on the tip of the Peninsula, Macuro is accessible by boat (two hours from Güiria) and by a new road from Güiria (20 km paved, the remainder passable by 4WD). It was around here that Columbus made the first recorded European landing on the continent on 5 August 1498. Locals like to believe the landing took place at Macuro, and the town's official new name is Puerto Colón. There is a small **Museo de Macuro** on Calle Bolívar, 1 block from **Posada Beatriz**; ask here about walking tours and boat trips. A big party is held here every year on 12 October to mark the official 'discovery' of America. Restaurants only open at weekends. There are also a few basic shops and a pharmacy. The boat to Güiria leaves at 0500, arrive early, US$1.50 per person.

The beach is unattractive but the coast on the north side of the peninsula is truly wonderful; crystal-clear water and dazzling sands backed by dense jungle. A highly recommended trip for the adventurous is the hike to **Uquire** and **Don Pedro** on the north coast; four to six hours' walk, places to hang a hammock or pitch a tent. **Note** This part of the peninsula is a national park; you need a permit from Inparques in Caracas.

Where to stay

Araya

$ Araya Mar
El Castillo, T0293-437 1382/
T0414-777 3682.
Hot water, good restaurant, arranges car and boat tours to the Salinas and around Araya, parking. Good restaurant serves Venezuelan food. Recommended.

$ Araya Wind
Beside the Fortaleza in front of beach,
T0293-437 1132.
Some rooms with bath, cold water.

$ Lagunasal
C El Progreso, T0293-437 1290/
T0424-849 9730.
Modern posada, 100 m from the dock, with good services.

Carúpano

$$-$ Hotel Euro Caribe Internacional
Av Perimetral Rómulo Gallegos, T0294-331 3911, www.eurocaribehotel.com.
Well located, some rooms with sea view, attentive staff, parking, good Italian restaurant.

$$-$ La Colina
Av Rómulo Gallegos 33, behind Hotel Victoria, T0294-332 2915.
Restaurant on terrace, beautiful view, comfortable rooms. Recommended.

$ Lilma
Av Independencia, 3 blocks from Plaza Colón, T0294-331 1361.
Hot water, restaurant, *tasca*, cinema.

$ Victoria
Av Perimetral Rómulo Gallegos, T0294-331 2832, hotelvictoria@hotmail.com.
Safe but basic, hot water.

Playa Copey

$ Posada Casa Blanca
Av Principal, 5 mins from Posada Nena, T0294-331 6896, www.posadacasablanca.com.
Hot water, safe, good family atmosphere, private stretch of beach illuminated at night, Spanish restaurant, German spoken, discounts for long stays.

$ Posada Nena
1 block from the beach, T0294-331 7297, www.venezuela-vacaciones.com.
Hot water, games room, good restaurant, public phone, good service, German spoken, owner Volker Alsen offers day trips to Cueva del Guácharo, Mochima, Medina and other Venezuelan destinations. Recommended.

Caripe

$$-$ Finca Agroturística Campo Claro
At Teresén, T0292-414 9409, www.haciendacampoclaro.com.
Cabins for 4-15 people with cooking facilities and hot water, also rooms ($), restaurant for residents, horse riding.

$$-$ Samán
Enrique Chaumer 29, T0292-545 1183, www.hotelsaman.com.
Also has more expensive suites, comfortable, pool, parking, not so welcoming to backpackers.

Río Caribe

As well as those listed, there are other posadas and private, unmarked pensions; ask around.

$$ Posada Caribana
Av Bermúdez 25, T0294-263 3649, www.parquenivaldito.com.
Beautifully restored colonial house, tastefully decorated, a/c or fan, restaurant, bar, excursions. Ask about posada at Playa Uva.

$ La Posada de Arlet
24 de Julio 22, T0294-646 1290.
English and German spoken, bar, arranges day trips to local beaches. Recommended.

$ Pensión Papagayos
14 de Febrero, 1 block from police station, opposite liceo, T0294-646 1868.
Charming house and garden, shared bath with hot water, use of kitchen, nice atmosphere, owner Cristina Castillo.

$ Posada Shalimar
Av Bermúdez 54, T0294-646 1135, www.posada-shalimar.com.
Francisco González speaks English, very helpful, can arrange tours to and provide information about local beaches and other areas. Beautiful rooms situated around pool have a/c. Recommended.

San Juan de las Galdonas

$$ Playa Galdonas
T0294-332 2915.
Overlooking the main beach, hot water, bar/restaurant, swimming pool, English and French spoken, arranges boat tours to Santa Isabel and beaches.

$ pp Habitat Paria
T0294-511 9571, www.soaf.info/hp/.
With breakfast and supper, huge, splendid, zodiac theme, fan, bar/restaurant, terraces, garden. The posada is right behind Barlovento beach on the right hand side of San Juan. Can arrange boat tours. Recommended.

$ Posada Las Tres Carabelas
T0294-511 2729/0416-894 0914, lastrescarabelas3@gmail.com.
Fans and mosquito nets, restaurant, wonderful view, owner is knowledgeable about local area.

Outside Río Caribe

$$ Hato Río de Agua
T0294-332 0527.
Rustic cabins with fans, private bathrooms, restaurant on a buffalo ranch (see above), price includes breakfast and tours of dairy factory.

$ pp Hacienda Posada Aguasana
T0416-607 1913/ T0414-304 5687, www.posadaaguasana.com.
Attractive rooms with fans near hot springs, price includes breakfast and dinner. 3-7 packages available, with and without transfers.

Güiria

$ Plaza
Esq Plaza Bolívar, T0294-982 0022.
Basic, restaurant, luggage store.

$ Timón de Máximo
C Bideau, 2 blocks from plaza, T0294-784 1776.
Hotel with good criollo restaurant. Recommended.

$ Vista Mar
Valdez y Trincheras.
Hot water, fridge, restaurant.

Macuro

$ Posada Beatriz
C Mariño y Carabobo.
Basic, clean, with bath, fan.

Restaurants

Araya

Eat early as most places close before 2000. Hamburger stalls around the dock and 2 *panaderías*.

$ El Timonel de Fabi.
Tasca across from dock.
Venezuelan food, karaoke.

$ Eugenía
In front of Posada Helen.
For good-value meals.

$ Las Churuatas de Miguel
On the beach near dock.
Fish and typical food.

Carúpano

$$-$ El Fogón de La Petaca
Av Perimetral on the seafront.
Traditional Venezuelan dishes, fish.

$$-$ La Madriguera
Av Perimetral Rómulo Gallegos, in Hotel Eurocaribe.
Good Italian food, some vegetarian dishes, Italian and English spoken.

$ Bam Bam
Kiosk at the end of Plaza Miranda, close to seafront.
Tasty hotdogs and hamburgers.

$ El Oasis
Juncal in front of Plaza Bolívar. Open from 1700.
Best Arabic food in Carúpano.

$ La Flor de Oriente
Av Libertad y Victoria, 4 blocks from Plaza Colón. Open from 0800.

Arepas, fruit juice and main meals, good, large portions, good, food, reasonable prices, very busy at lunchtime.

Other options include the food stalls in the market, especially the one next to the car park, and the *empanadas* in the Plaza Santa Rosa.

Caripe

$$ Tasca Mogambo
Next to Hotel Saman.
Good, local food.

$$ La Trattoria
C Cabello.
Wide variety of good food, popular with locals and tourists.

Río Caribe

$$ Mi Cocina
On the road parallel to Av Bermúdez, 3 mins' walk from Plaza Bolívar.
Very good food, large portions.

Güiria

Everywhere is closed Sun, except for kiosks on Plaza Bolívar.

$$ El Limón
C Trinchera near C Concepcion.
Good value, outdoor seating.

$$ Rincón Güireño
Corner of Plaza Sucre.
Good for breakfast (also rents rooms, $).

Transport

Araya

Ferry Cumaná–Araya car ferry, *La Palita* (Naviarca), T0293-432 0011/0293-431 5577, 3 times a day, US$0.10 pp, US$0.50-1 per car. To get to ferry terminal take taxi in Cumaná, US$1 (avoid walking; it can be dangerous). Alternatively, take a *tapaíto* (passenger ferry in a converted fishing boat, leave when full, crowded, stuffy, US$0.10) to Manicuare and *camioneta* from there to Araya (15 mins). Return ferries from Araya depart from main wharf at end of Av Bermúdez.

Carúpano

Air The airport is 15 mins' walk from the centre, US$1 by taxi. Check with **Rutaca** (*T0501-788 2221*), which occasionally offers flights to Caracas through Porlamar.

Bus To **Caracas**, US$2.50, 9 hrs, to Terminal de Oriente. For other destinations *por puestos* are a better option, eg **Cumaná**, US$2, 2 hrs, **Puerto La Cruz**, US$2, 4 hrs (Mochima/Santa Fé), **Güiria**, US$1.50, 3 hrs. They run more frequently and make fewer stops. Buses do not go from Carúpano to Caripe, you have to take a *por puesto* to **Cariaco**, US$0.50, then another to **Santa María**, US$1, then another to Caripe, US$0.75.

Caripe

Bus Terminal 1 block south of main plaza. For **Carúpano**, take *por puestos* to Santa María and Cariaco (see above), similarly for **Río Caribe** and **Las Aguas de Moisés**. To get to **Cumaná**, go to Santa María and catch transport from there. Bus to **Maturín** several daily, 2½ hrs, US$1.75; Maturín–**Caracas** costs US$2.25, 7½ hrs. *Por puestos* run from Maturín to Ciudad Bolívar.

Cueva del Guácharo

Bus Frequent from **Caripe** to the caves. If staying in Caripe, take a *por puesto* (a jeep marked Santa María-Muelle), at 0800, see the caves and waterfall and catch the Cumaná bus which goes past the caves between 1200 and 1230. Taxis from Caripe US$1, hitching possible. *Por puesto* from Cumaná US$2.50, 2 hrs. Private tours can be organized from Cumaná for about US$8 pp, with guide.

Río Caribe and San Juan de las Galdonas

Bus Direct from **Caracas** (Terminal del Oriente) to Río Caribe , US$2.50, 10 hrs, and from **Maturín**, US$1. *Por puesto* **Carúpano**–Río Caribe, US$0.75, or taxi US$3. Buses depart Río Caribe from the other Plaza Bolívar, 7 blocks up from pier. Jeep Carúpano–San Juan de las Galdonas 1100, 1½ hrs; *camioneta* from Río Caribe from stop near petrol station, 0600 till 1300, US$1.50.

Güiria

Bus Depart Plaza Sucre, at top end of C Bolívar to **Maturín** (0400, US$1.50, 6 hrs), **Caripito**, **San Félix**, **Cumaná**, US$1.35, Puerto La Cruz, US$1.50, and **Caracas**, US$3.

Ferry To **Macuro** daily 1100-1200 from the Playita, US$1-2, return 0500, 2 hrs. To **Trinidad** The ferry between Chaguaramas, Trinidad, and **Güiria**, operated by **Pier 1 Cruises**, www.pier1tt. com, was suspended indefinitely. Check with Pier 1 Cruises for resumption of service. Should the ferry run again, note that visas can't be arranged in Güiria, should you need one. Check all formalities in advance in Caracas or at another Trinidad and Tobago consulate.

Margarita is the country's main Caribbean holiday destination and is popular with both Venezuelans and foreign tourists. The island's reputation for picture-postcard, white-sand beaches is well deserved. Some parts are crowded but there are undeveloped beaches and colonial villages. Porlamar is the most built-up and commercial part of the island while Juan Griego and La Restinga are much quieter.

Despite the property boom and the frenetic building on much of the coast and in Porlamar, much of the island has been given over to natural parks. Of these the most striking is the **Laguna La Restinga**.

The western part, the **Peninsula de Macanao**, is hotter and more barren, with scrub, sand dunes and marshes. Wild deer, goats and hares roam the interior, but 4WDs are needed to penetrate it. The entrance to the Peninsula de Macanao is a pair of hills known as **Las Tetas de María Guevara**, a national monument covering 1670 ha. There are mangroves in the **Laguna de las Marites** natural monument, west of Porlamar.

Isla de Margarita

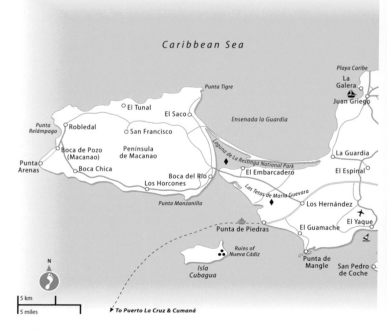

Other parks are **Cerro El Copey**, 7130 ha, and **Cerro Matasiete y Guayamurí**, 1672 ha (both reached from La Asunción). The climate is exceptionally good and dry. Roads are good and a bridge links the two parts. Nueva Esparta's population is over 437,000, of whom 185,000 live in Porlamar. The capital is La Asunción.

Porlamar

Most of the island's high-rise hotels are at Porlamar which is 20 km from airport and 28 km from Punta de Piedra, where ferries dock. Porlamar's beaches are nothing special, but it makes up for what it lacks in this department with its shops (see Shopping, below). At Igualdad y Díaz is the **Museo de Arte Francisco Narváez**, which has some good displays of the work of this local sculptor and other Venezuelan artists. At night everything closes by 2300.

The **Bella Vista** beach is busy but clean and has lots of restaurants lining the seafront. **Playa Concorde** is small, sheltered and tucked by the marina. **Playa Morena** is a long, barren strip of sand for the Costa Azul hotel zone east of the city. **La Caracola** is a popular beach for a young crowd.

Essential Isla de Margarita

Finding your feet

The capital of the island is La Asunción, on the eastern side. Porlamar, to the south, is the most developed area. If you're seeking sun and sand, then head for the north coast towns where the beaches tend to be lined with low-rise hotels and thatched restaurants. A 22-km sandbar known as La Restinga joins the eastern part of Margarita to the barren Península de Macanao via a road bridge.

Getting there and around

There are many national, international and charter flights to Isla de Margarita. There are also ferries from La Guaira (Caracas), Puerto La Cruz and Cumaná. Car hire is a good way of getting around (see Transport, page 123). Women should avoid walking alone at night on the island and after dark no one should go to the beaches(except El Yaque, see below).

South coast

Playa El Yaque, on the south coast near the airport, is a mecca for wind- and kitesurfers (see What to do, below). The winds are perfect from mid-June to mid-October and the water is shallow enough to stand when you fall off. After dark it becomes an open-air disco and is the safest beach on the island at night. Most visitors come on package deals and therefore accommodation is expensive, but cheaper places to stay can be found. There is no public transport; a taxi from Porlamar costs US$5. **Cholymar** travel agency will change money and there is a *casa de cambio* in the **Hotel California**.

Tip...

It is advisable to reserve ahead, especially in high season, to get the best value for accommodation.

Boats go from Punta de Piedra, El Yaque and La Isleta to the **Isla de Coche** (11 by 6 km), which has 4500 inhabitants and one of the richest salt mines in the country (see Transport, below). They also go, on hire only, to **Isla de Cubagua**, which is totally deserted, but you can visit the ruins of **Nueva Cádiz** (which have been excavated). Large private yachts and catamarans take tourists on day trips to Coche.

Pampatar

For a more Venezuelan atmosphere go northeast to Pampatar, which is set around a bay favoured by yachtsmen as a summer anchorage. Pampatar has the island's largest fort, **San Carlos de Borromeo**, which was built in 1662 after the Dutch destroyed the original. Jet skis can be hired on the clean and pretty beach. A fishing boat can be hired for 2½ hours, four to six passengers; shop around for best price; it's good fun and makes for a worthwhile fishing trip.

La Asunción

The capital, La Asunción, is located a few kilometres inland from Porlamar. It has several **colonial buildings**, a **cathedral**, and the **fort of Santa Rosa** ⓘ *Mon 0800-1500, the rest of the week 0800-1800*, which features a famous bottle dungeon. There is a **museum** in the Casa Capitular, and a good local **market**, worth browsing for handicrafts. Nearby is the **Cerro Matasiete** historical site, where the defeat of the Spanish on 31 July 1817 led to their evacuation of the island.

Eastern and northern beaches

Playa Guacuco, reached from La Asunción by a road through the Guayamurí reserve, is a local beach with a lot of surf, fairly shallow, palm trees, restaurants and car park. Playa Parguito further up the east coast is best for surfing (strong waves; full public services).

Playa El Agua has 4 km of white sand with many kiosks and shady restaurants on the beach and on Calle Miragua. The sea is very rough in winter (dangerous for children), but fairly shallow; beware the strong cross current when you are about waist deep. This beach gets overcrowded at Venezuelan holiday times. The fashionable part is at the south end. The beach is 45 minutes by bus from Porlamar. See also www.playaelagua.info.

Manzanillo is a picturesque bay between the mountains on the northeast point of the island with apartments, beach houses and good places to eat (cheaper than Playa El Agua). Playa Escondida is at the far end. Puerto Fermín/El Tirano is where Lope de Aguirre, the infamous conquistador, landed in 1561 on his flight from Peru.

The coast road is interesting, with glimpses of the sea and beaches to one side. There are a number of clifftop lookout points. The road improves radically beyond Manzanillo, winding from one beach to the next. **Playa Puerto la Cruz** (wide and windy) adjoins **Pedro González**, with a broad sweeping beach, running from a promontory (easy to climb) to scrub and brush that reach down almost to the water's edge. **Playa Caribe** is a fantastic curve of white sand with moderate surf. Chairs and umbrellas can be hired from the many beach bars.

Juan Griego is further west, a fast-expanding town whose pretty bay is full of fishing boats. The little fort of La Galera is on a promontory at the northern side, beyond which is a bay of the same name with a narrow strip of beach lined with many seafront restaurants.

La Restinga

This is the 22-km sandbar of broken seashells that joins the eastern and western parts of Margarita. Behind the Restinga is the eponymous **national park**, designated a wetland of international importance. More than 100 species of bird live here, including the blue-crowned parakeet, which is endemic to Margarita. There are also marine turtles and other reptiles, dolphins, deer, ocelots, seahorses and oysters. *Lanchas* can be taken into the fascinating lagoon and mangrove swamps to the beach from landing stages at the eastern end (US$2 for 30 minutes, US$12 for an hour trip in a boat taking five, plus US$2.50 entrance fee to park). Bus from Porlamar US$1. On La Restinga beach you can look for shellfish in the shallows (sun protection is essential) and delicious oysters can be bought here.

Península de Macanao

The Península de Macanao, over the road bridge from La Restinga, is mountainous, arid, barely populated and a peaceful place to get away from the holidaymakers on the main part of Isla Margarita. It also has some good beaches that are often deserted and is a good place for horse riding. **Punta Arenas** is a very pleasant beach with calm water and is the most popular. It has some restaurants, chairs and sunshades. Further on is the wilder **Playa Manzanillo**. It's best visited in a hire car as public transport is scarce. **Boca del Río**, near the road bridge, has a **Museo Marino** ⓘ *T0295-291 3231, www.museomarino.com, daily 0900-1630, US$0.75, US$0.50 children and seniors*, which has interesting collections of marine life, organized by ecosystem, and also features a small aquarium.

Tourist information

Cámara de Turismo
2da Entrada Urb Jorge Coll, Av Virgen del Valle, Qta 6, Pampatar, T0295-262 0683, www.ctene.org.
Private company, have free maps and are very helpful.

Corpotur
T0295-262 2322, Av Jóvito Villalba, Centro Artesanal Gilberto Menchini, Los Robles, www.corpoturmargarita.gob.ve.
The state tourism department.
Travel agencies can also provide a tourist guide to Margarita. The best map is available from Corpoven. See also www.islamargarita.com and http://margaritaislandnews.blogspot.co.uk.
Many offices close for lunch.

Where to stay

Porlamar
Many luxury hotels are grouped in the Costa Azul suburb east of Porlamar, but they now pepper most of the northeast coast of the island. Most hotels and tour operators work on a high season/low season price system. High season prices (Christmas, Easter and Jun-Aug) can be up to 35% higher. Flights and hotels are usually fully booked at this time. In low season, bargaining is possible.

$$$-$$ Bella Vista
Av Santiago Mariño, T0295-261 7222, www.hbellavista.com.
Large hotel with all services, pool with sea views, beach, car hire, travel agency, French restaurant, and restaurant serving *comida criolla*.

$$-$ Imperial
Av Raúl Leoni, via El Morro, T261 6420, www.hotelimperial.com.ve.
Modern, best rooms have sea view, parking, balcony, safe, restaurant, parking, English spoken.

$$-$ Margarita Princess
Av 4 de Mayo, T0295-263 6777, www.hotelmargaritaprincess.com.ve.
Large, comfortable rooms, balcony, restaurant, small pool.

$$-$ María Luisa
Av Raúl Leoni entre Campos y Fermín, T0295- 261 0564, www.hotelmarialuisa.com.ve.
With a pool and some beach views.

$ For You
Av Santiago Mariño, T0295-263 8635, foryouhotel@hotmail.com.
Modern, bland rooms but good service, roof restaurant, bar.

$ Posada Casa Lutecia
Final C Campos Cedeño y Marcano, T0295- 263 8526, posadacasalutecia@cantv.net.
Lovely bright rooms with personal touch, French-owned, café with outdoor seating near beach.

South coast

$$ El Yaque Motion
Playa El Yaque, T0416-596 5139 (English, German), T0416-596 5139 (Spanish), www.elyaquemotion.com.
400 m from beach. German-run, popular with wind- and kitesurfers (lessons and equipment hire available), well-established, kitchen, laundry, roof terrace, cheaper with shared bath, rents

3 apartments for 4-8 people, English spoken, good.

$ Sail Fast Shop
Playa El Yaque, T0295-263 3449, herbert@ sail-fast.com.
Basic rooms 300 m from the beach, ask for Herbert Novak at the Sail Fast Shop opposite Hotel Yaque Paradise. Rooms with private bath, some with a/c, kitchen facilities.

La Asunción

$$ Ciudad Colonial
C La Margarita, T0295-416 7647, isbeeu@ cantv.net.
Upmarket apartments minimum 4 people, swimming pool, accepts credit cards, restaurant.

$ Posada Restaurant Ticino Da´Rocco
Crucero de Guacuco, vía Playa El Agua, C San Onofre, sector Camoruco, T0295-242 2727, posadaticino@gmail.com.
Pool, restaurant, accepts credit cards.

Eastern and northern beaches
Playa Guacuco

$$ Guacuco Resort
Vía Playa Guacuco, T0295-242 3040, www.guacucoresort.com.
Stylish, comfortable apartments for up to 4 people with balcony or terrace, 1 km from the beach and 300 m off the road, self-catering, tranquil, beautiful tropical gardens with birds, spa, pool and bar.

Playa El Agua
Most posadas are on C Miragua, which is near the beach.

$$$-$$ Coco Paraíso
Av Principal, T0295-249 0117/ 0414-092 2403, www.cocoparaiso.com.ve.
Pleasant, large rooms, pool, 3 mins from beach, English and German spoken.

$$ Costa Linda
C Miragua, T0295-249 1303/415 9961, www.hotelcostalinda.com.
Lovely rooms in colonial-style house, relaxing, safe, pool, restaurant and bar, accepts credit cards, English and German spoken.

$$ Margarita Tropical Villa
C Díaz Ordaz, T0295-249 0558, www. casatrudel.com.
Canadian/Venezuelan-run, small place, patio with hammocks, 5 mins from beach, Wi-Fi, king-size beds, use of kitchen, hot water shower, minimum booking 4 nights.

$$-$ Doña Romelia
Av 31 de Julio (1 km before Playa Manzanillo), 10-min walk to Playa El Agua, T0295-249 0238.
Very attractive rustic-style hotel, bright rooms with balconies and hammocks, nice pool area and garden. Well-run, helpful staff. Recommended.

$ Chalets de Belén
Miragua 3, T0295-249 1707, jesush30@ yahoo.com.
2 chalets for 4 and 6, kitchen, good value, parking, no hot water, also 2 double rooms (with discounts in the low season).

$ Hostería El Agua
Av 31 de Julio vía Manzanillo, T0295-249 1297.
Simple, hot water, safe, restaurant/bar, on roadside 4 mins' walk from beach, English spoken.

Juan Griego

$$ The Sunset Posada Turística
T0295-253 2168, losavila@verizon.net, on Facebook.

Apartments sleep 4-8, good value, some with beachfront balconies.

$ Hostel El Caney
Giulliana Torrico 17, Rue Guevara, T0295-253 5059, http://elcaney.free.fr.
Shared kitchen, small pool, English and French spoken, weekly rentals.

$ Patrick's
El Fuerte, T0295-253 6218, www.hotelpatrick.com.
Good travellers hostel, rooms with fine sunset views, excellent restaurant and bar, near beach. English spoken, will arrange salsa and Spanish lessons. Recommended.

Península de Macanao

$$ Makatao
T0412-092 7187, www.makatao.com.
Run by Dr Alexis Vásquez, price includes transfer, food, some therapies, natural drinks and lodging in the singular rooms. The doctor runs health, 'eco-relax' and therapy programs, and there are mud baths at the *campamento*.

Restaurants

Porlamar
The upmarket dining is in Urb Costa Azul on Av Bolívar. There are plenty of eating places on Campos and 4 de Mayo.

$$ La Casa del Mero
Av Raúl Leoni.
Good place for a cocktail on the water, serves seafood, steaks and chicken.

$$ La Pimienta
Cedeño entre Campos y Fermín.
Good seafood.

$ Dragón Chino
Av Principal, 4 de Mayo.
Great Chinese.

$ El Pollo de Carlitos
Marcano y Martínez.
Pleasant location, good food.

$ El Punto Criollo
Igualdad near Hotel Porlamar.
Excellent-value *comida margariteña*.

Bars and clubs

Porlamar
Several bars in the Centro Comercial Costal Azul.

South coast
Several beach bars in Playa El Yaque; best bar is **Los Surf Piratas**, drinks and dancing from 2130.

Festivals

Many religious festivals, including **19 Mar** at Paraguachí (**Feria de San José**, 10 days); **26 Jul** at Punta de Piedras; **31 Jul** (Batalla de Matasiete) and **15 Aug** (**Asunción de la Virgen**) at La Asunción; **1-8 Sep** at El Valle; **4-11 Nov** at Boca del Río, **4-30 Nov** at Boca del Pozo; **5-6 Dec** at Porlamar; **27 Dec-3 Jan** at Juan Griego. See map page 116 for locations.

Shopping

Porlamar
Margarita's status as a duty-free zone attracts Venezuelan shoppers, who go in droves for clothing, electronic goods and other items. Street sellers lay out their handicrafts on Av Santiago Mariño in the afternoon. When buying jewellery, bargain, don't pay by credit card (surcharges are imposed) and get a detailed guarantee of the item. Av Santiago Mariño and surroundings are the place for designer labels, but decent copies can be found on Blv Guevara and

Blv Gómez and around Plaza Bolívar in the centre. For bargains on denims, T-shirts, shorts, swimming gear and bikinis, take a bus to Conejeros market (from Fraternidad, Igualdad a Velásquez).

Pampatar
Centro Comercial La Redoma, *Av Jovito Villalba*. A good small mall for food, clothing, medicines, and more. Also has a cyber café.

What to do

Porlamar
Language schools
A useful website worth visiting is www. insel-margarita-venezuela.de.
Centro de Lingüística Aplicada, *Corocoro Qta, Cela Urb, Playa El Angel between Porlamar and Pampatar, T0295-262 8198, http://cela-ve.com.*

Sailing

The motor yacht **Viola Festival** can be hired for mini cruises to the island of Coche, contact **Festival Tours** (*C Marcano, CC Paseo Terrazul, loc P1-8, Costa Azul, T0295-267 0552*). There are other yachts offering island cruises, fishing trips, etc.

Eastern and northern beaches
Tour shops in **Playa El Agua** are the best places to book scuba diving and snorkelling trips – most go to Los Frailes, a small group of islands to the north of Playa Agua, and reputedly the best diving and snorkelling in Margarita, but it's also possible to dive at Parque Nacional La Restinga and Isla Cubagua. Prices from US$75 pp for an all-inclusive full day (2 dives). Snorkelling is about two-thirds the price of scuba diving.
Enomis Divers, *Av 31 de Julio, CC*

Turístico, Playa El Agua, loc 2, sector La Mira, T0295-249 0366, www.divemargarita. com. PADI school, diving trips, many programmes and certifications offered.

South coast
Sailboards, **kite surf** and **kayaks** can be hired on Playa El Yaque from at least 5 well-equipped companies, who also offer lessons. An hour's lesson costs US$55. English, German, French and Portuguese spoken. Enquire at **El Yaque Motion** (see Where to stay, above) for more information about wind- and kite-surfing. See also www. velawindsurf.com. A 20-min boat ride to Isla Coche leaves from next door to **El Yaque Motion**, a recommended spot for advanced kiters. Rescue service available at Playa El Yaque.

Península de Macanao
Horse riding
You can ride on the peninsula at **Ranch Cabatucan** (2 km from Guayacancito on the road to Punta Arenas, T0295-808 5147, www.cabatucan.com).

Transport

Porlamar
Air There are too many flight options to list here – check with local offices for details. **Gen Santiago Mariño Airport**, between Porlamar and Punta de Piedras, has the international and national terminals at either end (*www.aeropuerto-margarita.gob.ve*). Taxi from Porlamar US$3.50, 20-30 mins. All national airlines have routes to **Margarita**. Many daily flights to/from **Caracas**, 45-min flight; tickets are much cheaper if purchased in Venezuela. To **Canaima** and to **Los Roques** with LTA.

Bus Local Buses and *por puestos* serve most of the island, buses US$0.25-50, *por puestos* minimum fare US$1, few services at night when you should take a taxi anyway.

Long distance Several bus companies in Caracas sell through tickets from **Caracas** to Porlamar, arriving about midday, US$1.75. Buses return to Caracas from La Paralela bus station in Porlamar.

Car hire Several offices at the airport and at the entrance to **Hotel Bella Vista**, others on Av Santiago Mariño. Check the brakes, bodywork and terms and conditions of hire thoroughly. Scooters can also be hired. Motor bikes may not be ridden 2000-0500. **Note** Fill up before leaving Porlamar as service stations are scarce. Roads are generally good and most are paved. Signposts are often non-existent. Free maps are confusing, but it's worth having one with you. Avoid driving outside Porlamar after dark. Beware of robbery; park in private car parks.

Ferry From **Puerto La Cruz** to Margarita (**Punta de Piedras**) **Conferry** (*Guanta terminal, Puerto La Cruz, freefone T0501-2663 3779, or T0281-267 7221, www. conferry.com*). Price varies according to class of seat, 4 a day(check times, extra ferries during high season). Fast ferry Guanta–El Guamache terminal, 3 hrs, passengers US$2.25 from mainland to island, US$4.50 return, over-60s and children under-13 about half price (proof of age required), slow ferry, 5 hrs, to Punta de Piedras also takes vehicles. Conferry from Punta de Piedras to Isla Coche, US$1.10 return. **Conferry** office in **Porlamar** (*Av Terranova con Av Llano Adentro, T0295-263 9985, Mon-Fri 0800-1730, Sat 0800-1200*).

Gran Cacique, 2-3 fast ferries a day Puerto la Cruz–Punta de Piedras, US$3-3.50 one way, also takes cars, US$5.25-7.25, and motorbikes, US$3.15-4, T0281-263 0935 (Puerto La Cruz ferry terminal), T0295-239 8339 (Punta de Piedras, or Av Santiago Mariño, Edif Blue Sky, loc 3, Porlamar, T0295-264 2945). It is most advisable to book in advance, especially if travelling with a car or motorbike during high season. To get to terminal in Puerto La Cruz, take 'Bello Monte' *por puesto* from Libertad y Anzoátegui, 2 blocks from Plaza Bolívar. From **Cumaná** ferry terminal, El Salado, **Gran Cacique**, T0293-433 0909, 2-3 a day, US$2.50-3 one way (children 3-7 and over-60s half price), and **Naviarca**, T0293-433 1209, continuous service, US$1.75 one way for passengers (children 3-7 and over-60s half price), motorcycles US$1.55-2.35, cars US$3.50. **Navibus**, T0295-500 6284, www.navibus.com.ve, has 2 sailings a day from Puerto la Cruz and Cumaná US$2.50 and 2 respectively (children 2-7, over-60s and disabled half price), motorcycles US$3.55 and 2.50, cars US$4.75-5.75 and US$3.50-4.

Taxi Taxi for a day is US$3.50 per hr, minimum 3 hrs. Always fix fare in advance; 20% extra after 2100 and on Sun. Taxi from Porlamar to Playa El Agua, US$3.

> **Tip...**
>
> Ferries are very busy at Saturday, Sunday and Monday. Buying tickets can be a complex business with a lot of confusing queuing. Cars are checked by SENIAT for their legality and to prevent the smuggling of tax-free goods to the mainland.

the Caribbean of your imagination

★The turquoise and emerald lagoons and dazzling white sands of the Archipelago de Los Roques make up one of Venezuela's loveliest national parks. For lazing on an untouched beach, or for snorkelling and diving amid schools of fish and coral reefs, these islands cannot be beaten. Diving and snorkelling are best to the south of the archipelago.

Essential Los Roques

Access and information

National park entry BsF254 for 15 days (US$1.30 at the SIMADI exchange rate), children under four and seniors over 65 free. Prices are subject to change. You can pay in dollars, but it is not known at what exchange rate. Camping is free, but campers need a permit from Inparques (T0212-273 2811 in Caracas, or the office on Plaza Bolívar, Gran Roque, Monday-Friday 0830-1200 and 1400-1800, weekends and holidays 0830-1200 and 1430-1730); also the small office by the runway where you pay the entry fee. See also www. los-roques.com, www.losroques.org and www.consejocomunallosroques. org. Look out for the excellent *Guía del Parque Nacional Archipiélago Los Roques* (Ecograph, 2004).

When to go

The average daytime temperature is 29°C with coolish nights. The islands tend to be very busy in July and August and at Christmas. At other times the islands are best visited midweek, as Venezuelans swarm here on long weekends and school holidays, after which there is litter on every island. Low season is Easter to July.

The islands of Los Roques, with long stretches of white beaches and over 20 km of coral reef in crystal-clear water, lie 166 km due north of La Guaira; the atoll, of about 340 islets and reefs, constitutes a national park of 225,153 ha. There are many bird nesting sites (eg the huge gull colonies on Francisqui and the pelicans, boobies and frigates on Selenqui); May is nesting time at the gull colonies. For information about the conservation of the marine environment, visit https:// fundacionlosroques.wordpress.com.

This is one of the least visited diving spots in the Caribbean. There are at least seven main dive sites offering caves, cliffs, coral and, at Nordesqui, shipwrecks. There are many fish to be seen, including sharks at the caves of Olapa de Bavusqui. Prices are higher than the mainland and infrastructure is limited but the islands are beautiful and unspoiled.

Gran Roque

Gran Roque (population 1200) is the only permanently inhabited island. The airport is here, as is the national guard, a few grocery stores, public phones (offering expensive internet), a bank with an ATM (but take cash from the mainland), medical facilities, dive shops, a few restaurants and accommodation. There is nowhere to change traveller's cheques. Park

Headquarters are in the scattered fishing village. Tourist information is available from the very helpful **Oscar Shop**, directly in front as you leave the airstrip. Boat trips to other islands can be arranged here or at posadas (round trip US$10-35, depending on distance), which are worthwhile as you cannot swim off Gran Roque.

Other islands

You can negotiate with local fishermen for transport to other islands you will need to take your own tent, food and (especially) water. You may also have to take your own snorkeling equipment, unless it is provided by your package tour operator. **Madrisqui** has a good shallow beach and joins Pirata Cay by a sandspit. **Francisqui** is three islands joined by sandspits, with calm lagoon waters to the south and rolling surf to the north. You can walk with care from one cay to the other, maybe swimming at times. There's some shade in the mangrove near the bar at La Cueva. **Crasqui** has a 3-km beach with beautiful water and white sand. **Cayo de Agua** (one hour by fast boat from Gran Roque) has an amazing sandspit joining its two parts and a nice walk to the lighthouse where you'll find two natural pools.

> **Tip...**
>
> You will need strong sunblock as there is no shade on the islands and an umbrella is recommended.

Listings Los Roques

Where to stay

In most places on Islas Los Roques, breakfast and dinner are included in the price.

There are over 60 posadas on Gran Roque. Those listed below are all here.

$$$ pp El Botuto
On seafront near Supermercado W Salazar, T0416-622 0061, www.posadaelbotuto.com.
Nice airy rooms with fan, good simple food, locally owned. Trips to other islands and watersports arranged.

$$$ pp Piano y Papaya
Near Plaza Bolívar towards seafront, T0414-281 0104, www.losroques.com.
Very tasteful, run by Italian artist, with fan, $$ pp for bed and breakfast, credit cards and TCs accepted, Italian and English spoken, laundry service.

$$$ pp Posada Acquamarina
C 2 No 149, T0412-310 1962, www.posada-acquamarina.com.
All-inclusive, rooms have a/c, private bathrooms with hot water, terrace. Owner Giorgio very helpful, speaks Italian and some French, can arrange flights from Caracas. Excursions to other islands.

$$$ pp Posada Caracol
On seafront near airstrip, T0237-414 5566, www.caracolgroup.com.
Delightful, full-board with excursions, credit cards and TCs accepted, Italian and English spoken, good boats.

$$$ pp Roquelusa
C 3 No 214, behind supermarket,
T0212-287 0517.
A cheaper option, basic, with cold
water, a/c.

$$ pp Posada Doña Magalis
Plaza Bolívar 46, www.magalis.com.
Simple place, locally owned, with a/c,
cheaper with shared bath, includes trips
to other islands, soft drinks, breakfast
and dinner, delicious food, mostly fish
and rice.

What to do

Many posadas arrange water sports
such as windsurfing and kitesurfing
(especially good at Francisqui), diving,
sailing and fishing.

Diving
For health reasons you must allow 12 hrs
to elapse between diving and flying
back to the mainland. Lots of courses
and packages available. **Cayo de Agua**
and **Francisqui** recommended for
snorkelling. Boats and equipment rentals
can be arranged.
Ecobuzos, *3 blocks from the airstrip,*
T0295-262 9811/0416-595 0464, www.
ecobuzos.com. Very good, new
equipment, modern boats, experienced
dive masters. PADI courses (US$250) and
beginner dives available.

Sailing
Fully equipped yachts can be chartered
for US$200-400 per night for 2 people,
all inclusive, highly recommended as a
worthwhile way of getting some shade
on the treeless beaches. Ask at **Angel
& Oscar Shop**, or see websites such as
www.los-roques.com, http://losroques.
mobi or www.roques.com.

Transport

Air Flights from **Maiquetía** or
Porlamar. **LTA** (*www.tuy.com*), **Chapi Air**
(*T0212-355 1349, reservacioneschapiair@*
gmail.com), **Blue Star** (*T0412-310 1962,*
www.bluestar.us) and **Los Roques
Airlines** (*T0414-332 0055, www.*
losroques-airlines.com) all fly from
Maiquetía (Aeropuerto Auxiliar) once
a day, 40 mins, up to US$285 round
trip, more expensive if booked outside
of Venezuela. Tax of about US$10 is
payable. Some carriers charge more
at weekends. Remember that small
planes usually restrict luggage to 10
kg. They offer full-day (return flight,
meals and activities) and overnight
packages. It's best to buy a return to
the mainland as buying and confirming
tickets and finding offices open on the
islands is difficult.

Canaima &
the Orinoco Delta

In Parque Nacional Canaima, one of the largest national parks in the world, you'll find the spectacular Angel Falls, the highest in the world, and the mysterious 'Lost World' of Roraima (see page 153). Canaima is the tourist centre for the park, but indigenous communities are now accepting tourists as well. The historic Ciudad Bolívar on the Río Orinoco is a good starting place for the superb landscapes further south. To the east, beyond the industrial city of Ciudad Guayana, the Orinoco Delta is also developing as a tourist destination.

The region of Guayana, south of the Orinoco River, constitutes half of Venezuela, comprising rounded forested hills and narrow valleys, rising to ancient flat-topped tablelands on the borders of Brazil. These savannahs interspersed with semi-deciduous forest are sparsely populated. So far, communications have been the main difficulty, but a road that leads to Manaus passes through Santa Elena de Uairén on the Brazilian frontier (see page 147). The area is Venezuela's largest gold and diamond source, but its immense reserves of iron ore, manganese and bauxite are of far greater economic importance.

Best for
Adventure ▪ Isolation ▪ Scenery

beautiful and historical colonial town

Ciudad Bolívar is on the narrows of the Orinoco, some 300 m wide, which gave the town its old name of Angostura, 'The Narrows'. It is 400 km from the Orinoco Delta. It was here that Bolívar came after defeat to reorganize his forces, and the British Legionnaires joined him. At Angostura he was declared President of the Gran Colombia he had yet to build and which was to fragment before his death. With its cobbled streets, pastel buildings and setting on the Orinoco, it is one of Venezuela's most beautiful colonial towns.

Towards Ciudad Bolívar

Ciudad Bolívar can be reached easily by roads south from Caracas and Puerto La Cruz. The Caracas route, via Valle de la Pascua, and the Puerto La Cruz route, via Anaco, meet at **El Tigre**, which has good hotels and services. From the Llanos, from **Chaguaramas** turn south through Las Mercedes (hotel $) to **Cabruta**, 179 km,

Ciudad Bolívar

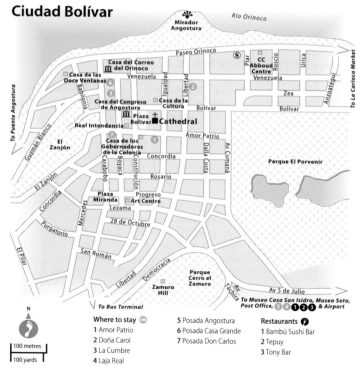

Where to stay
1 Amor Patrio
2 Doña Carol
3 La Cumbre
4 Laja Real
5 Posada Angostura
6 Posada Casa Grande
7 Posada Don Carlos

Restaurants
1 Bambú Sushi Bar
2 Tepuy
3 Tony Bar

100 metres
100 yards

road in very bad shape, daily bus to Caracas, US$2.25, basic hotel. Then take a ferry from opposite the airport to **Caicara** (car ferry 1½ hours, *lanchas* for pedestrians 25 minutes). An 11.2-km bridge across the Orinoco is being built between Cabruta and Caicara (due to open in 2016). Alternatively, from San Fernando de Apure take a bus to **Calabozo** and *por puesto* to **El Sombrero**, where you can catch the Ciudad Bolívar bus.

Sights

At the Congress of Angostura, 15 February 1819, the representatives of the present day Venezuela, Colombia, Panama and Ecuador met to proclaim Gran Colombia. The building, on **Plaza Bolívar**, built 1766-1776 by Manuel Centurión, the provincial governor, houses a museum, the **Casa del Congreso de Angostura**, with an ethnographic museum in the basement. Guides give tours in Spanish only. Also on this plaza is the **Cathedral** (which was completed in 1840), the **Casa de Los Gobernadores de la Colonia** (also built by Centurión in 1766), the **Real Intendencia**, and the **Casa de la Cultura**. Also here, at Bolívar 33, is the house where General Manuel Piar, the Liberator of Guayana from the Spanish, was held prisoner before being executed by Bolívar on 16 October 1817, for refusing to put himself under Bolívar's command. The restored **Plaza Miranda**, up Calle Carabobo, has an art centre. The present legislative assembly and **Consejo Municipal** are between Plaza Bolívar and Plaza Miranda. In 1824, when the town was still known as Angostura, a Prussian physician to Bolívar's troops invented the famous bitters; the factory moved to Port of Spain in 1875.

Museum at **Casa del Correo del Orinoco** ⓘ *Paseo Orinoco y Carabobo, Mon-Fri 0930-1200, 1430-1700*, houses modern art and history exhibits of the city. **Museo Casa San Isidro** ⓘ *Av Táchira, Tue-Sun 0900-1700, free, knowledgeable guides*, is a colonial mansion where Simón Bolívar stayed for two weeks. It has antique furniture and an old garden. **Museo de Arte Moderno Jesús Soto** ⓘ *Av Germania, 0930-1730, weekends and holidays 1000-1700, free, guide in Spanish only,* is located some distance from the centre in pleasant gardens. It has works by Venezuela's celebrated Jesús Rafael Soto and other modern artists from around the world. Recommended. The best views of the city are from **Fortín El Zamuro** ⓘ *C 28 de Octubre y Av 5 de Julio, daily except Mon, free, guides available*, dating from 1902, strategically located at one of the tallest points of the city.

The Paseo Orinoco skirts the riverbank and heads west out of town; it is a relaxing place to stroll but unsafe after dark. Speedboats go across the river to the small, picturesque town of **Soledad** (US$0.25, one way, five minutes) on a journey that offers great views of colonial centre, the bridge and the river itself. Security can be an issue at either end; don't cross at night. There are no other passenger boat services. The **Angostura Bridge** can be seen from the waterfront paseo. This is the first bridge across the Orinoco, 1668 m long, opened in 1967, again with great views (cyclists and walkers are not allowed to cross, you must flag down a car or truck).

West of the centre is **El Zanjón**, an area of vegetation typical of the region. East is **Parque El Porvenir**, with botanical gardens (entrance on Calle Bolívar), but it is unsafe to wander unless accompanied by staff. Outside the airport is the *Río Caroní* aeroplane, which Jimmy Angel landed on top of Auyán Tepuy (see page 136).

Listings Ciudad Bolívar *map p129*

Tourist information

Dirección de Turismo
Av Bolívar, Quinta Yeita 59, T0285-632 2362, www.e-bolivar.gov.ve. Mon-Fri 0800-1200, 1400-1730.
Helpful, English spoken.

Where to stay

$$ Posada Casa Grande
C Boyacá 8, T0285-632 4639, www. cacaotravel-venezuela.com (the HQ of Cacao Travel is here).
A handsome colonial building converted to a tasteful 4-star hotel. Well-attired rooms overlook a central patio upstairs there's a rooftop terrace with a bar and small pool. Professional service, good meals by prior arrangement, breakfast included. Recommended.

$ Amor Patrio
Amor Patrio 30, T0414-854 4925, www.posadaamorpatrioaventura.com.
A simple, friendly guesthouse with a tranquil little patio. 5 rooms have fan and shared bathroom, a/c is extra. No Wi-Fi but an internet terminal is available. Also laundry service and tours. Run by Gerd Altmann, German and English spoken. Recommended.

$ La Cumbre
Av 5 de Julio, T0285-632 7709, www.holacumbre.com.
Secluded hill-top retreat with commanding views. Rooms are large and simple, some overlook the town and Orinoco river below. Resort-style facilities include a great pool, restaurant, bar, and terraces, maybe noisy at weekends. Take a taxi, you can't walk.

$ Laja Real
Av Andrés Bello y Jesús Soto, opposite airport, T0285-632 7911, www.hotellajareal.com.
A reasonable 1980s hotel, good for early morning flights, excellent pool (small charge for non-residents), sauna, gym, parking, restaurant.

$ Posada Angostura
Same contact details as Posada Casa Grande above, also on C Boyacá.
Handsome rooms in old colonial house, some rooms have river view, hot water, travel agency, unwelcoming service. Excellent food.

$ Posada Don Carlos
C Boyacá 26 y Amor Patrio, just 30 m from Plaza Bolívar, T0285-632 6017, www.posada-doncarlos.com.
Stunning colonial house. 6 private double rooms with a/c, or 4 cheaper rooms with fan and shared facilities. Breakfast and dinner available, lovely patio, bar, tours. Good vibe, helpful, popular. Recommended.

$ Posada Doña Carol
Libertad 28, T0285-634 0989, jmaury2008@hotmail.com.
Basic and hospitable guesthouse with a mixture of rooms, including one large quadruple with an outdoor patio-balcony. Very helpful, can prepare meals, organize bus tickets, tours. Communal fridges, refreshments and Wi-Fi.

Outside town

$ Posada La Casita
Av Ligia Pulido, Urb 24 de Julio, T0285-617 0832, www.posada-la-casita.com.
Beautiful leafy grounds at this secluded hotel, also home to a small private zoo. Lodging is in spacious and immaculately clean apartments or in tasteful garden *casitas*. Amenities include pool, laundry service, hammocks, food and drink at extra cost. Free pick-up from airport or bus terminal (ring in advance), free shuttle service into town. The owner runs **Gekko Tours.** German and English spoken, helpful. Prices in euros.

Restaurants

Many restaurants close at 1700.

$$ Bambú Sushi Bar
Av 5 de Julio, inside Hotel La Cumbre, take a taxi.
Authentic sushi rolls served up on a breezy hill overlooking the city. In the same hotel, **Restaurante El Mirador**, serving grilled fish and meat, isn't bad either.

$$ Tepuy
Av Andrés Bello y Jesús Soto, opposite airport and inside Hotel Laja Real.
Slightly formal place with very attentive service. Good pasta with prawns, as well as meat, chicken and fish, wines and cocktails.

$$ Tony Bar
Av Táchira y Mario Briceño Iragory.
Very good stone-baked Italian-style pizzas, pastas, chicken, and general *típico* fare. Service isn't stellar, but the food makes up for it. A few blocks from the airport, but easiest to jump in a taxi. Recommended.

$$-$ Mercado La Carioca
Octava Estrella y Paseo Orinoco, on the banks of the river. Daily from 0600-1500.
The best place for eating tasty local food. Great view. Various stalls and excellent local food with a range of prices.

$ Mirador Angostura
Paseo Orinoco.
Un-pretentious *comida criolla* with views over the river.

Cafés and fast food
Several fast-food restaurants around **Museo de Arte Moderno Jesús Soto**.

Café Estilo
Av Andrés Bello, opposite Laja Real Hotel and very near airport. Open 0900-1200, 1500-1900.
Boutique and café with home-made sweets, comfortable, spotless. Run by very nice elderly couple. Recommended.

Tip...

Tours, usually starting from Ciudad Bolívar (see What to do, below), can be made into the area south of the Río Orinoco from Maripa, travelling on the Río Caura. These include visits to indigenous villages, river bathing, jungle treks to waterfalls with explanations of wildlife and vegetation.

What to do

Competition is stiff in Ciudad Bolívar. Do not agree to, or pay for a tour in the bus station or on the street. Always ask to be taken to the office. Always ask for a receipt (and make sure that it comes on paper bearing the company logo) and only take a tour that starts in Ciudad Bolívar. If you fall prey to a con artist, make a *denuncio* at the police station and inform genuine travel agents.

Ciudad Bolívar is the best place to book a tour to Canaima, but you will pick up cheaper deals for trips to Roraima and the Gran Sabana from Santa Elena. Most agents in Ciudad Bolívar sell tours run by just a handful of operators, but sometimes add commission. Always ask who will be running the actual tour; it may be cheaper to book from them directly. Get independent recommendations on standards of guiding, food, time-keeping, etc. For 3-day/2-night tours to Canaima including flights, you pay around US$220-400 pp depending on accommodation, or US$110-290 for 1-day tour that includes flights to Canaima, flight near the Angel Falls, and activities around Canaima lagoon (price depends on the activities) and food (see page 139 for flights to Canaima).

Bernal Tours, *T0285-632 6890, T0414-854 8234 (mob in Spanish), T0414-899 7162 (in English), www.bernaltours.com*. Agency is run by descendents of Peruvian adventurer Tomás Bernal from Arequipa. They use indigenous guides and their own ecolodge at Canaima lagoon overlooking the falls.

Gekko Tours, *run by Pieter Rothfuss at airport (also Posada La Casita), T0285-632 3223, T0414-854 5146, www.gekkotours-venezuela.de*. Established family business with 18 years of experience.

Soana Travel, *run by Martin Haars at Posada Don Carlos, Boyacá 26, T0285-632 6017, T0414-864 6616, www.posada-doncarlos.com*. English and German spoken. Professional and reliable.

Tiuna Tours, *at airport, T0416-686 1192, tiunatoursca@gmail.com*. Cheapest

option for Canaima, have a camp that takes 180 people.

Transport

Ciudad Bolívar
Air It's possible to fly to **Canaima** independently, but an organized tour is highly recommended. Several flights leave daily with **Transmandú** (*T0285-632 1462, www.transmandu.com*), **Sundance Air** (*Gekko Tours, T0285-632 3223*) and, less frequently, with other charter airlines. One-way tickets cost around US$100; try to book at least 24-48 hrs in advance. A 20-person charter to Santa Elena can be arranged with **Transmandú**, subject to weather conditions. Flights to **Caracas**, 5-6 a week, 1 hr with **Rutaca**.

> **Tip...**
>
> Puerto Ordaz/Ciudad Guayana is a busier flight hub and some tours start from there. Taxi to Ciudad Guayana US$5; to historic centre US$1.20.

Bus Terminal at junction of Av República and Av Sucre. Left luggage. To get there take bus marked Terminal going west along Paseo Orinoco (US$0.15). Buy bus tickets in advance. Hourly to **Caracas** US$2.50-3, 8-9 hrs. 10 daily to **Puerto La Cruz**, US$1.35, 5 hrs. 1 daily to **Cumaná**, US$1.55, 7 hrs . Daily to **Valencia**, via Maracay, US$3.5.25, 8-9 hrs. **El Dorado** US$1.65. To **Santa Elena de Uairén** with several companies, **Occidente** and **Línea Los Llanos** recommended for comfort, US$3, 12-13 hrs. To **Ciudad Guayana** hourly from 0700, US$0.50 1½ hrs. 2 daily to **Caicara**, US$1.55 (including 2 ferry crossings), 7-8 hrs, with **Coop Gran Mcal**

Sucre. 2 daily to **Puerto Ayacucho**, US$2.65, 10-12 hrs with **Línea Amazonas** or **Coop Gran Mcal Sucre**, take food.

Taxi US$1.20 to virtually anywhere in town. US$1 from bus station to town centre.

☆Canaima National Park, a UNESCO World Heritage Site since 1994, is one of the most unspoilt places on earth. At over three million hectares, it is the second largest national park in Venezuela, the sixth largest on the planet. It is a world apart, with its fantastic table mountains, waterfalls which include the world's highest (Angel Falls), caves, deep forests and indigenous cultures.

Canaima Camp

At Canaima Camp, the Río Carrao tumbles spectacularly over Ucaima, Golondrina and Hacha Falls into the lagoon, which has beautiful tannin-stained water with soft beige beaches. It's a lovely spot, but it also has the air strip and is the centre of operations for river trips to indigenous areas and to Angel Falls. The falls are named after Jimmie Angel, the US airman who first reported their existence in 1935. Two

Parque Nacional Canaima

Canaima · Taraipa · San Salvador de Paúl · Río Carrao · Piedra del la Virgen · San Isidro/km 88 · Danto Falls · GUYANA · Angel Falls · Auyán Tepuy (2560m) · Kaváč · Kamarata · Luepa · Monumento al Soldado Pionero · Torón-Merú · Kavanayén · Kamoirán · Karuari-Merú · Iboribó · Chinak-Merú · Kama Merú · Parque Nacional Canaima · Quebrada Arapán · San Francisco de Yuruaní · San Ignacio de Yuruaní · Quebrada de Jaspe · Río Caroní · Santa Elena de Uairén · Paraitepuí · El Pauji · Icabarú · El Abismo · BRAZIL · To Boa Vista · To Paraitepuí & Mount Roraima

N

20 km
20 miles

Guyana claimed by Venezuela

years later he returned and crash landed his plane, the *Río Caroní*, on top of Auyán Tepuy. The site is marked with a plaque. The sheer rock face was climbed in 1971 by three Americans and an Englishman, David Nott, who recounted the 10-day adventure in his book *Angels Four* (Prentice-Hall). Hugo Chávez said that the falls should be called by an indigenous name Kerepakupai Merú. A second indigenous name is Parekupa Vena.

Excursions There is a famous 'tunnel' between Sapo and Sapito Falls (where Río Carrao passes behind Isla Anatoliy), where one can walk behind the huge waterfall – a must for any visitor. It is essential to be accompanied by a guide. The easiest way to get there is from Tomás Bernal Camp on Isla Anatoliy (five minutes boat ride from Canaima Camp). It's a 25-minute walk from there. Plastic raincoats are usually provided by the guide, or wear a swim suit. Wrap your camera and other belongings in a plastic bag. No matter what, you will get completely soaked in the middle of the tunnel. The path behind the waterfall is extremely slippery and should be taken only by the reasonably fit. Wrap your hand in an extra plastic bag, so it's not cut by the rough rope. When taking photos from behind the wall of water, experiment with camera speeds for the best effects.

Warning There is one more, invisible, waterfall on Canaima Lagoon, at the opposite end from Canaima Camp. It is called Salto Ara. The lagoon is a terrace and at Salto Ara all the water goes down one step. It is invisible from the surface, the only indicator is foam rising as if from nowhere. This fall is extremely dangerous do not swim or take a boat near it. This is where Tomás Bernal, the Peruvian discoverer of the above tunnel, lost his life in 1998 after the engine of his boat broke down. He is buried on Isla Anatoliy.

★**Trips to the Angel Falls**
Administered by Inparques, Av Guayana, Edif Centro Empresarial Alta Vista, p 8, Puerto Ordaz, Ciudad Guayana, T0286-966 2033.

The Angel Falls, the highest in the world (979 m – its longest single drop is 807 m), 70 km downriver from

ON THE ROAD

The rise and falls of Jimmy Angel

Right up there with Hiram Bingham and Colonel Fawcett as one of the true greats of South American exploration is Jimmy Crawford Angel. Born in 1899 in the small mining town of Springfield, Missouri, he gave his name to the highest waterfall in the world.

This particular Angel gained his wings early on in life. Legend has it that he made his first proper flight at the age of 14. He then served in the First World War, under age, in the Canadian Flying Corps, breaking records for the highest flight, highest landing and most loops. After the war he drifted in and out of various humdrum jobs running the mail down through Mexico; training pilots in Shanghai; herding reindeer in Canada for the Hudson Bay Company. He even appeared as a stunt flyer in Howard Hughes' movie Hell's Angels. His real claim to fame would come later, though.

It all began in Panama City in 1921, and a chance meeting with a gold prospector who spoke of a river of gold in the Guayana Highlands and asked Jimmy to fly him there. On 12 May they flew out of Panama for Cartagena in Colombia, and from there onto Maracaibo, Caracas, San Fernando de Apure, south up the Río Caroní then westwards along the Río Carrao. They had no instruments and no map but eventually made it to the promised river, somewhere near Auyán Tepuy. Angel described it as "a hell of a place to land a plane". The pair successfully panned the river for gold, limited only by the weight they could safely take on board.

For years afterwards, Jimmy Angel flew over the area, trying to relocate the 'river of gold'. Early in 1935, he set out on yet another expedition, this time with the backing of a New York company. He flew with his chief investor and a couple of prospectors. On 25 March 1935, he piloted his single-engined Cessna up a narrow canyon near Auyán Tepuy and saw for the first time the monumental cascade of water that would later bear his name.

Angel's accounts of this historic sighting were dismissed as wild exaggeration back in Caracas, but he found the falls again two years later, this time crash-landing his plane, a Flamingo called El Río Caroní, on the summit of Auyán Tepuy. The entire party, including his wife, Marie, had to walk for 12 days through the forest, finally arriving at the mission settlement of Kamarata.

However, it was not until 1949 that an overland expedition, led by the US journalist Ruth Robertson, reached the base of the falls and established scientifically what Jimmy Angel had claimed all along – that he had discovered the highest waterfall in the world, 979 m from summit to base.

In June 1956, back in Panama, Jimmy crashed a plane. Not an unusual occurrence for a man dedicated to flying, but one that proved fatal. He suffered a stroke and fell into a coma, later dying in hospital on 8 December 1956.

Canaima, are best reached by plane to Canaima from Ciudad Bolívar or Ciudad Guayana. Trips by boat upriver to the Angel Falls operate May-January, depending on the level of the water in the rivers. Boats literally fly up and down river over the boulders (not for faint-hearted), but even during the rainy season you may have to get out and push in places. Most trips starting from Canaima make an overnight stop on one of the islands, continuing to the falls the next day. More relaxing, with more stops at beauty spots, are 44-hour, 'three-day' trips. Ask at Inparques (see above) if you need a *permiso de excursionistas* to go on one tour and come back with another, giving yourself more time at the falls. You may have to pay extra to do this, up to US$10 (take all food and gear). Trips can be arranged with agencies in Ciudad Bolívar (see above) or at Canaima airport. All *curiaras* (dugouts) must carry first aid, life jackets, etc. Take wet weather gear, swimwear, mosquito net for hammock and insect repellent and a plastic bag to protect your camera/day bag. The light is best on the falls in the morning.

The cheapest way to fly over the falls is on scheduled flights from Ciudad Bolívar. From Canaima a 45-minute flight costs around US$100 per person and does some circuits over and alongside the falls; departures only if enough passengers.

Kamarata

The largest of the tepuis, **Auyán Tepuy** (700 sq km) is also one of the more accessible. Kamarata is a friendly indigenous settlement with a Capuchin mission on the plain at the east foot of the tepuy. It has a well-stocked shop but no real hotels; basic rooms can be found for under US$10 per person, camping also possible at the mission (mosquito nets necessary and anti malarial pills advised). Take food, although there is one place to eat, and locals may sell you dinner. The whole area is within the Parque Nacional Canaima.

Pemón families in Kamarata have formed co-operatives and can arrange *curiaras*, tents and porters for various excursions see What to do, below.

Kavác

About a two-hour walk northwest of Kamarata, this is an indigenous-run resort consisting of a dozen thatched huts (*churuatas*) for guests, a small shop, and an excitingly short airstrip serviced by Cessnas from Ciudad Bolívar, Santa Elena, and Isla Margarita; flights from the north provide excellent views of Angel Falls and Auyán Tepuy. There is a vehicle connection with Kamarata but it is expensive because all fuel has to be flown in.

The prime local excursion is to **Kavác Canyon** and its waterfall known as La Cueva, which can be reached by joining a group or by setting out early west up the Río Kavác. A natural jacuzzi is encountered after a 30-minute wade along the sparkling stream, after which the gorge narrows dramatically until the falls are reached. Go in the morning to avoid groups of day-trippers from Porlamar. The sun's rays illuminate the vertical walls of the canyon only for a short time around 1100. Be prepared to get wet; swimwear and shoes with good grip, plus a dry change of clothing are recommended; also insect repellent, as there is a mosquito and midge invasion around dusk. Late afternoon winds off the savannah can make conditions chilly. Most visitors to Kavác are on tours from Canaima, or elsewhere, so it may be difficult to book lodging at the camp (basic rooms or hammocks). If you go independently, take food with you. There is an entry charge for visitors.

Uruyén
South of Auyán Tepuy and west of Kamarata, Uruyén is similar to Kavác, only smaller and more intimate. It also has a beautiful canyon and is the starting point for treks up Auyán Tepuy. The camp is run by the Carvallo family. See also www. angelconservation.org/lodges.html.

Listings Canaima and Angel Falls

Where to stay

Canaima
Most lodges and camps are booked up by package tour companies.

$$$ Wakü Lodge (Canaima Tours)
T0286-962 0559, www.wakulodge.com.
The best option in Canaima, 4-star luxury, romantic, comfortable, a/c, good food, right on lagoon, free satellite/ Wi-Fi internet for guests. Specializes mainly in all-inclusive packages. Recommended.

$$ pp Campamiento Canaima
T0289-540-2747, www.venetur.gob.ve.
Run by **Venetur** as a luxury resort with 105 rooms, restaurant, meeting room. Superb views of the lagoon.

$$ pp Campamiento Ucaima Jungle Rudy
T0289-808 9241, T0286-952 1529 in Puerto Ordaz, www.junglerudy.com.
Run by daughters of the late 'Jungle' Rudy Truffino, full board with a variety of tour packages, 1-hr walk from Canaima above Hacha Falls, bilingual guides.

$$ pp Parakaupa Lodge
5 mins from airport, on southwestern side of lagoon, Caracas T0212-287 2015.
Attractive rooms with bath, hammocks views over the lagoon and falls, restaurant, full board.

$$ pp Tapuy Lodge
50 m from Canaima beach, T0212-993 2939 (reservations), www.casatropical.com.ve.
Next to the beach with expansive views of the mountains. Rooms are pleasant and include bath and a/c. Facilities include restaurant and bar. Attentive service and good reputation. One of the best. Recommended.

$ Camp Wey Tepuy
In the village, T0414-989-6615, www.weytepuy.com.ve.
Cheap and basic with some reported deficiencies. Fan, shower, bar, a range of tours available.

$ Kusari
Close to Parakaupa Lodge, near airport, T0286-962 0443.
Basic but clean, with bath, fan, food available, ask for Claudio at **Tienda Canaima**.

Camping and hammocks
Camp for free in Canaima, but only around the *fuente de soda*; fires are not permitted. No tents available for hire. Otherwise, best place to rent a

hammock or camp is at **Campamento Tomás Bernal (Bernal Tours)** on Isla Anatoliy, T0414-854 8562 Spanish, T0414-899 7162 English, www.bernaltours.com. Camp has capacity for 60 hammocks. Also 4 beds in open for elderly travellers, 4 rooms with private bath. Clean bathrooms. Package ($$$ pp) includes flight, bilingual guide, hammock, mosquito repellent, all meals, boat trip across lagoon, raincoat. Bernal Tours also has a camp on Ratoncito Island by Angel Falls.

Campamento Tiuna (Tiuna Tours) has camping space and lodging ($ pp). Some families in the village rent hammocks ($ pp).

Restaurants

Canaima
Food is expensive at the lodges. A cheaper option is **Simon's** restaurant in the village which is used by many agencies. It is advisable to take food, though there are various stores, both on the west side, **Tienda Canaima**, or in the indigenous village, selling mainly canned foods. A *fuente de soda* overlooks the lagoon. There is an expensive snack bar at the airport selling basic food, soft drinks and coffee; also souvenir shop.

What to do

Canaima
You can do walking expeditions into the jungle to indigenous villages with a guide, but negotiate the price. Other excursions are to the Mayupa Falls, including a canoe ride on the Río Carrao (US$18, half day), to Yuri Falls by jeep and boat (US$15, half day); to Isla Orquídea (US$25, full day, good boat ride, beach barbecue); to Saltos de Sapo and Sapito (3 hrs, US$10).

Guides in Canaima

Fierce competition at the airport but agencies pretty much offer the same thing at the same price. Some package tours to Canaima are listed under Caracas and Ciudad Bolívar Tour operators. Agents may tell you that guides speak English some do, but many don't.
Bernal Tours (*see Camping and hammock, above*).
Excursiones Kavác, *T0414-857 8560, 0416-285 9919*. Several local companies use or otherwise recommend Excursiones Kavác as a well-structured and economical option. In Canaima, they operate a basic lodge, Campamento Churúm, along with a rustic camp near the falls.
Kamaracoto Tours and **Tiuna Tours** for trips to Salto Sapo, Kavác, Salto Angel; they will also help with finding accommodation.

Kamarata
Macunaima Tours (Tito Abati), **Excursiones Pemón** (Marino Sandoval), and **Jorge and Antonio Calcaño II** run local tours.

For details on climbing Auyán Tepuy and many other tours in the region, contact **Kamadac** in Santa Elena, run by Andreas Hauer (T0289-995 1408, T0414-094 4341, www.abenteuer-venezuela.de).

Transport

Canaima
Air There are flights from **Caracas** to Canaima with **Conviasa**, but these require a change in Puerto Ordaz. Many travelers prefer to go independently

to **Puerto Ordaz** or **Ciudad Bolívar** and have their chosen tour operator or lodging organize onward flights to Canaima.

The flight to Canaima from **Ciudad Bolívar** is spectacular and takes 1 hr each way, overflying mining towns of San Isidro and Los Barrancos, as well as the vast artificial lake at Guri and the Yuri Falls. For more information see page 133.

Kamarata

Air Transmandú from **Ciudad Bolívar** (2 hrs).

Kavác

Air A day excursion by light plane to Kavác from **Canaima** (45 mins' flight) can be made with any of the tour operators at the airport, US$100. There are also flights from **Ciudad Bolívar** with **Transmandú**. Trips from Ciudad Bolívar can be arranged for 5 days/4 nights including Kavác and Angel Falls for US$300-500.

Ciudad Guayana and the Orinoco Delta

take a boat trip into a watery world

Ciudad Guayana

In an area rich in natural resources 105 km downriver from Ciudad Bolívar, Ciudad Guayana was founded in 1961 with the merger of two towns, San Félix and Puerto Ordaz, on either bank of the Río Caroní where it spills into the Orinoco. Today, they are technically a single city, but most locals to refer to them as if they were separate settlements. Ciudad Guayana is hot, humid, sprawling and futuristic. Its wide avenues, lack of sidewalks and public transport reflect the functional vision of the US-owned Orinoco Mining Company, which had its headquarters here and was nationalized in 1976. The city lacks any aesthetic charm and is unsuitable for casual strolling.

East of the Caroní is the commercial port of **San Félix** and the Palúa iron-ore terminal. It is a very dangerous part of the city and there is no reason for you to visit it. Across the Caroní by the 470 m concrete bridge is the wealthier settlement of **Puerto Ordaz** (airport), the iron-ore port connected by rail with the Cerro Bolívar open-cast iron mine. The second bridge across the Río Orinoco, Puente Orinoquia, 3156 m long, was opened in Ciudad Guayana in 2006.

Excursions Unlike elsewhere in Venezuela, there is little emphasis on arts and culture. However, beyond the urban functionality are some pleasant parks, all well kept and free to enter. Just up the Caroní at Macagua, some truly beautiful cataracts called Salto Llovizna are in the **Parque Nacional La Llovizna** ⓘ *open from early morning till 1630, taxi, US$2*, which covers 26 islands

> **Tip...**
>
> Visitors should be particularly careful while exploring Ciudad Guyana it is surrounded by some desperately poor neighbourhoods. Violent crime, including rape, is unfortunately very common. And so is police unwillingness to answer 171 calls, let alone to investigate.

separated by narrow waterways and connected by 36 footbridges. Also in the park are hydroelectric plants, but these do not spoil the views of the larger and smaller falls, diverse fauna, including monkeys, and magnificent plants growing from the falling water. There are several trails. A facility on the **hydroelectric dam** ① *Tue-Sun 0900-2100*, houses an ecological museum, art exhibitions and displays on the dam's construction, and a café. Near La Llovizna, the iron-tinted waterfall in the pretty **Parque Cachamay** (about 8 km from centre, near the **Guayana Hotel**; closes 1700) is worth a visit. A third park, adjoining Cachamay, is **Loefling Wildlife Park**, with tapirs, capybaras and capuchin monkeys.

Los Castillos, supposedly where Sir Walter Raleigh's son was killed in the search for El Dorado, are two old forts down the Orinoco from San Félix (one hour by *por puesto*, US$1, or take a tour).

Tucupita

A worthwhile side trip along asphalted roads can be made to Tucupita, on the Orinoco Delta. Though capital of Delta Amacuro state and the main commercial centre of the delta, there's a one-horse feel about it. **Tourist office** ① *Parque Central de Tucupita Módulos II y III, Av Mons A García de Espinosa, by the Terminal de Pasajeros*. Tourists should go there first for tour information.

For a three- to four-day trip to see the delta, its fauna and the indigenous Warao people, either arrange boats through the tourist office (see above). Boats are not easy to come by and are expensive except for large groups. Bargain hard and never pay up front.

Excursions often only travel on the main river, not in the *caños* where wildlife is most often seen. To avoid disappointment, be sure to determine where your guide intends to take you before you leave. If the river level rises after a downpour, arrangements may be cancelled. On all trips agree in advance exactly what is included, especially that there is enough food and water for you and your guide. Hammocks and mosquito repellents are essential.

Barrancas

An interesting and friendly village, founded in 1530, Barrancas is one of the oldest villages in the Americas, but its precolonial past dates back to 1000 BC. Situated on the Orinoco, it can be reached by road from Tucupita (63 km), or from Maturín. It has two basic hotels ($). The village has a large community of Guyanese people who speak English. It is possible to take a boat to the Warao villages of **Curiapo** and **Amacuro** (near the Guyana border), check at harbour.

Where to stay

Ciudad Guayana
The following options are in Puerto Ordaz:

$$$ Venetur Orinoco
Av Guayana, Parque Punta Visat, T0286-713 1000, www.venetur.gob.ve.
It overlooks La Llovizna in Parque Cachamay, far from centre, great location but poor value. Get one of the newer rooms with a good view.

$$ Doral Inn Hotel
C Neverí, opposite the airport, T0286-952 6803, doralinn@bolivar.travel.
A good option for early-morning flights. Generic rooms are massive and spotless with white marble floors, a/c, cable TV, and Wi-Fi. Next door, **Hotel Mara** is good too, but twice the price.

$ Casa del Lobo
Of Wolfgang Löffler of Lobo Tours, C Zambia 2, Africana Manzana 39, T0286-961 6286, www.lobo-tours.de.
Homely posada with room for 8 people, free transfer from airport. 'El Lobo' speaks English and German.

$ Posada Turística Alonga
Urb La Corniza, Av Canadá, manzana 10, casa 14, T0286-923 3154, posadaalonga@hotmail.com.
Family-run posada in a quiet residential area, see Facebook.

$ Residencias Tore
C San Cristóbal y Cra Los Andes, T0286-923 1389.
Ecologically aware hotel with solar-heated water, restaurant, laundry and Wi-Fi. Simple, pleasant, quiet rooms have TVs and sparkling bathrooms.

Tucupita

$ Pequeño
La Paz, T0287-721 0523.
Basic but clean, fan, good value, safe, stores luggage, orchid garden, popular, closes at 2200.

$ Saxxi
On main road into Tucupita, 10 mins from centre, T0287-721 2112, www.deltaorinocomis palafitos.com.
Comfortable, hot water, a/c, bar/restaurant, disco Fri-Sat, pool. Also has camps **Mis Palafitos** and **Orinoco Bujana Lodge**, **$$**, T0287-721 1733. All-inclusive.

Restaurants

Ciudad Guayana
There are plenty of restaurants and cafés on Cras Tumeremo and Upata, off Av Las Américas. Fast-food and upmarket eateries in Ciudad Comercial Altavista.

El Arepazo Guayanés
C La Urbana, Puerto Ordaz, T0286-922 4757.
The oldest and best *areparía* in Ciudad Guyana, open 24 hrs.

Mall Orinokia
On Av Guayana, Altavista, close to the bus terminal.
Huge, super-modern shopping mall with restaurants, cafés and travel agencies. Multi-screen cinema.

Mi Rinconcito
Across the street from Mall Orinokia (Altavista), T0286-962 1554.
Famous for its *cachapas* and live music at the end of the week.

What to do

Ciudad Guayana

Lobo Tours, *see Casa del Lobo, Where to stay.* Wolfgang Löffler will tailor his tours to fit your demands. Trips organized to the Gran Sabana and Orinoco Delta, but will put together other excursions. Very helpful, all-inclusive, excellent cooking. English and German spoken.

Tucupita

Some boat owners visit hotels in the evenings looking for clients and may negotiate a price. Ask Pieter Rothfuss at **Gekko Tours/Posada La Casita** in Ciudad Bolívar about a trip through the southern part of the delta and into the Sierra Imataca highlands. The following (and **Mis Palafitos** – see **Hotel Saxxi**) are registered with the tourist board and have insurance (this does not necessarily guarantee a good tour):

Aventura Turística, *C Centurión 62, T0414-879 5821, and at bus station, a_t_d_1973@hotmail.com, www. hosteltrail.com/atd.* 2 camps in the northern part of the delta, all-inclusive tours, English and French spoken.

Tucupita Expeditions, *opposite hospital, T0295-249 1823, T0414-789 8343, www. orinocodelta.com.* 2- to 5-night tours to lodges and camps in the delta.

Transport

Ciudad Guayana

Air Daily flights from Puerto Ordaz to **Caracas**, **Maracaibo**, **Porlamar** and short-haul destinations. Walk 600 m to gas station on main road for buses to San Félix or Puerto Ordaz.

Bus Terminals at San Félix and close to Puerto Ordaz airport; long-distance buses at both. Public transport in Ciudad Guayana is very limited. Free local buses are infrequent. Minibuses are fast and cheap; San Félix–Puerto Ordaz, US$0.30; buses run until 2100. Several buses daily to **Santa Elena de Uairén** (via El Callao), US$2.50, 10 hrs, night buses with **Los Llanos** and **Occidente** recommended for comfort, but you'll miss the scenery. **El Callao** (US$1), **Tumeremo** (US$1), **El Dorado** (US$1.25) and Km 88 with Turgar. **Ciudad Bolívar** US$0.50, 1 hr. 8 daily to **Caracas**, US$3, 10 hrs. 8 daily to **Puerto La Cruz**, US$1.75, 6 hrs. 2 daily to **Cumaná**, US$2, 8 hrs. To **Tucupita**, US$1, 3 hrs, leaving from San Félix bus terminal with **Expresos Guayanesa**, booking office opens 1 hr before departure, be there early, passport check just before Tucupita. San Felix bus terminal is not a safe place, especially at night.

Car hire Many agencies at airport. A car is very useful here, eg for local excursions, or taking a road trip through the Gran Sabana to Brazil.

Taxi San Félix–Puerto Ordaz US$1 minimum, Puerto Ordaz–airport US$1.50, San Félix bus terminal-Puerto Ordaz bus terminal US$1.75, bus terminal-centre US$1.50, centre–San Félix bus terminal US$1.50.

Tucupita

Bus *Por puesto* from **Maturín** US$2.50, 2-3 hrs; bus to Maturín, US$1, 3-4 hrs, **Expresos Guayanesa**, US$1.50 with **Expresos Los Llanos** recommended. 2 daily to **San Félix**, US$1, see above. 2 daily to **Caracas**, US$2.60, 12-13 hrs.

Barrancas

Bus Tucupita–Barrancas, US$0.50, return at 0945 and 1700.

Ciudad Guayana to Santa Elena de Uairén

cross the great savannah to reach Brazil

Travelling south from Ciudad Guayana to the Brazilian border is popular with Venezuelans, as well as for overland travellers heading in or out of Brazil via Boa Vista. The road to the border at Santa Elena de Uairén passes across the beautiful Gran Sabana and is paved, with all bridges in place.

To Tumeremo

South from Ciudad Guayana Highway 10 is a four-lane *autopista* as far as **Upata**. Buy provisions opposite the petrol station. At 18 km beyond **Guasipati** is **El Callao** on the south bank of the Río Yuruari, off the highway, a small, clean, bright town whose renowned pre-Lenten carnival has a touch of calypso from British Caribbean immigrants who came to mine gold in the late 19th century (all prices rise for carnival). The town has many jewellery shops and restaurants.

On another 41 km is **Tumeremo** (Population 24,300), which is recommended as the best place to buy provisions and gasoline, all grades at a normal price (better than El Dorado).

Essential Gran Sabana

Getting around

A 4WD is only necessary off the main road, especially in the rainy season. You may need spare tanks of gasoline if spending a lot of time away from the main road (eg in Kavanayen and El Paují) and have a gas-guzzling vehicle. Carry extra water and plenty of food. Small eating places may close out of season. There are Guardia Nacional checks at the Río Cuyuní (Km 8), at Km 126, and at San Ignacio de Yuruaní (Km 259), and a military checkpoint at Luepa (Km 143); all driving permits, car registration papers, and ID must be shown. See also Driving in Venezuela, page 173.

Advice

In the towns as far as El Dorado, there are hotels, but many cater for local business, legitimate or otherwise, and for short-stay clients. Water is rationed in many places and hot water in hotels is rare south of Ciudad Guayana, except in the better hotels of Santa Elena. Towns usually have a bank, but don't rely on it for getting money. Camping is possible but a good waterproof tent is essential. A small fee is payable to the *indígenas* living around Kaui, Kama and similar villages (see also under Parque Nacional Canaima). Insect repellent and long-sleeved/trousered clothes are needed against *puri-puri* (small, black, vicious biting insects) and mosquitoes (especially in El Dorado, at Km 88 and at Icabarú). See www.lagransabana.com.

ON THE ROAD

The search for El Dorado

Sir Walter Raleigh will forever be associated with the introduction of tobacco to Elizabethan England in the early 1580s from the newly settled province of Virginia in the United States. But Raleigh was also obsessed with the idea of finding the mythical golden city of El Dorado. By the time of his voyage to South America in 1595 he was already 40 years old, out of favour with Queen Elizabeth and deep in debt. His motivation for undertaking such a risky venture may have been to restore his damaged reputation but he was also determined to bring an end to the Spanish domination of the region.

Raleigh's interest in El Dorado had been fired by a certain Spanish gentleman, Don Pedro Sarmiento de Gamboa, an old American campaigner who had been captured by two pirate ships owned by Raleigh and brought to England, where he told Raleigh of El Dorado, which he claimed was an empire of Inca refugees from Peru.

Raleigh believed El Dorado to be in the Guayana Highlands, on the shores of a lake, at a point roughly 150 miles south of the confluence of the Caroní and Orinoco rivers. This belief was fostered by another Spaniard, Don Antonio de Berrio.

In May 1595, Raleigh reached the Venezuelan mainland on the Paría peninsula and found a suitable entrance into the great Orinoco Delta at a place now called Boca Bagre, or Catfish Bay. The expedition progressed up the river, but lasted no more than a few months. It effectively ended at the confluence of the Orinoco and Caroní Rivers when an encounter with the chief of the local Pemón tribe led Raleigh to abandon his search. The chief told him of the occupation of Guayana by a strange and powerful tribe who had migrated into the region early in the 16th century. The chief warned Raleigh that they may have been Incas with an inpregnable outpost, defended by 3000 troops. Raleigh withdrew, and it saved him the indignity of having his theory proved wrong.

His obsession was not over, however. Indeed, it could be said that Raleigh lost his head over El Dorado – literally. In 1617 he secured Royal permission for a second voyage to the New World, despite being imprisoned in the Tower of London for his alleged part in a conspiracy against King James I. The second expedition was a fiasco and Raleigh returned to England not only a broken man, but also facing certain death. He had broken his promise to the king of not engaging in battle with the Spanish during the expedition and was duly beheaded on 29 October 1618.

El Dorado

This hot, dirty and noisy town is 76 km from Tumeremo, 278 km from Ciudad Guayana, and 7 km off the road on the Río Cuyuní. On a river island is the prison made famous by Henri Charrière/Papillon's stay there in 1945. El Dorado's economic mainstay is its gas station (daily 0800-1900).

El Dorado to Santa Elena de Uairén

The turn-off to El Dorado is marked Km 0; distances are measured from here by green signs 2 km apart. The wall of the **Gran Sabana** looms above Km 88 (also called **San Isidro**), where gasoline and expensive supplies can be bought. The highway climbs steeply in sharp curves for 40 km before reaching the top. The road is in very good condition and presents no problem for conventional cars. 4WDs may be better in the wet season (May-October). At Km 100 the huge **Piedra de la Virgen** is passed before the steepest climb (La Escalera) enters the beautiful **Parque Nacional Canaima** (see page 134).

The landscape is essentially savannah, with clusters of trees, moriche palms and bromeliads. Typical of this area are the large abrupt tepuis (flat-topped mountains or mesas), hundreds of waterfalls, and the silence of one of the oldest plateaus on earth. At Km 119 (sign can only be seen going north) a short trail leads to the 40 m **Danto ('Tapir') Falls**, a powerful fall wreathed in mosses and mist. The falls are close to the road (about five minutes slippery walk down on the left-hand side), but not visible from it. The **Monumento al Soldado Pionero** (Km 137) commemorates the army engineers who built the road from the lowlands, finally opened in 1973; barbecues, toilets, shelters are now almost all in ruins. Some 4 km beyond is **Luepa**; everyone must stop at the military checkpoint a little way south. There is a popular camping place at Luepa, on the right going south. You may be able to rent a tent or you can hang a hammock in an open-sided shelter (very cold at night, no water or facilities, buy meals from a tour group, but pricey). The Inparques station at Luepa has guestrooms for visitors of Inparques, but they may let you stay for a small fee. You can camp at a site on Río Aponwao on the left hand side of the road going south.

Some 8 km beyond Luepa, a poor, graded gravel road leads 70 km west to **Kavanayén** (little traffic, best to have your own vehicle with high clearance, especially during the wet season, take snacks; the road can be cycled but is slow, lots of soft, sandy places). Accommodation is at the Capuchin mission, $, also in private homes. One of the two grocery stores will prepare food, or the restaurant opposite serves cheap breakfasts and dinners, order in advance.

The settlement is surrounded by tepuis. Off the road to Kavanayén are the falls of **Torón Merú** and **Chinak-Merú** (also called Aponwao), 105 m high and very impressive. Neither is a straightforward detour, so get full instructions before setting out. Chinak-Merú is reached via the Pemón village of **Iboribó**. A day's walk west of Kavanayén are the lovely falls on the **Río Karuay**.

For the remaining 180 km to Santa Elena de Uairén few people and only a few Pemón indigenous villages are to be seen. San Juan and San Rafael de Kamoiran and **Rápidos de Kamoiran** are passed. The 5-m Kawí Falls on the **Kaüi** River are at Km 195, while at Km 201.5 are the impressive 55 m high **Kama Merú** falls (US$1 to walk to bottom of falls). Also a small lake, handicrafts, a small shop, canoe trips. Cabins and *churuatas* can be rented, also camping. Buses can be flagged down going south or north three times a day; check times in advance.

At Km 237 the Río Arapán cascades over the charming **Quebrada Pacheco** (Arapán Merú); pools nearby where you can swim. Tour groups often stop here. A path up the opposite side of the main falls leads to an isolated natural pool 20 minutes' walk away, in the middle of the savannah. **Warning** Do not go beyond the red line at Pacheco there is a hidden fall which has claimed lives. There is a Campamento at Arapán. Next is **Balneario Saro Wapo** on the Río Soruapé (Km 244), a good place for swimming and picnics, natural whirlpool, restaurant, 10 minutes downriver is a natural waterslide. At Km 250 is the Pemón village of Kumarakapai, San Francisco de Yuruaní (see page 153), whose falls (Arapena-merú) can be seen from the bridge, followed, 9 km of bends later, by the smaller **San Ignacio de Yuruaní** (strict military checkpoint; excellent regional food).

A trail at Km 275 leads to the **Quebrada de Jaspe** where a river cuts through striated cliffs and pieces of jasper glitter on the banks. Visit at midday when the sun shines best on the jasper, or at 1500 when the colour changes from red to orange, dazzlingly beautiful.

Santa Elena de Uairén

This booming, pleasant frontier town was established by Capuchin Monks in 1931. The mid-20th-century **cathedral** ① *daily 0530-1900, Mass Mon-Sat 0630 and 1830, Sun 0630 and 2030*, built from local stone, is a famous landmark. Thanks to its relaxed atmosphere and many hotels, Santa Elena is an agreeable place in which to spend time. It has Arab and Chinese communities and you are as likely to hear Portugese spoken as you are Spanish.

Border with Brazil

The 16 km road to the border is paved. The entire road links Caracas with Manaus in four days with hard driving; see Northern Brazil, in Brazil chapter, for a description of the road from the border and Brazilian immigration formalities. Modern customs and immigration facilities are at the border and the crossing is straightforward on both sides (for more information, see Transport, page 152). Staff at the **Ministry of Justice** and the **Guardia Nacional headquarters** ① *T0289-960 3765/995 1189/995 1958*, have been recommended as helpful with entry and exit problems. You can get a visa at the **Brazilian consulate** ① *Edif Galeno, C Los Castaños, Urbanización Roraima del Casco Central, T0289-995 1256; open 0800-1400*. The **Brazilin consulate in Ciudad Guyana** ① *Cra Tocoma, Edif Eli-Alti, of 4, Alta Vista, Ciudad Guyana, T0416-183 6135, 0900-1200, 1400-1800*, is helpful, visa issued promptly.

For entry to Venezuela, some nationalities who cross the border from Boa Vista, Brazil, need a visa. It is not required by western Europeans, whose passport must be valid for a year, but check with a consulate before leaving home. A yellow fever vaccination certificate is required. Ask well in advance for other health requirements (eg malaria test certificate). Entering by car, keep photocopies of your licence, the Brazilian permission to leave and Venezuelan entry stamp. Allow two hours for formalities when crossing by private vehicle and don't cross during the lunch hour.

> **Tip...**
>
> Note that banks in Ciudad Guyana will not exchange Brazilian reais.

Fresh fruit and vegetables may not be brought into Venezuela. There are frequent road checks when heading north from Santa Elena. SENIAT (the customs authority) has its Aduana Principal Ecológica outside the town and there may be up to eight more thorough searches, mainly for drugs. Luggage will be sealed before loading into the bus hold in Santa Elena. These checks may mean you arrive in Ciudad Bolívar after dark. There is no public transport on the Venezuelan side, hitch or take a taxi from Brazil.

ATMs are unlikely to accept non-Venezuelan credit cards. Try shops in the centre, C Urdaneta, for dollars cash, or Brazilian reais. Try at border with Brazilians entering Venezuela. Ask the bus driver on the Santa Elena-Boa Vista bus the best place for favourable bolívares/reais rates in Santa Elena at Sucre y Perimetral; in Brazil at the first stop after the border. Check with travellers going in the opposite direction what rates should be.

El Pauji

A road leaves the highway 8 km south of Santa Elena and after passing through a tunnel of jungle vegetation emerges onto rolling savannah dotted with tepuis. The road has been considerably improved and has been paved for 20 km. The rest is graded, but deteriorating. It can take between two to four hours to reach El Pauji. Take advice before setting out, as rain can rapidly degrade the road. At Km 8 is a Guardia Nacional checkpoint at Paraitepuí, waterfall nearby.

El Pauji, 17 km further on, is an agricultural settlement with a growing foreign population. It is a lovely area, with good walking. Excellent sights **Chirica Tepuy**, huge, beautiful, jet black, set in rolling savannah; **Río Surucún**, where Venezuela's largest diamond was found; **Salto Catedral** (61 km off the road), beautiful small hollow, lovely falls, excellent swimming (camping, shop); **Salto La Gruta**, impressive falls; and **Pozo Esmeralda**, 1.5 km outside El Pauji towards Icabarú (400 m south of road), fine rapids, waterfall you can stand under and pools. At Los Saltos de Pauji are many powerful falls; going from El Pauji towards Santa Elena, before crossing the first bridge, take track on left for about 500 m. A good walk is to the small hill, 2 km from El Pauji beyond the airfield; views from the crest over **El Abismo**, the plunging escarpment marking the end of Gran Sabana highlands and the start of the Amazon rainforest. It takes an hour to reach the top, and the walk is highly recommended. Guides, though not necessary, are in the village. A recommended guide is German-speaking Marco. Small campsite (lovely early morning or sunset).

Apiculture is the main activity of El Pauji and there's an **International Honey Festival** every summer. The honey made in this area is delicious; buy it at the shop in El Pauji or Salto Catedral.

Where to stay

To Tumerem

$ Andrea
Plaza Miranda, Upata, T0288-221 3656.
Decent rooms, a/c, hot water, fridge
in some rooms. Credit cards accepted,
Chinese restaurant, safe parking, good.

El Dorado to Santa Elena de Uairén

$$ pp La Barquilla de Fresa
*At Km 84.5. Book via Alba Betancourt in
Caracas T0288-808 8710, T0426-991 9919.*
English and German spoken.
Birdwatching tours; inventory of bird
species here has reached more than 300
species. Full board lodging, reservations
and deposit required.

Santa Elena de Uairén

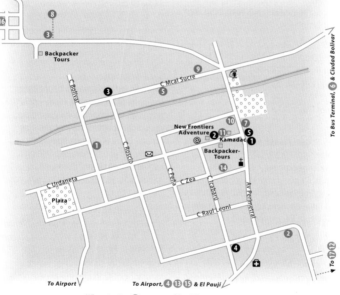

Where to stay
1 Augusta
2 Cabañas Friedenau
3 Cabañas Roraima
4 Gran Sabana
5 Jaspe
6 Kiamantí
7 La Posada Aventura &
  Adventure Tours
8 Las 5 Jotas
9 Los Castaños
10 Lucrecia
11 Michelle
12 Tavarúa
13 Temiche Camp
14 Tres Naciones
15 Villa Apoipó
16 Villa Fairmont
17 Ya-Koo Ecological Camp

Restaurants
1 Alfredo's
2 Café Goldrausch &
  Michelle
3 El Ranchón Criollo
4 Panadería Gran Café
5 Venezuela Primero

Rápidos de Kamoiran

$ Campamento Rápidos de Kamoiran
Km 172, T0289-540 0009, www.
rapidosdekamoiran.blogspot.com.
Clean, with fan, well-kept, cold water,
also has camping, also restaurant,
gasoline, and picnic spot by rapids.

Santa Elena de Uairén

$$-$ Cabañas Friedenau
Av Ppal de Cielo Azul, off Av Perimetral,
T0289-995 1353, see Facebook.
Self-contained chalets, nice grounds,
vegetarian food, parking, transfer to
Puerto Ordaz, bikes, horseriding, trips
to Roraima (see below), English spoken.
Recommended.

$$-$ Gran Sabana
Carretera Nacional Via Brasil, 10 km
from border, T0289-995 1810,
www.hotelgransabana.com.
Large resort-style hotel with 58 rooms,
one of the most upscale in town but
past its heyday. Pool, parking, café, tours.

$$-$ Posada L'Auberge
C Urdaneta, T0289-995 1567,
www.l-auberge.net.
Brick-built guesthouse with good rooms
and shared balcony, a/c, Wi-Fi, cable TV,
hot water, parking, tourist information.
Family-run. Recommended.

$$-$ Villa Fairmont
Urb Akurimá, T0289-995
1022, at north edge of town,
www.lagransabana.com/villafairmont.
Large place up on a hill with pool,
jacuzzi, restaurant, parking, bar.
Reasonable rooms but check
before accepting.

$ Kiamantí
Outside town 1 km from bus
terminal, T0289-995 1952,
http://kiamanti.blogspot.com/.
Very simple little cabins, full board, fan,
hot water, parking, pool.

$ Lucrecia
Av Perimetral, T0289-995 1105,
near old terminal.
Motel-style lodgings with a small pool,
parking and restaurant. Rooms have a/c
or fan, hot water, cable TV, Wi-Fi. Helpful.

$ Michelle
C Urdaneta, T0289-416 1257,
www.hosteltrail.com/posadamichelle.
Popular backpacker place, helpful. Basic
rooms have fan, hot water, Wi-Fi. Shower
and changing room available if you're
waiting for a night bus.

$ Villa Apoipó
On the road to the airport, turn left at
the Hotel Gran Sabana, T0289-995 2018,
www.lagransabana.com/villapoipo.
Very nice rooms, hot water, fan. For
groups but will take independent
travellers if you ring ahead. Use of
kitchen or full board. Bunk beds or
hammocks available in large *churuata*.

$ Ya-Koo Ecological Camp
2 km on unpaved road to Sampai
community, up mountain behind Santa
Elena, T0289-995 1742, www.ya-koo.com.
Cabañas in beautiful 10-ha site, full
board, spacious rooms, hot water,
natural pool. Cheaper in low season.
Recommended if you have a car.

El Paují

$$-$ pp Campamento Amaribá
3.5 km outside El Paují on road from
Santa Elena, transport available from
airstrip, T0424-254 9161, amaribapauji@
yahoo.com.

Comfortable cabins with mosquito nets, good facilities, full board, kitchen, tours arranged, very hospitable. Also dance, healing and therapy centre.

$ Campamento El Paují
3.5 km outside El Paují on road from Santa Elena, transport available from airstrip, T0289-995 1431, T0426-691 8966, dianalez@gmail.com, or contact through Maripak.
Beautiful cabins with spectacular views over the Gran Sabana, food available, camping US$6 per tent. Recommended.

$ Cantarana tourist camp
25 km from town, T0415-212 0662 (in Caracas T0212-234 0255), www.gran-sabana.info.
Basic, breakfast and dinner included, owners, Alfonso and Barbara Borrero, speak German, English and Spanish, waterfall and lovely surroundings.

$ Maripak
Near the airstrip and small store, T0414-772 3070, www.maripak.com.ve, or reserve in Caracas T0212-234 3661.
Cabins for 2/3 with bath, meals extra, good food, tours, camping.

$ Weimure
2 km out, outside El Paují on road from Santa Elena, pauji0@yahoo.com.
Beautiful cabin close to river, dynamic architect owner.

Restaurants

Santa Elena de Uairén
Several restaurants on Mcal Sucre. The local river fish, Lau Lau, is good. Avoid seafood.

$ Alfredo's
Av Perimetral, at the end of C Urdaneta.
Tasty pizzas at good prices.

$ Peixada e Restaurant Do Léo
C Zea, between C Peña and C Icabarú.
Unpretentious Brazilian barbeque with chicken, sausages and chorizos, pay by weight, also a good selection of salads for vegetarians. Recommended.

$ Tumá Serö
A cheap and bustling gastronomic market where you can pick up wholesome arepas, soup, pizzas, burgers.

$ Venezuela Primero
Av Perimetral.
Dated interior but often recommended for its chicken, meat and fish.

Gran Sabana Deli
C Bolívar, T0289-995 1158.
A large café with pavement seating selling good hot coffee, imported ham, cheese, salami, fresh bread, olives, cakes, and pastries.

What to do

Santa Elena de Uairén
Santa Elena is the most economical place to book tours of the Gran Sabana, Roraima, and other tepuis. Many interesting attractions lie along the highway and can be covered in an undemanding day-trip. Trips to Roraima typically last 5-6 days, but it can be done in 4. An all-inclusive package (transport, guide, sleeping bag, mattress, map, food, tent, and porter) costs about US$550 for two people (less if the tour is priced in BsF). There are cheaper options depending on how much equipment of your own you carry.
Alvarez Treks, *office in the bus station, T0414-385 2846, www.saltoangelrsta.com.*
An excellent range of Gran Sabana tours by Francisco Alvarez. The 'traditional'

tour is physically undemanding, follows the highway, a good trip for families and seniors. The moderately demanding 'non-traditional' tour offers a more intimate experience of the landscape with hikes through rivers and rainforests. The combination tour offers a bit of both, while the Extreme Tour is a 6-hr day with stops at waterfalls and swimming holes; 4-people minimum. Also tours of Roraima, Angel Falls, Los Llanos, and the Orinoco Delta. Knowledgeable, helpful, recommended.
Backpacker Tours, *C Urdaneta, T0289-995 1430, T0414-886 7227, www. backpacker-tours.com*. 1- to 5-day, all-inclusive jeep tours through the Gran Sabana, visiting little-known falls in the Kavanayen area. Trekking to nearby Chirikayen Tepuy, 3-4 days, and to Roraima (minimum 4 persons), plus more. German and English spoken. Recommended. Also own $ Posada.
Kamadac, *C Urdaneta, T0289-995 1408, T0414-094 4341, www.abenteuer-venezuela.de*. Run by Andreas Hauer, tours of Gran Sabana, all-inclusive tour to Roraima, and also more adventurous tours to Auyán Tepuy from which Angel Falls cascades, difficult. Recommended.
Roberto's Mystic Tours, *Urdaneta, casa 6, T0289-416 1081, www.mystictours. com.ve*. As the author of several books about Roraima and the Gran Sabana, Roberto is very knowledgeable about the local environment and culture. His tours include a complete briefing of the region's ecological, botanical and energetic properties. Excellent tours, very helpful, highly recommended.
Ruta Salvaje, *C Mcal Sucre, at the junction opposite the petrol station, T0289-995 1134, www.rutasalvaje. com*. Well-established adventure tour specialists offering white-water

rafting, parapenting and paramotoring, traditional and non-traditional day tours of the Gran Sabana, treks to Roraima, and tours of Angel Falls.

Transport

To Tumeremo
Bus From Upata to **Ciudad Bolívar**, US$1; to **San Félix** (Ciudad Guayana), US$0.35; to **Santa Elena**, US$2.50.

Tumeremo
Bus To **Caracas**, US$3.65. To **Ciudad Bolívar**, US$1.50, 6 a day, 6½ hrs. To **Santa Elena**, 8-10 hrs, with **Líneas Orinoco**, 2 blocks from plaza. **El Dorado**, US$0.35, 1½ hrs.

El Dorado
Bus All buses stop on main plaza. From **Caracas**, **Expresos del Oriente**, at 1830 daily, US$3.50-4, 14½ hrs (925 km). The **Orinoco** bus links with **Ciudad Bolívar** (6 hrs, US$1.65) and **Santa Elena**, as does **Transmundial** (better, leaving 1100, US$1.65 to **Santa Elena**, US$1.65 to **San Félix**, 4 hrs).

El Dorado to Santa Elena de Uairén
Km 88 (San Isidro)
Bus Frequent *por puestos* from **El Dorado** to Km 88, 1 hr, US$1. Most non-luxury buses stop at the petrol station to refuel. Or get a ride with jeeps and trucks (little passes after 1030).

Santa Elena de Uairén
Air Airport, 8 km from the centre. Scheduled flights from Caracas with **Conviasa** only (unreliable); infrequent charters from **Ciudad Bolívar** subject to weather conditions.

Bus The bus terminal on road to Ciudad Bolívar is 2-km/30 mins' walk from town, taxi US$1. Get to terminal 30 mins in advance for SENIAT baggage check for contraband. From **Caracas** there are direct buses (eg **Expresos Los Llanos**), US$4.25, or you can go to Ciudad Bolívar or to Ciudad Guyana and then take a bus direct to Santa Elena. 10 buses daily from Santa Elena to **Ciudad Bolívar**, US$3, **Expresos Los Llanos** and **Expresos Occidente** recommended for comfort, 10-12 hrs. 10 daily to **Ciudad Guayana** and **San Félix**, US$2.50, 10-11 hrs.

To the border The best way to reach the border is with a *por puesto* taxi, US$1. They depart from the intersection of C Roscio and C Icabarú. Check that they drop you at the 2 immigration offices, 750 m apart, before going onward to the town of Pacaraima, where you can pick up connections to Boa Vista. Alternatively, from the bus station, there are 3 buses daily to **Boa Vista**, US$3, 4 hrs, **Eucatur**.

El Paují
Road From **Santa Elena** by jeep, US$3 if full, more if not, daily at around 0600-0700 and 1500-1600 from Plaza Bolívar. Also at **Panadería Gran Café**, C Icabarú. To get further than El Paují, 4WD vehicle is necessary **Cantarana**, US$5, and **Icabarú**, US$6.

Mount Roraima
conquer the 'Lost World'

An exciting trek is to the summit of Mount Roraima (altitude 2810 m), at one time believed to be the 'Lost World' made famous by Arthur Conan Doyle's novel. 'Roroima' is a word in the indigenous Pemón language meaning 'The great blue-green'. Due to the tough terrain and extreme weather conditions, this hike is only suitable for the fit. Supplies for a week or more should be bought in Santa Elena. If a tour company is supplying the food, check what it is first; vegetarians may go hungry.

San Francisco de Yuruaní
The starting point is this Pemón village, 9 km north of the San Ignacio military checkpoint (where you must register). There are three small shops selling basic goods but not enough for Roraima hike. Meals are available and tents can be hired, about US$10 each per day, quality of tents and stoves is poor; better equipment is available in Santa Elena.

Paraitepui
The road to Paraitepui (which is signposted), the nearest village to the mountain, leaves the highway 1 km south of San Francisco. It is in good condition, with three bridges; the full 25 km can be walked in seven hours. You can sleep for free in the village if hiring a guide; camping is permitted. Few supplies are available; a small shop sells basics. The villagers speak Tauripán, the local dialect of the Pemón linguistic group, but now most of them also speak Spanish.

Climbing Roraima

The foot trail winds back and forth on a more direct line than the little-used jeep track; it is comparatively straightforward and adequately marked descending from the heights just past Paraitepui across rolling hills and numerous clear streams. The goal, Roraima, is the mountain on the right, the other massive outcrop on the left is Mata Hui (known as Kukenán after the river which rises within it). If leaving the village early in the day, you may reach the Río Cuquenán crossing by early afternoon (good camping here). Three hours' walk brings you to a lovely bird-filled meadow below the foothills of the massif, another perfect camping spot known as *campamento base* (10 hours to base camp from Paraitepui). The footpath now climbs steadily upwards through the cloud forest at the mountain's base and becomes an arduous scramble over tree trunks and damp rocks until the cliff is reached. From here it is possible to ascend to the plateau along the 'easy' rock ledge which is the only route to the top. Walkers in good health should take about four hours from the meadow to the top. The summit is an eerie world of stone and water, difficult to move around easily. There are not many good spots to camp; but there are various overhanging ledges which are colourfully known as 'hoteles' by the guides. Red painted arrows lead the way to the right after reaching the summit for the main group of these. A marked track leads to the survey pillar near the east cliff where Guyana, Brazil and Venezuela meet; allow a day as the track is very rough. Other sights include the Valley of the Crystals, La Laguna de Gladys and various sinkholes.

The whole trip can take anywhere between five days and two weeks. The dry season for trekking is November-May (with annual variations); June-August Roraima is usually enveloped in cloud. Do not remove crystals from the mountain; on-the-spot fines up to US$100 may be charged. Thorough searches are made on your return. Take your rubbish back down with you.

Listings Mount Roraima

Where to stay

San Francisco de Yuruaní

$ Arapena Posada
T0241-866 4339 or 0414-422 7227.
Small and basic, information on treks and adventure tourism.

$ El Caney de Yuruaní
T0416-289 2413.
Clean, basic rooms, fan, restaurant.

Camping
Permitted just about anywhere, free. Plenty of mosquitos at night.

Climbing Roraima
Camping
Full equipment including stove is essential (an igloo-type tent with a plastic sheet for the floor is best for the summit, where it can be wet), wear thick socks and boots to protect legs from snakes, warm clothes for the summit (much mist, rain squalls and lightning at night) and effective insect repellent – biting *plaga* (blackflies) infest the grasslands. The water on the summit and around the foot of Roraima is very pure, but as more do the trek, the waters are becoming dirtied. Bring bottled water or

ON THE ROAD
The Land that Time Forgot

Roraima is the most famous of all the tepuis in Guayana, and for a good reason. Arthur Conan Doyle's novel, *The Lost World* was based on the accounts of Everard Im Thurn, who was the first explorer ever to climb to the summit of Roraima, in 1884. On his return, he gave a series of lectures, which inspired Conan Doyle to write of a strange and mysterious land lost in time and inhabited by prehistoric creatures.

But Conan Doyle's imaginings may not be so far fetched. Scientists have called these tepuis ecological islands – or islands in time. These separated from the surrounding land two billion years ago and unique species of plant have been found on their wild, marshy summits. New sub-species of fauna, too, have been discovered.

Indeed, one of the legendary old pioneers of Canaima, Alexander Laime, who lived in a hut below Auyán Tepuy, claimed he had seen prehistoric creatures near the summit. He made a sketch, and it turned out that they looked uncannily like plesiosaurs, aquatic mammals of the Jurassic period, which were thought to have been extinct for nearly 100 million years.

It's true that when you reach the top of Roraima, you do experience a strange, eerie sensation – almost as if you had travelled far back in time. So, perhaps a question you should be asking any potential guide is "how fast can dinosaurs run?"

a purifier for the savannah. Fires must not be lit on top of Roraima, only gas or liquid fuel stoves. Litter is appearing along the trail; please take care of the environment.

What to do

Climbing Roraima
Guides and tours
The National Guard requires all visitors to have a guide beyond Paraitepui; you will be fined. Go with a guide or tour operator from Santa Elena or from San Francisco; ask at **Arapena**, or **El Caney de Yuruaní**. Those hired on the street or in Paraitepui have no accident insurance cover. Guides can help for the hike's final stages (easy to get lost) and for finding best camping spots. Guides in San Francisco de Yuruaní cost US$15 a day, more if they carry your supplies. Check the camping gear for leaks, etc, and be clear about who is providing the guide's food.

Spanish-speaking guides in Paraitepui cost US$10 a day. The **Ayuso** brothers are the best-known guides. Ask for El Capitán; he is in charge of guides. Parking at Inparques US$1.

Transport

San Francisco de Yuruaní
Bus From **Santa Elena** bus will let you off here and pick up passengers en route northwards (no buses 1200-1900). Jeep to **Paraitepui** US$30. Cheapest is Oscar Mejías Hernández, ask in village.

Background
Venezuela

History

Conquest and colonial rule

Venezuela was the first of Spain's New World colonies to be explored. On his third voyage to America, in 1498, Columbus first set foot on the continent, somewhere in the south of the Paria peninsula, then explored the delta region of the Orinoco and the coast of the Paria peninsula. The following year, another expedition headed by Amerigo Vespucci and Alonso de Ojeda, covered the same route, then sailed along the northern coast to Lake Maracaibo. Here, the lakeside dwellings built on stilts in the shallow waters were sarcastically compared to a miniature Venice, giving the country the name 'Little Venice', or Venezuela.

Though the first to be 'discovered', Venezuela was the last to be conquered and developed. The new colony was held in low regard by the Spaniards, due to the considerable environmental barriers to effective colonization and also the lure of other regions such as Mexico and Peru, which were wealthier in both human and material resources. Compared to the Incas, or the Chibchas of neighbouring Colombia, the indigenous people of Venezuela were primitive. The most advanced groups were the farming tribes of the Andes and the northeast coast. Most backward were the nomadic hunting and fishing tribes of Lake Maracaibo and the Llanos. In the central coastal region were both nomadic and agricultural groups. Many of these tribes were cannibalistic and most of them warlike.

For the first half of the 16th century, Spanish interest was confined to the exploitation of pearls, gold and slaves on the northeast coast and off the adjacent islands, such as Cubagua and Margarita. A few small settlements were founded, such as Cumaná, but these were abandoned as soon as profits dwindled and local indigenous resistance grew too fierce.

In 1528, interest moved to the western part of the country, when Charles V mortgaged the whole colony to the German banking house of Welser. After two decades in hopeless search for El Dorado, the enterprise collapsed and Venezuela returned once more to Spanish control.

During the second half of the 16th century, subjugation of the indigenous peoples proved slow and difficult. Separate wars had to be waged against every scattered tribe and, as a low-priority colony, Venezuela could not secure royal troops. Geographical obstacles added to these problems. But the Spanish persevered.

By 1545 the only settlement of note was Coro, but by the end of the century there were 20 towns dotted around the Caribbean coast and the Andes, and these regions were effectively occupied by Spanish farmers. Caracas, founded in 1567, was the most prosperous city and province. Conquest was far from complete by the end of the 16th century, however. The Llanos and Maracaibo basin were still inhabited by nomadic tribes.

The colonial government and administration was characterized by factionalism and decentralization. The colony was, during this period, generally under the rule of more important neighbouring areas, such as the Audiencia of Santo Domingo during the 16th and 17th centuries and, in the 18th century, the Viceroyalty of Bogotá. Neither, however, exercised any real control over the remote government in Caracas. By the same token, Caracas did not exercise much influence over the other six provinces. These were ruled by their own *cabildos* (municipal councils) which, throughout the colonial period, successfully resisted any attempts to bring them under the control of a central authority.

The colonial economy

As a relatively isolated colony, Venezuela developed a diversified, self-sufficient economy during the colonial period. The first colonists produced their own staple foods such as maize, beans, wheat and beef. By the end of the 16th century the country began to grow highly valued tropical crops such as tobacco, sugar, cocoa and indigo. And by the early 17th century it was actually exporting cattle hides.

Such potentially lucrative trade, however, was initially exploited not by Spain but by its European competitors, despite being illegal. English and French privateers and smugglers were regularly using Venezuelan ports by the end of the 16th century. At the turn of the century Dutch merchant fleets began exploiting the salt pans on the northeast coast and soon after began supplying black slaves in exchange for cacao and tobacco.

During the 18th century Spain attempted to exert control over Venezuela's trade. To this end they set up a monopoly trading company, the Real Compañía Guipuzcoana (better know as the Caracas Company), in 1728. The Basque company was granted not just economic control but also political power over the country. For half a century the company was successful in limiting foreign competition, developing cacao, cotton and hide production for export, and encouraging domestic manufacturing. Success, though, came at the expense of the Venezuelan people. Widespread dissatisfaction and resistance forced relaxation of the monopoly in 1781, and a few years later the Caracas Company disappeared. From then until the end of the colonial period, illegal non-Spanish traders prospered once more. The colonists also profited from their new-found commercial freedom.

The struggle for independence

Venezuela may have played a minor role during Spanish colonial rule in Latin America, but it was the catalyst for the whole independence movement in South America. The spirit of liberty had long thrived in the cabildos and the *criollos* who dominated these local governing bodies resisted Spain's efforts to tighten her political grip on the colony in the late 18th century. The antagonism between the criollo and the Spanish colonial officials contributed more than anything else to the break with Spain, but the principal cause of the independence movement was the conquest of the Iberian peninsula by Napoleon Bonaparte in 1808-1810. The *criollos* took the opportunity to assume control themselves. In 1810 the *criollos* of Caracas deposed the Spanish governor, and were followed by the other six provinces, who then set up a governing junta. On 5 July 1811 they declared Venezuela independent and began drawing up a new constitution for the new nation. However, this first move towards independence was not supported by the majority *pardo* (mestizo) class. They viewed with suspicion the transfer of political power to the already dominant *criollo* class. As a result, except in Caracas, the *pardos* fought on the side of the royalists until late into the war.

The initial revolutionary activities were dominated by Francisco de Miranda, the main precursor of the Spanish American independence movement. But even this brilliant young *criollo* could not prevent the fall of the first republic, less than 10 months after the declaration of independence, in the face of growing royalist opposition. The patriot demise was hastened by a massive earthquake on 26 March 1812, which razed the patriot cities to the ground but left the royalist strongholds untouched. This was, of course, seized on by the clergy as proof of divine disapproval of the rebellion against the Spanish crown.

With the collapse of the first republic, the leadership of the patriots passed to Simón Bolívar, a young man destined to become the father of Venezuela. He had fled to Colombia after defeat, but returned in 1813 at the head of an invading expedition, declaring a 'war to the death' with the Spanish and their supporters. By August of that year, his victorious army had reached Caracas, where he was proclaimed Liberator of his country.

But complete liberation was still a long way off. The Spanish forces were still strong on the coast and the *pardos* of the Llanos had not yet been converted to the patriot cause. The royalists had won them over with promises of racial equality and war profits. In less than a year, Bolívar and his patriots were driven from the capital. So the second republic fell in 1814 as suddenly as the first.

In exile once more, Bolívar realized he would need the support of the majority of the *pardos*, as well as foreign help, as Spain was no longer occupied in Europe. In December 1816 he launched yet another campaign, this time from the northeast. Soon after, the same fierce *llanero* plainsmen who had chased Bolívar from Caracas in 1814, turned on their leader Boves and on Spain. Under a new leader, José Antonio Páez, they raised the flag of freedom in their headquarters, the isolated city of Angostura on the Orinoco River (now appropriately renamed Ciudad Bolívar). Here also, the much sought after European aid began to flow in. By mid-1819 The Liberator was ready to resume the offensive. By August his army had climbed over the Andes and freed Colombia. The way was now clear for the final conquest of Venezuela.

In June 1821 Spanish resistance was decisively broken at the Battle of Carabobo. Venezuela was free, but at a considerable cost. She had suffered more than any other Latin American country. During 11 years of warfare the country had lost one quarter of its population and the economy was left in ruins.

It would be another nine years before a truly independent status was achieved.

BACKGROUND
Simón Bolívar – Liberator

There isn't a Venezuelan village or town worth its salt that doesn't have a Plaza Bolívar at its centre. Simón Bolívar is so revered in Latin America in general, and in Venezuela in particular, that streets, currencies and even a country have been named after him.

Bolívar was largely responsible for the liberation from Spanish colonial rule of an area of land of about 5,000,000 sq km and which now comprises modern Venezuela, Colombia, Panama, Ecuador, Peru and Bolivia.

Simón Bolívar was born on 24 July 1783. He was by birth part of the *gran cacao*, the richest white land-owning families of colonial Caracas. He obviously enjoyed the privileges of the criollo class but was acutely aware that neither he nor the poorest of slaves were completely free. In the colonial Venezuela, *criollos* were still barred from public office and trade and it was their cause he initially championed.

Bolívar was educated privately in Caracas and Europe, where he read the works of Hobbes, Locke and the Enlightenment philosophes and he was clearly influenced by the American and French revolutions. On one of his travels to Europe he met the famous explorer and scientist, Alexander von Humboldt who believed that South America was ripe for independence but lacked the person to bring it about. For the last 20 years of his life he struggled ceaselessly to remove Spanish rule from South America.

He was not a tall man, at only 1.68 m The Spanish General Pablo Morillo was amazed that the 'little man on a mule' who had come to sign a peace treaty with the Spanish in 1820 after the decisive battle of Boyacá, was Simón Bolívar. As well as being a great soldier and thinker, he was known to swear like a trooper and would enjoy a good ball or fiesta. He was also renowned as being a passionate lover who had a number of stormy relationships, the most important being that with Manuelita Sáenz, an Ecuadorian This side of The Liberator is brilliantly depicted in Gabriel Garcia Marquez's novel *The General in his Labyrinth*.

Bolívar achieved his goal but failed in his desire to unite Venezuela, Colombia and Ecuador into a single independent nation Gran Colombia. Many of his former allies, particularly the *llanero* José Antonio Páez and General Francisco de Paula Santander, who later became presidents of Venezuela and Colombia respectively, turned against him. But what finally broke him was the murder of his closest friend and best general, José Antonio Sucre.

In 1830, weary of the bitter rivalries between *caudillos* who had carved up South America for their own ends, Bolívar lamented "America is ungovernable. Those who serve the revolution, plough the sea. The only thing to do in America is to emigrate." He was trying to do just that when he died of tuberculosis, virtually alone and penniless aged only 47 on his way to take a boat to Europe.

After Independence

Despite being at the heart of Simón Bolívar's cherished Gran Colombia (together with Ecuador, Colombia and Panama), Venezuela under General Páez became an independent nation in 1830, before Bolívar's death. Páez was either president, or the power behind the presidency from 1831 to 1848, a time of stability and economic progress. In the second half of the 19th century, though, the rise of the Liberal Party in opposition to the ruling Conservatives led to conflicts and social upheaval. In 1870 a Liberal politician-general, Antonio Guzmán Blanco, came to power. Even though his term was peaceful, it marked the entry of the army into Venezuelan politics, a role which it did not relinquish for almost a century.

20th century

In the first half of the century presidents of note were Juan Vicente Gómez (1909-1935), a brutal but efficient dictator, and Isaías Medina Angarita, who introduced the oil laws. There was much material progress under the six-year dictatorship of General Marcos Pérez Jiménez (1952-1958), but his Gómez-like methods led to his overthrow in January 1958. A stable democracy has been created since, with presidential elections every five years. Carlos Andrés Pérez of the centre-left Democratic Action party (AD) took office in 1974, presiding over a period of rapid development following the first great oil-price rise, and was succeeded in 1979 by Luis Herrera Campins of the Christian Democratic party, Copei. Jaime Lusinchi of Democratic Action was elected president in 1983, to be followed by Carlos Andrés Pérez, who began his second term in 1989.

1990s instability and economic crisis

Pérez' second term was marked by protests against economic adjustment and growing levels of poverty. In 1992 there were two unsuccessful coup attempts by military officers, including Colonel Hugo Chávez Frías, who became president by legitimate means in 1999. Among reforms designed to root out corruption, the Supreme Court and Central Bank were given greater independence. Both bodies were instrumental in the decision that Pérez himself be tried on corruption charges in 1993. The president was suspended from office, arrested and, after two years of house arrest, was found guilty in May 1996. An interim president, Senator Ramón José Velázquez, took office until the presidential elections of December 1993, in which Rafael Caldera, standing as an independent, was re-elected to office (as a member of Copei, he was president 1969-1974). Many of his aims, such as improvement in social conditions, tax reform and the control of inflation, had to be postponed, even reversed, in favour of solving an economic and financial crisis which began in 1994. This helped him to conclude an agreement with the IMF, but caused public protest at declining salaries and deteriorating public services.

Modern Venezuela

Presidential elections in December 1998 were won by Hugo Chávez, by an overwhelming majority. On taking office in February 1999, Chávez called for a complete overhaul of Venezuela's political system in order to root out corruption and inefficiency. He obtained special powers from Congress to reduce the budget deficit and diversify the economy away from oil. These were first steps towards his aim of eradicating poverty and restoring real incomes, which had fallen by two-thirds in 15 years. He set up a constituent assembly which drew up a new constitution and 70% of the electorate approved it in a plebiscite in December 1999. New elections, scheduled for May 2000 but postponed until the end of July as the electoral commission failed to make the necessary preparations, were won comfortably by Chávez. Opposition parties did, however, increase their share of seats in Congress as the middle and upper classes supported Chávez' main challenger, Francisco Arias Calderón, while the president held on to his heartland in the poverty-stricken slums.

The 2002 coup

Through 2001 and into 2002 Chávez succeeded in antagonizing dissident military officers, the business sector, the Roman Catholic Church and the press. The middle classes, office workers and trades unionists blamed him for mismanaging the economy. Pro- and anti-Chávez street demonstrations became a regular event in Caracas. When Chávez tried to reform PDVSA, the state oil company, replacing executives with his own allies, the value of the bolívar slumped against the dollar and oil workers went on strike. This led to a 48-hour general strike in early April and, during the protests, 16 people were killed. On 12 April it was announced that Chávez had been replaced as president after being arrested by the military high command. His successor was businessman Pedro Carmona, who dissolved Congress and cancelled the constitution, only to resign a day later in the face of pro-Chávez demonstrations equally as strong as those that had ousted the president. On 14 April, Chávez was restored to office, but society remained deeply polarized. The opposition coalition, made up of the business sector, the main trades union and the private media, kept up its pressure on Chávez. Calls for early elections were backed by the US, but the government insisted that the first poll to be held would a mid-term referendum in August 2003, as required by the constitution if sufficient voters requested it.

By the end of 2002, the political situation had deteriorated to such a degree that a general strike call was met with massive support. It lasted two months and cost Venezuela some US$6 billion as the oil industry was paralyzed, the banking sector shut down and the bolívar plummeted to record lows against the dollar. Chávez stood firm, the strike eventually ended, but the demand for a mid-term referendum did not evaporate. This was eventually held and Chávez won comfortably.

Subsequent opinion polls showed that the majority of Venezuelans supported the changes Chávez instituted in political participation, economic benefits for the poor and social reform, despite the fierce debates within and outside Venezuela over the true meaning of Bolivarian democracy. Consequently, there was little danger of Chávez losing the presidential elections of December 2006.

In early 2008 Chávez brought in a new economic team to tackle, among other problems, rapidly rising inflation, stimulated mainly by oil profits being pumped into the economy for infrastructure projects and food subsidies. In an effort to increase oil revenues and restrict non-essential imports, the bolívar was devalued to a two-tier official exchange rate in January 2010. The exchange rate for essential imports (eg food and medicines) was further devalued on 1 January 2011 and another full-scale devaluation took place in February 2013. In 2012 and 2013 inflation remained stubbornly high, between 25 and 30% (the highest in Latin America), still largely because of the cost of food.

Having first applied for membership of Mercosur in 2006, Venezuela was eventually admitted in June 2012. Paraguay had opposed Venezuelan membership, but when the other members suspended Paraguay after the deposition of President Lugo, that objection was removed. Chávez' attendance at the Mercosur ceremony at the end of July 2012 was the first official foreign trip he made since he was diagnosed with cancer in mid-2011. From the outset, that single issue overshadowed just about everything in Venezuela. In July 2011 Cuban surgeons removed a tumour from his pelvic area and several other operations followed. The president revealed little about the precise nature of the cancer and the true state of his health was the subject of much speculation. Nevertheless, he stood for reelection in October 2012, running against the opposition's elected candidate, Henrique Capriles Radonski, governor of Miranda state. Chávez won with a comfortable majority, but his illness prevented him from being inaugurated in January 2013. All the debate about the constitutional position of the president-elect finally came to an end when, on 5 March 2013, he succumbed to the illness that he had fought for almost two years. His death meant that new elections had to be called. These were held in April 2013 and were won by Chávez' chosen successor, Nicolás Maduro, by the slimmest of margins over Henrique Capriles.

Chávez and Bolivarian Revolution

Hugo Chávez Frías (1954-2013), president of Venezuela from 1999 to 2013, was undoubtedly the most high-profile Latin American politician of the early 21st century. Outspoken critic of globalization and neoliberalism he tirelessly promoted Latin American unity and democratic socialism. Under his leadership, Venezuela pulled out of the World Bank and IMF (after paying off its debts) and key industries were nationalized. Critics at home and abroad called him populist, even a tyrant. Supporters stressed that his rule was fully democratic, with almost every important change decided by referendum.

Under Chávez, Venezuela allied itself not only with Latin American nations sympathetic to his vision of the Bolivarian Alliance for the

Americas (ALBA – integration based on social welfare and equity rather than trade liberalization), for example Cuba, Bolivia, Ecuador and Nicaragua, but also with Iran, China and Russia. His model of 21st-century socialism included the removal of Latin America from the US sphere of influence and wresting power for the unrepresented people from the hands of the oligarchies that have controlled the region. The main methods included the supply of cheap oil, transcontinental infrastructure projects and forging ties with indigenous movements and opposition parties in other countries. At the other extreme, relations with the US were bitterly strained, particularly during the George W Bush presidency (but not so badly as to affect sales of Venezuelan oil), with Chávez unceasingly vocal in his disgust at US foreign policy.

On the social front, the Chávez government promoted alternative models of economic development, combating poverty, malnutrition, illiteracy and disease. Subsidized food stores, well-equipped hospitals and schools and a model housing scheme for low-income families were established. Land was returned to indigenous groups.

Post-Chávez Venezuela faced huge challenges. These included the political divisions between the many Venezuelans helped by the programmes mentioned above and the privately owned media and others determined to discredit the Bolivarian Revolution. The government was accused repeatedly of not listening to grievances and of corruption. Police brutality and Venezuela's high crime rates (including homicide – the highest in the world according to some statistics) were of great concern. Capriles' improved showing in the second election of 2013 should have given the opposition heart, but even though the various groups combined in a coalition called the Mesa de la Unidad Democrática (MUD) they could not find a unified voice with which to confront the government. In the first quarter of 2014 a series of prolonged, violent demonstrations, sparked by student protests at high crime rates, shortages of basic goods and other economic difficulties, failed to bring about change. Neither the antagonistic approach, favoured by, for example, Leopoldo López, leader of Voluntad Popular (arrested in February 2014) and María Corina Machado, a deposed deputy, nor the moderates' tactic of seeking talks with the government had any effect. In August 2015 López was still in prison. In May of that year he went on hunger strike to protest against what he called the government's authoritarianism. Also on hunger strike was Daniel Ceballos, ex-mayor of San Cristóbal de Táchira, but Ceballos and former Chávez aide-turned-critic, retired general Raúl Baduel, were released in August. Meanwhile, María Machado was suspected of being involved in a plot to assassinate Maduro and in February 2015, Antonio Ledezma, mayor of Caracas, was arrested on charges of conspiracy in an attempted coup that was prevented by armed forces loyal to the government.

The president stated that the coup attempt was backed by the US (a charge that was strenuously denied), who, he said, was also waging "economic war" against Venezuela through support for the opposition and its alleged efforts to cause chaos and discontent through shortages of staple goods, among other activities. Relations with the US deteriorated in December when the US Congress approved sanctions against seven officials who were said to have directed human rights abuses during the early 2014 riots. The majority of Latin American countries denounced the sanctions and President Obama faced much criticism at the Summit of the Americas in Panama in April 2015. Maduro and Obama met briefly at the Summit, but Obama did not attend Maduro's speech. US and Venezuelan officials did however meet for talks in Haiti in June to try to reduce tensions between the two countries.

Legislative elections were due to be held on 6 December 2015 and many polls indicated that the ruling PSUV (United Socialist Party of Venezuela) might fare very badly. In mid-year Maduro's own popularity rating stood at little over 20%. At root were the economic problems which not only provoked fierce opposition, but also caused rifts within the PSUV on how to tackle inflation, reduce subsidies and end the supply problems and imbalances caused by multiple exchange rates. These problems were exacerbated by the fall in global oil prices to about US$45 a barrel in August 2015 and a dramatic fall in the price of gold, another important export, which threatened to undermine social spending. The 2015 budget had stated that social spending programmes would be maintained on the strength of inflation falling from its 2014 level of 68.5%, GDP growth of 3% and a slight fall in unemployment. The slump in oil and gold prices undermined all that and, in the absence of official data, analysts put inflation at over 100% in mid-2015 and expected GDP to decline by 6-7% over the year. A new exchange regime was introduced in February, which added a free-floating rate of 170 bolívares to the dollar to the existing fixed rates of 6.30 and 12.80, but by August a black market rate of almost BsF 600 showed there was no confidence in the currency. While the government considered the reforms needed to turn the economy round, saying they would be introduced after the December elections, the general public had to endure queues at supermarkets for basic goods, arbitrary price hikes for transport, looting and further difficulties which had the inevitable effect of eroding support for Maduro and his administration.

Government

Under the Constitution of 1999, the president holds office for six years and may stand for immediate reelection. There are 23 states, a Capital District and federal dependencies of 72 islands. There is one legislative house, a chamber of deputies with 165 members who are elected every five years, with three seats reserved for indigenous peoples. All elected officials are eligible for unlimited reelection.

Culture

People

Population was 29.3 million in 2015. Population growth was 1.39%; infant mortality rate 18.91 per 1000 live births; literacy rate 96.3%; GDP per capita US$17,700 (2014). A large number are of mixed Spanish and indigenous origin. There are some pure Africans and a strong element of African descent along the coast, particularly at the ports. The arrival of 800,000 European immigrants, mostly in the 1950s, greatly modified the racial make-up in Venezuela. Despite its wealth, Venezuela still faces serious social problems. Many rural dwellers have drifted to the cities; one result of this exodus is that Venezuelan farmers do not provide all the food the nation needs and imports of foodstuffs are necessary, even for items such as beans and rice. A very small proportion of the population (150,000) is *indígena*. Among the best-known are the Yanomami, who live in Amazonas, and the Bari in the Sierra de Perijá (on the northwest border with Colombia). An indigenous reserve gives the Bari effective control of their own land, but this has not prevented infringement from mining, plantation or settlers. Other groups include the Wayuu (in the Guajira), the Panare and the Piaroa.

Arts and crafts

Venezuela has a rich heritage of arts and crafts due to its mixture of African, European and indigenous cultures. The different regions of the country are another factor forming separate centres of *artesanía* even within one geographical area such as the Andes. The Spanish conquest led to the introduction of the potter's wheel and the pedal loom to already sophisticated indigenous craftsman.

Ceramics The Andes is probably the most developed zone with Táchira and Mérida both having different styles. The use of oxidizing substances and high-temperature ovens results in well-finished pottery with designs particular to the region. The state of Lara is another good centre as is Isla de Margarita, especially the village of Cercado. Handmade pots, earthern jars and other utensils can also be seen in Amazonas and other indigenous areas.

Clothing The Guajiros of Maracaibo make good sandals and long flowing dresses called *mantas* for sale in local markets. They first used cotton but after the Spanish conquest the use of wool began to appear in their textile products. Bags made from soft weaves from the heart of the *cumare* or *moriche* palm can also be bought in Puerto Ayacucho. Hats made from palm fibres can be found in many parts of the country. The hammocks made by the Warao of the Orinoco Delta are regarded as both ornate and practical.

Basketware Baskets are made in various designs from *chiquichique* palm and other fibres by indigenous groups along the whole length of the Orinoco. The Yanomami of Amazonas are particularly known for their fine baskets.

Woodcarving Carvings are widely sold whether life-size ones of birds and reptiles or replicas of indigenous boats or religious statues. Barinas in the Llanos is a good place to find carvings of the local wildlife. Ritual masks, such as those used in Miranda by the *diablos danzantes,* are to be found in parts of the country.

Musical instruments One of the most popular string instruments made in Venezuela is the cuatro influenced by the Renaissance guitar popular in the 16th century in Europe. The African influence has resulted in the coastal tradition of making drums from trunks and skin. Another percussion instrument often found are the popular maracas still used in modern music. Pan pipes can also be found amongst the wind instruments made in the country.

Music

While Venezuela and Colombia are famously at odds, musically they share much in common, both in their folk traditions and in their national obsessions with salsa, a style born from Cuban rhythms in the back streets of New York but kidnapped by these two nations who have made it their own. Venezuela gave the world Oscar d'León, a former motor mechanic from Caracas with an irrepressible smile who made his name dancing and playing upright bass with Cuban-influenced son band, La Dimensión Latina in the 1970s. He has since become one of the biggest salsa acts in the world, with a host of imitators. Caracas' clubs and bars are filled with imitation Oscar d'León big bands and singers.

If Venezuela has a national music it is *llanera*, sung by cowboy troubadours from the sweeping grasslands, accompanied by harp, guitar and percussion. In its most refined form, as played by the likes of stetson-clad nonagenarian Juan Vicente Torrealba, *llanera* sounds like a fusion between calypso, easy listening and classical music, whilst mainstream, popular *llanera's* syrupy songs are closer to Mexican mariachi music.

Venezuelans enjoy salsa as much as other Hispanic peoples around the Caribbean, but they are also very keen on their own music, whether rustic 'folk' or urban 'popular'. The virtuoso harpist Juan Vicente Torrealba (see above) has performed with his group Los Torrealberos since 1947, usually with Mario Suárez as vocal soloist. Another famous singer is Simón Díaz. Outstanding among the folk groups who strive for authenticity are Un Solo Pueblo, Grupo Vera and Grupo Convenezuela. Choral and contrapuntal singing of native music in a more sophisticated style has also been perfected by Quinteto Contrapunto and Serenata Guayanesa.

Land & environment

Venezuela has a land area of 912,050 sq km and 2800 km of coastline on the Caribbean Sea with many islands. The Andes run up northeastwards from Colombia, along the coast eastwards past Caracas, ending up as the north coast of the Caribbean island of Trinidad. In the northwest corner is the Maracaibo basin. South of the Andean spine is the vast plain of the Orinoco which reaches the sea near the Guyana border and to the southeast of that are the ancient rocks known as the Guayana highlands.

The Andes are highest near the Colombian border where they are known as the Sierra Nevada de Mérida. Beyond, they broaden out into the Segovia highlands north of Barquisimeto, and then turn east in parallel ridges along the coast to form the Central highlands, dipping into the Caribbean Sea only to rise again into the northeastern highlands of the peninsulas of Araya and Paria. This region has an agreeable climate and is well populated with most of the main towns. The Maracaibo lowlands are around the freshwater lake of Maracaibo, the largest lake in South America (12,800 sq km). Considerable rainfall feeds the lake and many rivers flow through thick forest to create swamps on its southern shore. The area is dominated by the oil-producing fields on both sides of the lake and beneath its surface. To the west, the Sierra de Perijá forms the boundary with Colombia and outside the lake to the east is the most northerly point of the country, the peninsula of Paraguaná, virtually desert.

The Llanos, as the Orinoco plains are called, cover about one-third of the country. They are almost flat and are a vast cattle range. The Orinoco river itself is part of Latin America's third largest river system. Many significant rivers flow from the Andes and Guayana highlands to join the Orinoco, whose delta is made up of innumerable channels and thousands of forest-covered islands. The Guayana highlands, which take up almost half the country, are south of the Orinoco. This is an area of ancient crystalline rocks that extend along the top of the continent towards the mouth of the Amazon and form the northern part of Brazil. In Venezuela they are noted for huge, precipitous granite blocks known as tepuis, many of which have their own unique flora, and create many high waterfalls including the Angel Falls, the world's highest.

Practicalities
Venezuela

Getting there

All countries in Latin America (in fact across the world) officially require travellers entering their territory to have an onward or return ticket and may at times ask to see that ticket. Although rarely enforced at airports, this regulation can create problems at border crossings. In lieu of an onward ticket out of the country you are entering, any ticket out of another Latin American country may sometimes suffice, or proof that you have sufficient funds to buy a ticket (a credit card will do).

Flights from Europe
The choice of a departure point for Venezuela is limited to Madrid and one or two other cities (Paris for instance). There are no direct flights from London so you'll need to travel via mainland Europe, the USA or another Latin American country, such as Brazil or Argentina.

Flights from North America
Where there are no direct flights, connections can be made in the USA, Buenos Aires or São Paulo. The main US gateways with direct flights to Caracas or Marcaibo are Miami, Houston, Atlanta and New York. If buying airline tickets routed through the USA, check that US taxes are included in the price. Flights from Canada are mostly via the USA.

Flights from other areas
Likewise, flights from Australia and New Zealand are best through the USA except for the Qantas/LAN route from Sydney and Auckland to Santiago, and Qantas' non-stop route Sydney to Santiago, from where connections can be made. But there are no direct flights from Santiago to Venezuela.

Departure tax

Airport tax International passengers do not pay airport tax at Maiquetía International Airport (Caracas) as it is included in the price of tickets. At all other airports, a tax of BsF 85 (US$0.45) is levied on domestic flights, BsF 406 (US$2.10 at Simadi rate) on international flights, which must be paid after check-in and before proceeding to security. The rate changes annually, for the latest check www. aeropuerto-maiquetia.com.ve and http://baer.gob.ve. Exit stamps are payable by overland travellers at some borders. Correct taxes are not advertised and you may be overcharged. Under 2s do not pay tax.

Getting around

Air

Venezuela's most important cities are served by domestic flights from Caracas. The most extensive coverage is offered by state-owned carrier **Conviasa** ⓘ *www.conviasa.aero*. Other lines include **Aeropostal** ⓘ *www.aeropostal.com*, **Aserca** ⓘ *www.asercaairlines.com*, **Avior** ⓘ *aviorair.com*, **Rutaca** ⓘ *www.rutaca.com.ve*, **Laser** ⓘ *www.laser.com.ve*, and **Venezolana** ⓘ *www.ravsa.com.ve*. **LTA (Aereotuy)** ⓘ *www.tuy.com*, connects Caracas with Porlamar, Los Roques and camps at Boral (Maturín) and Arekuna (Canaima). None of Venezuela's airlines is great. Lost luggage, delays and cancellations without compensation are common. Beware of overbooking during holidays, especially at Caracas airport; check in at least two hours before departure. If you book a ticket online with a credit card, you may be told at check-in that your tickets is 'reserved but not purchased'. Check with your card company that you have not been charged twice. It is essential to reconfirm all flights, international and domestic, 72 hours in advance.

Road

Buses on most long-distance routes come in three standards, *tradicional*, *ejecutivo* and *bus-cama*. Fares are set by the authorities and you should see them posted on bus office windows, or in the *Gaceta Oficial*. There are numerous services between the major cities and many services bypass Caracas. Buses stop frequently, but there may not always be a toilet at the stop. For journeys in air-conditioned buses take a sleeping bag or similar because the temperature is set to freezing. This is most important on night journeys, which otherwise are fine. Also take earplugs and eyemask to protect against the loud stereo and violent Hollywood screenings. For journeys longer than six hours, it is essential to buy your ticket in advance, although they may not always be available until the day of departure. Sometimes hoteliers and tour operators have inside connections which can save a lot of hassle.

The **colectivo taxis** and **minibuses** (jitneys), known as *por puesto*, seem to monopolize transport to and from smaller towns and villages. For longer journeys they are normally twice as expensive as buses, but faster, often breaking local speed limits. They are sometimes an unreliable and risky mode of transport, but great places to meet the locals, learn about the area and discuss politics. If first on board, wait for other passengers to arrive. Do not take a *por puesto* on your own unless you want to pay for the whole vehicle. Outside Caracas, town taxis are relatively cheap, and they are becoming popular for tourists and locals, for security reasons. Phone *Líneas de Taxi* and ask for interstate trip fares.

Hitchhiking (*cola*) is not recommended as it is unsafe. It is illegal on toll roads and, theoretically, for non-family members in the back of pick-up trucks. Avoid hitchhiking around Guardia Nacional posts (see also Safety, below).

Driving in Venezuela

Road The four-lane *autopistas* are quite good, but generally roads are in poor shape. Potholes are often marked by a pile of stones or sticks left by road-users to highlight the danger. Road congestion and lengthy delays are normal during holidays. Traffic jams are common in Caracas and car parks crowded.

Safety As infrastructure is not improving and spare parts for cars are scarce and expensive, serious road accidents are common. The situation is not helped by reckless driving at extremely high speed. If you have an accident and someone is injured, you will be detained as a matter of routine, even if you are not at fault. Carry a spare tyre, wheel block, jack, water and the obligatory breakdown triangle. Use private car parks whenever possible. Car-jackings have soared in recent years, so be alert and try to drive in daylight and in populated areas.

Documents Minimum driving age is 18. A valid driving licence from your own country, or international driving licence (preferred) is required. Neither a *carnet de passages*, nor a *libreta de pasos por aduana* is officially required, but is recommended. You should also have copies of vehicle and insurance documents and passport with you at all times since stops at National Guard and local police checkpoints (*alcabalas*) are frequent. Drive slowly through these and stop to show your documents if instructed to do so. Before shipping your vehicle to Venezuela, go to a Venezuelan consul to obtain all necessary documentation. You must also go to a Venezuelan consul in the country in which you land your car if other than Venezuela.

Organizations Touring y Automóvil Club de Venezuela, Torre Phelps, p 15, of A y C, Plaza Venezuela, Caracas, T0212- 781 9743, www.automovilclubvenezuela. com, issues *libreta de pasos por aduana* and a separate form for taking a car only to Colombia. See www.automovilclubvenezuela.com/documentos.php.

Car hire It is a good idea to hire a car; many of the best places are off the beaten track. You need a credit card to rent a vehicle. Rates for a car start at about US$20 per day, not including insurance, collision damage waiver, taxes or GPS if you book in advance. This is based on a price in BsF, converted at the SIMADI rate (see Money). If you pre-book in dollars, the price may be higher.

Fuel 91 and 95 octane, unleaded, cost BsF0.70 and BsF0.097 a litre respectively; diesel, BsF0.048 a litre (Apr 2015). **Warning** There is a fine for running out of fuel.

Maps The best country map is International Travel Maps' *Venezuela Travel Reference Map*. They also publish *Caracas (Venezuela) ITM City Map* (Vancouver, Canada, www.itmb.ca). Also see Google Maps and the recently updated **Caracas Street Map** by www.dubbele.com, pre-loaded on your phone before you leave home (download can take time).

Essentials A-Z

Accident and emergency

Dial T171 for the integrated emergency system. **CICPC (Cuerpo de Investigaciones Científicas, Penales y Criminalísticas)**, Av Urdaneta entre Pelota y Punceres; Edif Icauca, mezzanina 2, Caracas, T0800-272 4224, www.cicpc.gob.ve. For registering crimes throughout the country.

Disabled travellers

In most of South America, facilities for the disabled are severely lacking. For those in wheelchairs, ramps and toilet access are limited to some of the more upmarket, or most recently built hotels. Pavements are often in a poor state of repair or crowded with street vendors. Most archaeological sites have little or no wheelchair access. Visually or hearing-impaired travellers are also poorly catered for, but there are experienced guides in some places who can provide individual attention. There are also travel companies outside South America who specialize in holidays which are tailor-made for the individual's level of disability. Disabled South Americans have to rely on others to get around, and foreigners will find that people are generally very helpful. The **Global Access – Disabled Travel Network** website, www.globalaccessnews.com/index.htm, is useful. Another informative site, with lots of advice on how to travel with specific disabilities, plus listings and links belongs to the **Society for Accessible Travel and Hospitality**, www.sath.org.

Electricity

120 volts, 60 cycles. Plugs are US-style 'A' and 'B' types, 2-pin flat and 2-pin flat with optional D-shaped earth.

Embassies and consulates

The Ministry of Foreign Affairs website is www.mppre.gob.ve. For Venezuelan embassies and consulates abroad and for all foreign embassies and consulates in Venezuela, see http://embassy.goabroad.com.

Health

See your GP or travel clinic at least 6 weeks before departure for general advice on travel risks and vaccinations. Try phoning a specialist travel clinic if your own doctor is unfamiliar with health in the region. Make sure you have sufficient medical travel insurance, get a dental check, know your own blood group and, if you suffer a long-term condition such as diabetes or epilepsy, obtain a **Medic Alert** bracelet (www.medicalert.org.uk).

Vaccinations and antimalarials
Confirm that your primary courses and boosters are up to date. It is advisable to vaccinate against polio, tetanus, typhoid, hepatitis A and, for more remote areas, rabies. Yellow fever vaccination is obligatory for most areas. Cholera, diphtheria and hepatitis B vaccinations are sometimes advised. Specialist advice should be taken on the best antimalarials to take before you leave.

Health risks

The major risks posed in the region are those caused by insect disease carriers such as mosquitoes and sandflies. The key parasitic and viral diseases are malaria, South American trypanosomiasis (Chagas' disease) and dengue fever. Be aware that you are always at risk from these diseases. **Malaria** is a danger throughout the lowland tropics and coastal regions. **Dengue fever**, which is widespread, is particularly hard to protect against as the mosquitoes can bite throughout the day as well as night (unlike those that carry malaria). In 2015 cases of the chikungunya virus, transmitted by the same mosquito that carries dengue, had been confirmed. Try to wear clothes that cover arms and legs and also use effective mosquito repellent. Mosquito nets dipped in permethrin provide a good physical and chemical barrier at night. **Chagas' disease** is spread by faeces of the triatomine, or assassin bugs, whereas sandflies spread a disease of the skin called **leishmaniasis**.

Some form of **diarrhoea** or intestinal upset is almost inevitable, the standard advice is always to wash your hands before eating and to be careful with drinking water and ice; if you have any doubts about the water then boil it or filter and treat it. In a restaurant buy bottled water or ask where the water has come from. Food can also pose a problem, be wary of salads if you don't know whether they have been washed or not.

There is a constant threat of **tuberculosis** (TB) and although the BCG vaccine is available, it is still not guaranteed protection. It is best to avoid unpasteurized dairy products and try not to let people cough and splutter all over you.

One of the major problems for travellers to the Andes in the west of Venezuela is **altitude sickness**. It is essential to get acclimatized to the thin air of the Andes before undertaking long treks or arduous activities. The altitude of the Andes means that strong protection from the sun is always needed, regardless of how cool it may feel.

Another risk, especially to campers and people with small children, is that of the **hanta virus**, which is carried by some forest and riverine rodents. Symptoms are a flu-like illness, which can lead to complications. Try as far as possible to avoid rodent-infested areas, especially close contact with rodent droppings.

If you get sick

Make sure you have adequate insurance (see below). Contact your embassy or consulate for a list of doctors and dentists who speak your language, or at least some English. Your hotel may also be able to recommend good local medical services.

Caracas

Clínica Avila, *Av San Juan Bosco con 6ta Transversal, Altamira, T0212-276 1111, www.clinicaelavila.com.*

Maracaibo

Hospital Coromoto, *Av 3C, No 51, El Lago, T 0261-790 0000.*

Mérida

Dr Aldo Olivieri, *Av Principal La Llanita, La Otra Banda, Centro Profesional El Buho, 09, T244 0805, T0414-374 0356, aldrolia250@cantv.net. Very good,* gastroenterologist, speaks English and Italian.

Further information

Centres for Disease Control and Prevention (USA), www.cdc.gov.
Department of Health advice for travellers, www.gov.uk/foreign-travel-advice.
Fit for Travel (UK), www.fitfortravel.scot.nhs.uk, a site from Scotland providing a quick A-Z of vaccine and travel health advice requirements for each country.
National Travel Health Network and Centre (NaTHNaC), www.nathnac.org.
Prince Leopold Institute for Tropical Medicine, www.itg.be.
World Health Organisation, www.who.int.

Insurance

We strongly recommend that you invest in a good insurance policy that covers you for theft or loss of possessions and money, the cost of medical and dental treatment, cancellation of flights, delays in travel arrangements, accidents, missed departures, lost baggage and lost passport. Be sure to check on inclusion of 'dangerous activities' if you plan on doing any. These generally include climbing, diving, skiing, horse riding, parachuting, even trekking. You should always read the small print carefully. Not all policies cover ambulance, helicopter rescue or emergency flights home.

There are a variety of policies to choose from, so it's best to shop around. Reputable student travel organizations often offer good-value policies. Travellers from North America can try the **International Student Insurance Service (ISIS)**, which is available through **STA**, T800-7814040, www.statravel.com. Companies worth trying in Britain include **Direct Line Insurance**, T0845-246 8704, www.directline.com, and the **Flexicover Group**, T0800-093 9495, www.flexicover.net. Some companies will not cover those over 65. The best policies for older travellers are through **Age UK**, T0845-600 3348, www.ageuk.org.uk.

Internet

The government has introduced a Wi-Fi for All programme, which is due to include connectivity in public areas. Nevertheless, internet connection, while common, is among the slowest in Latin America.

Language

The Constitution of Venezuela states that Spanish and languages spoken by Venezuela's indigenous people are all official. The majority of Venezuelans speak Spanish but at least 40 other languages are spoken too.

Without some knowledge of Spanish you will become very frustrated and feel helpless in many situations. English, or any other language, is absolutely useless off the beaten track. Some initial study, to get you up to a basic vocabulary of 500 words or so, and a pocket dictionary and phrase-book, are most strongly recommended   your pleasure will be doubled if you can talk to the locals.

Money

US$1= BsF 6.30 (Cencoex); US$1= BsF 12.80 (Sicad); US$1= BsF 199.57 (Simadi) (Jul 2015).
The unit of currency is the bolívar fuerte (BsF), introduced in 2008. There are coins for 1 bolívar fuerte, 50, 25, 12.5, 10, 5 and 1 céntimos, and notes for 2, 5, 10, 20, 50 and 100 bolívares fuertes. Have small coins and notes to hand, since in many

shops and bars and on public transport large notes may be hard to change.

Official and unofficial currency exchange

Venezuela has had an exchange control regime since 2003 to prevent capital flight. In Apr 2015, 3 official rates were in operation. Applicable to 'priority sectors' of food, medicine and staples, the official rate set by the Centro de Comercio Exterior (Cencoex) was US$1 = BsF 6.3. The **exchange rate** for lower priority items was the Sistema Complementario de Administración de Divisas (Sicad) set at US$1 = BsF 12.8. The 3rd official exchange rate, Simadi, was a brand new, floating forex system introduced in Feb 2015 which allows US dollars to be bought and sold according to supply and demand. In late Jul 2015 it stood at US$1 = BsF 199.57. This rate is available to tourists and is used for international credit card transactions, including at ATMs, and in approved cambios, such as Italcambio (www.italcambio.com – see website for branches). You must present your passport and a photocopy; daily limit US$300. Prices in this book have been calculated where possible on its basis.

Prices at anything other than the Simadi rate are extremely high, but since foreign visitors can use this rate they should not find the country expensive. At the time of writing, Simadi had not eliminated the 'parallel' (ie black) market in foreign currencies. According to unofficial reports this was around US$1 = BsF 678 in late Jul 2015, but since the unofficial exchange of dollars is illegal in Venezuela and since it is difficult for a visitor to find such a rate, the safest option is to use the Simadi rate. Whatever you decide to do, always consult a trusted and senior member of staff at a hotel or tour operator, never ask a stranger on the street. The unofficial rate can be checked on the internet before you enter Venezuela, but once inside the country you will find those websites blocked (search twitter instead). Remember, the parallel exchange is illegal and involves risk to the changer. You will also be fined if caught in the act.

You can investigate wiring money to a foreign-based account which will release cash in Venezuela, or, if you have friends living in Venezuela with an overseas bank account, sending money there.

Plastic, TCs, cash At the time of research, Simadi had been fully implemented and *casas de cambio* and most ATMs and credit card transactions were using it, although commission charges might apply. ATMs are widespread but highly unreliable and not recommended. Some require a Venezuelan ID number and you should speak to your card issuer about this before leaving home. Despite the security risks, it is best to bring all the cash you need for your trip in US dollars and change small amounts at a time. Only bolívares purchased officially can be converted back, up to 25% of the amount originally changed, and you will need the original exchange receipt. For money exchange and other services including travel, go to **Italcambio**, www.italcambio.com, the official government exchange office and take ID. Offices at Av Urdaneta, esq Animas a Platanal, Edif Camoruco, Nivel Pb, El Centro, T0212-565 0219 and others in the capital and around the country. Italcambio also at national and international terminals at airport (open public holidays).

Cost of travelling If using the Simadi rate, you will need a daily budget of around US$20-40 for 'mid-range' lodging and dining, depending on the region. On a basic budget, you can get by on less than US$15 per day. First class travel can be had for US$50-70 daily, often for much less, and multi-day treks and all-inclusive packages to Angel Falls and Roraima are quite reasonable. Please bear in mind that Venezuela's economic situation is extremely unpredictable. The new Simadi exchange mechanism signifies another massive devaluation of the BsF and it may raise an already high rate of inflation, rendering some prices in this book inaccurate. Exchange regulations are subject to change at any moment and you can check the three official rates at **Cencoex**, www.centrodecomercioexterior.com. At the time of writing it appeared that stability had not been brought to consumer markets so you may find shortages of basic shopping items. Before you travel, find out what the current situation is.

Opening hours

Generally speaking, Venezuelans start work early, and by 0700 everything is in full swing. Most firms and offices close on Sat
Banks Mon-Fri 0830-1530 only.
Businesses 0800-1800 with a midday break.
Government offices 0800-1200 are usual hours, although they vary. Officials have fixed hours, usually 0900-1000 or 1500-1600, for receiving visitors.
Shops Mon-Sat 0900-1300, 1500-1900..

Post

Post offices are run by **Ipostel**, whose main branch is at Urdaneta y Norte 4, near Plaza Bolívar, Caracas, see www.ipostel.gob.ve, for branches, Mon-Fri 0800-1630. (The Galerías Avila office is open Mon-Sun 1000-2100.) It has an overseas package service; packages should be ready to send, also at airport. **MRW**, throughout the country, T0800-304 0000, see www.mrw.com.ve, for branches. 24-hr service, more reliable than Ipostel.

Public holidays and festivals

Business travellers should not visit during Easter Week or Carnival. There are extra holidays only for banks which are set every year according to religious festivals, dates vary.
1 Jan New Year
Feb/Mar Carnival on the Mon-Tue before Ash Wednesday (everything shuts down Sat-Tue; book a place to stay in advance).
Easter Thu-Sat of Holy Week.
19 Apr Declaration of Independence.
1 May Labour Day
Early Jun Corpus Christi (8 weeks after Maundy Thursday) in San Francisco de Yare, 90 km from Caracas, some 80 male 'diablos' of all ages, dressed all in red and wearing horned masks, dance to the sound of their drums and rattles.
24 Jun Battle of Carabobo and the feast day of **San Juan Bautista**, celebrated on the central coast where there were once large concentrations of plantation slaves who considered San Juan their special saint; the best-known events are in villages such as Chuao, Cata and Ocumare de la Costa.
5 Jul Independence.

24 Jul Bolívar's birthday.

12 Oct Día de la Resistencia Indígena.

24 Dec-1 Jan From 24 Dec-1 Jan, museums are closed, most restaurants close 24-25 Dec (except for fast-food outlets) and there is no long-distance public transport on 25 Dec, while other days are often booked solid. On **New Year's Eve**, everything closes and does not open for at least a day.

Safety

Venezuelans are generally honest, helpful and hospitable people. The vast majority of visitors to the country do not encounter any problems, but you should be aware that street crime in big cities has soared in recent years. Most of the trouble occurs at night in poor barrios, but nonetheless caution is strongly advised when navigating the downtown and bus station districts of Caracas, Maracaibo and Valencia. Carry only as much money as you need, dress like the locals, don't wear jewellery or expensive sunglasses, don't take out smartphones in the street. During the day is mostly trouble-free, as long as you are aware of where you are going. Ask your hotel about any unsafe areas. It is not advisable to walk after dark always take a taxi from a well-marked, recognizable company with a number, or get someone to recommend a driver. This applies even to tourist centres like Mérida and Ciudad Bolívar. You will need

Take heed...

The British Foreign and Commonwealth Office currently advises against all travel to within 80 km of the Colombian border due to the risk of kidnapping by drug traffickers and paramilitaries.

to speak at least basic Spanish to be able to get yourself around. Few people in the street will speak English, and even fewer in rural areas.

Outside the big cities you will feel less unsafe, but still need to be careful in quieter rural areas. The more popular destinations (such as beaches and national parks) are used to having travellers. You still need to watch out for scams, cons and petty thieving. If you are seeking an isolated beach, make enquiries about which are safe beforehand.

Stay away from political rallies (unless you are there to join them) and protest marches, as they can turn violent.

Foreigners may find themselves subject to harassment or abuse, or to thorough police identity and body searches. Carry a copy of your passport and, if searched, watch the police like a hawk, in case they try to plant drugs to your bags. Do not photograph people without permission. Carry a mobile (but don't display it), keep the number of a trusted Venezuelan contact handy, and be prepared to call him or her, or your embassy if a police search becomes threatening.

Tax

VAT/IVA 12%.

Telephone *Country code +58*

Ringing long equal tones with equal long pauses. **Engaged** short equal tones, with equal pauses.

The national phone carrier is **CANTV**, which has offices country-wide, many of which also have internet. Everywhere there are independent phone offices, sometimes just tables, offering landline and mobile calls. Phone cards for local calls are sold in multiples of BsF 5. Mobile phone codes are generally 0412, 0414, 0416, or 0424. **Digitel**, **Movilnet** and **Movistar** are the main mobile providers. Visitors can use foreign phones with roaming, or purchase a local SIM card (phone must be unlocked).

Time *GMT-4*

4½ hrs behind GMT.

Tipping

Taxi drivers do not expect to be tipped. **Hotel porters**, US$1-2; **airport porters** US$4 per piece of baggage. **Restaurants** add 10% to bill for staff wages; tip a further 5-10%.

Tourist information

In charge of tourism is the **Ministerio del Poder Popular para el Turismo**, Av Francisco de Miranda con Av Principal de La Floresta, Edif Mintur (Frente al Colegio Universitario de Caracas), Chacao, Caracas, T0212-208 4651, www.venezuelaturismo.gob.ve and www.mintur.gob.ve. **Venetur**, Centro Empresarial Centro Plaza, Torre B, p 16, Los Palos Grandes, Caracas, T0500-TURISMO (887 4766), www.venetur.gob.ve, Mon-Fri 0900-1730, is the state-owned and operated travel agency, aimed at facilitating travel for nationals and foreigners, making reservations and arranging tours. In Caracas, go to **Corpoturismo**, Parque Central, Torre Oeste, p 35, 36 y 37, T0212-576 5696.

Outside Venezuela, contact Venezuelan embassies and consulates. Read and heed the travel advice at websites below.

Useful websites

www.gobiernoenlinea.gob.ve Government site.

www.venezuelatuya.com Tourism, history, geography, cuisine, traditions and more.

www.turismo.net.ve Tourism portal and related blog at **www.turismo.venezuela.net.ve**.

www.audubonvenezuela.org Site of the not-for-profit conservation organization.

Visas and immigration

Entry is by passport, or by passport and visa. Immigration forms are issued by airlines to visitors from all EU and other Western European countries, Australia, Canada, New Zealand, South Africa, USA and some South and Central American and most Caribbean countries. Forms are processed for an entrance stamp upon arrival. Valid for 90 days, entrance stamps cannot be extended. At some overland border crossings (including San Antonio) visitors are given only 30 days. Overstaying will lead to arrest and a fine when you try to depart. For citizens of some countries, tourist, transit, student, and business visas must be sought in advance. To check if you need a visa, see www.mppre.gob.ve. Requirements vary and include 2 passport photos, passport valid for 6 months, references from bank and employer, proof of foreign residence, demonstration of non-emigration to a consular official, proof of economic conditions, documentation of assets, and an onward or return ticket. The fee is US$30-43. For a 90-day extension go to the Servicio Administrativo de Identificación, Migración y Extranjería, **SAIME**, Av Baralt, Edif Mil, p 3, on Plaza Miranda in Caracas, T0800-SAIME00 or

T0800-724 6300, www.saime.gob.ve (go to Extranjería, Prórroga de Visa); take passport, tourist visa, photographs and return ticket; passport with extension returned at end of day. SAIME offices in many cities do not offer extensions. If coming from Manaus or travelling onward to other countries in Latin America, you will need a yellow fever inoculation certificate. Carry your passport with you at all times as police do spot checks and anyone found without ID is immediately detained. You may also be asked to provide passport number in some restaurants and shops. Military checkpoints are common, especially in border zones, where all transport is stopped and you may be searched very thoroughly. Have documents ready and make sure you know what entry permits you need; soldiers may not know rules for foreigners. Business visitors have to obtain a tax clearance certificate (*solvencia*) before they can leave. Do not lose the carbon copy of your visa as this has to be surrendered when leaving.

Weights and measures

Metric.

Index

Entries in bold refer to maps

FOOTPRINT

Features

DA   10/16 ✓

Footprint credits
Editor Nicola Gibbs
Production and layout Patrick Dawson
Maps Kevin Feeney
Colour section Angus Dawson

Publisher Patrick Dawson
Managing Editor Felicity Laughton
Administration Elizabeth Taylor
**Advertising sales and
marketing** John Sadler, Kirsty Holmes
Business Development Debbie Wylde

Photography credits
Front cover Vadim Petrakov/
  shutterstock.com
Back cover
Top Juniors/Superstock.com.
Bottom F1 ONLINE /SuperStock.com.

Colour section
Inside front cover Minden Pictures/
SuperStock.com; Philip Lee Harvey/
SuperStock.com; testing/Shutterstock.
com; Hemis.fr/SuperStock.com.
Page 1 F1 ONLINE/SuperStock.com.
Page 2 Prisma/SuperStock.com.
Page 4 Hemis.fr/SuperStock.com.
Page 5 Alice Nerr/Shutterstock.com;
Vadim Petrakov/Shutterstock.com;
Xinhua/Alamy.
Page 6 imageBROKER/SuperStock.com.
Page 7 Hemis.fr/SuperStock.com; Alice
Nerr/Shutterstock.com.
Page 8 age fotostock/SuperStock.com.
Duotone Page 18 Piccaya/Dreamstime.
com.

Printed in Spain by GraphyCems

Publishing information
Footprint Venezuela
2nd edition
© Footprint Handbooks Ltd
September 2015

ISBN 978 1 910120 12 5
CIP DATA A catalogue record for this
book is available from the British Library

® Footprint Handbooks and the
Footprint mark are a registered
trademark of Footprint Handbooks Ltd

Published by Footprint
6 Riverside Court
Lower Bristol Road
Bath BA2 3DZ, UK
T +44 (0)1225 469141
F +44 (0)1225 469461
footprinttravelguides.com

Distributed in the USA by
National Book Network, Inc.

Every effort has been made to ensure
that the facts in this guidebook are
accurate. However, travellers should still
obtain advice from consulates, airlines,
etc about travel and visa requirements
before travelling. The authors and
publishers cannot accept responsibility
for any loss, injury or inconvenience
however caused.